From Ring Shout to Bomba:

Ethnographic Perceptions and Approaches to Music and Religion in the Gullah/Geechee and Afro-Latin Diasporas

Anthony Luis Sanchez Cruz

Sceaud'or Press

Sceaud'or Press

Ethnographic photography by Maria Goretti Cruz

Map Illustration and book cover by Freddy Sanchez and Maria Goretti Cruz

Unless otherwise indicated, the block quotes featured in the contents of this book derive from "Public Domain" materials via governmental resources and informants who initially expressed their permission to have their words included as part of the publication.

Manufactured in the United States of America

978-0578-97038-7

In loving memory of my abuela,

Carmen Perez Velazquez

For motivating me to keep traditions alive

Table of Contents

List of Figures v

Introduction 1

Aspects of Researching Gullah/Geechee and Afro-Latin Cultures 6

Selected Culture Theories (and Their Problems).................................30

Addressing Misconceptions About the Gullah/Geechee and Afro-Latin America

....44

(Re)Interpreting Gullah/Geechee Culture, Religion, and Music.........70

Research on Afro-Latin Syncretic Religions and Music..........................84

Gullah/Geechee and Latin American Audio Recordings and Archives
....106

Aspects of Gullah/Geechee Culture in Popular Music..........................139

Moving Towards the Future: The Legacy of Gullah/Geechee and
Afro-Latin Cultures and Music...155

Works Cited 171

Appendices A-D...200-213

Acknowledgements..214

List of Figures

Figure 1: Habanera Rhythm ("café con pan")..17

Figure 2: Bomba Sica Rhythm...18

Figure 3: (Stylized) Bomba Dance 18

Figure 4: (Stylized) Bomba Dance with Drumming..18

Figure 5: Boone Hall Plantation Slave Quarters—Mt. Pleasant, South Carolina 45

Figure 6: Hamilton Plantation Slave Quarters—St. Simons, Georgia............45

Figure 7: Kingsley Plantation (Ruins)—Jacksonville, Florida.......................46

Figure 8: Gullah/Geechee Rice in Basket...55

Figure 9: "Parade of Flags" at St. Helena Island, South Carolina 55

Figure 10: "Walkway to Freedom" at Ft. Mose (1752 Estimated Location)—St. Agustune, Florida...59

Figure 11: Re-enactors at Ft. (During COVID-19)—St. Augustine, Florida 59

Figure 12: Ring Shout Rhythm..81

Figure 13: Praise House in Mitchelville, South Carolina 81

Figure 14: Church Sermon (Display) at Boone Hall Plantatation Slave Quarters—Charleston, South Carolina 82

Figure 15: African Drum—Possibly Batá, or Djembe.......................................84

Figure 16: Sra. Raquel Ayala (Right) at the Batey de Los Hermanos Ayala—Loiza, Puerto Rico..93

Figure 17: Vejigante Masks—Loiza, Puerto Rico

....93

Figure 18: Banner Commemorating the 2019 *Fiesta de Santiago Apóstol* and Tricentennial of the city of Loiza, Puerto Rico 93

Figure 19: Type of Shekere...102

Figure 20: Record Player (Photo by Lee Campbell on Unsplash) 107

Figure 21: Sound-Mixing Board (Photo by Filip Barna on Unsplash)..........139

Figure 22: Close-up of Choir at First African Baptist Church—Hilton Head, South Carolina 157

Figure 23: Interview with Zenobia Harper (Left) at Hopsewee Plantation—Georgetown, South Carolina..157

Figure 24: Ring Shout Performance by the Geechee Gullah Ring Shouters at RiceFest (Riceboro, Georgia) 158

Figure 25: Dancers at MOJA Festival—Charleston, South Carolina............167

Figure 26: Gullah/Geechee Dance 168

Figure 27: African Musicians in Concert—Conway, South Carolina............168

Introduction

"If oonuh ent kno weh oonuh dah gwine, oonuh should kno weh oonuh come fum."[1]

~Gullah Proverb

The work presented in this book discusses the Gullah/Geechee of the coastal southern United States and their connections to Afro-Latin communities by investigating aspects of their histories and music cultures. This research concentrates on the historical, religious, and musical links with the Gullah/Geechee in the United States and Afro-Latin cultures in Puerto Rico, Cuba, and Brazil. I consider this project as a reassessment that addresses the gaps or challenges the contemporary scholarship about the Gullah/Geechee and Afro-Latin communities with new or previously overlooked details.

This study involves acknowledging that researching history is not a static process. Perceptions of history change over time with the advent of new information that either adds to or critically questions past events with concrete information and factual evidence. Within the context of this current research, that process requires reframing colonialism: both the historical effects in the United States and from a global standpoint. That means demonstrating that this process has featured more than one colonizing country. I devote some research to explaining the Spanish, Portuguese, and British colonial practices and perceptions of Africans in the New World. Given the urgency of that specific topic in recent years, mainly in relation to slavery[2] in the United States, the research that I present explores the necessity for expanding upon the U.S. colonial historiography.

In addition to discussing musical aspects from the respective cultures, this research addresses the effects of audio recording

---

[1] This proverb roughly translates in English to: "If you do not know where you are going, you should know where you come from."

[2] I use this term in the book to refer to the institution of chattel slavery (ownership of another human being) in the United States and slavery as it was enforced in parts of Latin America and the Caribbean in the past. Whenever possible, to avoid misrepresentation and historical inaccuracy, I use the terms "enslaved" to refer to the *conditions* endured by the Gullah/Geechee and Afro-Latin people and "enslaver(s)" to refer to the people who committed these actions.

Geographical Regions with Gullah/Geechee or Afro-Latin Influences Covered in this Research

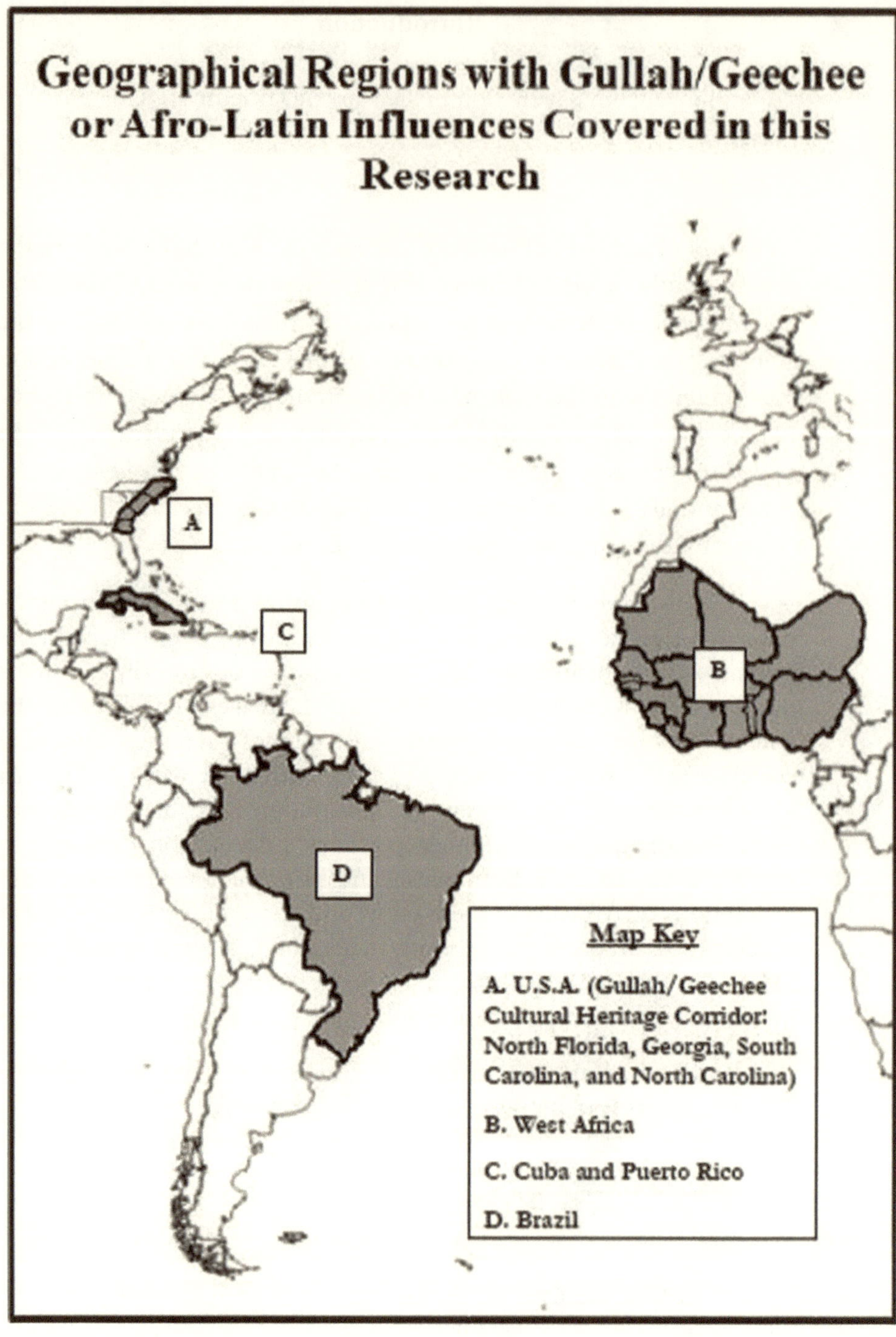

technologies on the Gullah/Geechee and Afro-Latin communities in relation to modernization by examining their applications within ethnomusicology, ethnography, and popular music. In doing so, I discuss aspects of cultural representation from different perspectives. By analyzing selected twentieth-century field recordings by Robert Winslow Gordon, the Lomax family, Lorenzo Dow Turner, Herbert Halpert, and others, I demonstrate how these researchers sought to transmit and preserve Gullah/Geechee and Afro-Latin oral musical traditions and narratives. In terms of popular music and the Gullah/Geechee, the investigation concentrates on selected songs and pieces where musicians and groups, primarily those outside of the culture, apply Gullah/Geechee music as creative and political inspiration: from the folk music revival of the 1950s and 60s, to digital sampling in the 1980s and 90s, to jazz and rap in the 2010s.

Taking these analyses into consideration, this book also examines the problems associated with using past Gullah/Geechee and Latin American audio recordings for archival and artistic purposes to promote authenticity and cultural visibility. Referring to the problematic theoretical literature concerning *transculturation* and *cultural appropriation* enables readers to further understand the misconceptions about these topics. Linking this information to the twenty-first century, I examine how music streaming services and radio stations help to expand the presence of these cultures for people within the communities and for the public. This research concludes by suggesting the creation of an interactive application/program for younger generations of people that concentrates on further preserving Gullah/Geechee and Afro-Latin audio recordings and culture without promoting exploitation and assimilation.

Scope of Study

This book represents years of gleaning credible sources via a series of discoveries and re-examining previously accepted information about the Gullah/Geechee and Afro-Latin cultures. When I began researching this topic in 2018, I intended to investigate the historiographical and cultural aspects by concentrating specifically on the music of the Gullah/Geechee in the United States and Afro-Puerto Ricans in Puerto Rico. The process changed drastically after realizing that I needed to expand the geographical scope to include more areas from Latin America and the Caribbean: primarily, the Anglophone (English-speaking), Hispanophone (Spanish-speaking) and Lusophone (Portuguese-speaking) regions. It also required recognizing that the

Gullah/Geechee cultural presence not only comprises areas like the Bahamas, Barbados, and Jamaica. They also have established themselves in countries like Cuba, Belize, and Brazil.

I also had to consider the possibility that certain countries and territories in Latin America and the Caribbean did not necessarily need to have *direct* cultural, religious, linguistic, or musical connections with the Gullah/Geechee. Given these details, it becomes more appropriate to establish a comparative survey of these cultures and demonstrate the effects of history, archiving, and preserving their identities. This study does not merely mention cultural similarities and differences at the surface level. It involves thinking critically about the respective histories and the geography of the Gullah/Geechee and previously specified areas of Latin America and the Caribbean.

The research presented here can function as a resource designed to expand the knowledge about the Gullah/Geechee and Afro-Latin American social, religious, and music cultures. While I discuss music in relation to the Gullah/Geechee and Afro-Latin American communities, I do so while also attempting to avoid using technical jargon to enable accessibility for readers outside of the musical field. The sources uncovered and used for this investigation refer to several cultures: British, Spanish, Brazilian Portuguese, and Gullah/Geechee. Most resources consulted in this book stem from primary and secondary sources from the 1980s to the 2020s and interview transcripts, where appropriate.

I have written extensively about the problems associated with perceiving documents and artifacts from older time periods as "definitive" and "accurate" sources of information.[3] Such materials should be treated as historical materials and constantly scrutinized for factual inconsistencies. The reason that I occasionally refer to older sources stems from comprehending how scholars and authors from certain eras thought or understood different cultures: often, in misguided or condescending terms. Whenever necessary, I discuss and apply extant and current theoretical literature that explores concepts of *transculturation* and *cultural appropriation*. Readers looking for more

---

[3] Anthony L. Sanchez, *The Puerto Rican Cuatro as a Device for Transculturation: A Contemporary Compositional Approach in Estampas de La Isla del Encanto.* University of Georgia, D.M.A. Dissertation. http://dbs.galib.uga.edu/cgi-bin/getd.cgi?userid=galileo&serverno=18&instcode=publ&_cc=1 (accessed December 30, 2019); *The Jíbaro and the Gaucho United in Music and Song* (English Translation), Vancouver, BC: Ditrie Marie Bowie, 2019.

detailed discussions about transculturation theory can consult my previous studies on the subject.[4]

Some readers might wonder: *Wait a minute. Shouldn't this book concentrate on religion and music? Why so much emphasis on history and culture theories? These topics are just random and unnecessary.* No, they are not. I include sections about culture theories and history because they have *everything* to do with what I uncover. These topics provide contexts about the Gullah/Geechee and Afro-Latin people and what they have experienced over the centuries. Discussing transculturation and cultural appropriation also helps because it provides examples of the different interpretations that scholars (and society) have about these cultures. To talk about Africanized religions and music without providing that contextual information would prove illogical.

With *that* clarification out of the way, I must provide another warning to readers throughout this investigation. Certain older sources demonstrate racial biases towards their topics by concentrating too much on the differences or "weirdness" of foreign cultures and practices. While such an approach would be considered by many as both juvenile and highly unprofessional in the twenty-first century, it is better to learn from the mistakes presented in such resources instead of immediately discarding and attempting to erase them from the collective cultural memory. One cannot and should not assume that the authors or scholars from previous centuries had acted apathetically towards foreign cultures. This is a point that I have referred to again and again in my previous research, and it deserves repeating for *this* study. Older sources about foreign cultures written by outsiders (specifically, scholars and folklorists from Europe and the United States) either aimed to educate or—in certain cases—entertain audiences about non-Western or marginalized communities via the ways that *outsiders* understood. Readers should not misinterpret this explanation as absolving such behavior. *From Ring Shout to Bomba* attempts to present historical balance by mentioning the many atrocities committed under colonization and racism in the past and their consequences in the twenty-first century.

---

[4] Sanchez 2017; Sanchez 2019

Aspects of Researching Gullah/Geechee and Afro-Latin Cultures

Correctly Signifying the Gullah/Geechee

It is imperative that I begin this study by mentioning how to properly address the Gullah/Geechee people in writing. Multiple resources about the Gullah/Geechee demonstrate different ways of spelling the name of the community. Some of the most frequent variants that I have encountered throughout this research use the following three types: "Gullah Geechee," "Gullah-Geechee," and "Gullah/Geechee." While the Gullah/Geechee Nation prefers the third variant with the backslash as the proper approach for naming the group of people, not everyone in the Gullah/Geechee community agrees with this choice. Althea Sumpter explicitly states in her ethnographic research that the spelling of this group does not use the backlash.[5] However, the backslash is applied in legal documents and when referring to the Gullah/Geechee Nation out of cultural respect. For the sake of consistency, I apply that spelling variant, unless it is spelled differently in other documents and resources.

The names "Gullah" and "Geechee" refer to groups of people from the United States of West African heritage and to their written and spoken language. "Gullah" often signifies the community of people who live in coastal South Carolina along the Cultural Heritage Corridor in the Sea Islands: a region of states extending from North Carolina to North Florida. The Gullah/Geechee, predominantly consisting of descendants of enslaved West Africans brought to the New World in the American Colonial Era, derived mainly from the coastal countries of Sierra Leone, Liberia, Guinea, Gola, and Angola among others. Their ancestors arrived via colonial enslavement and forts, like Bunce Island, which the British controlled from the eighteenth century until the early nineteenth century.[6] Sources

---

[5] Queen Quet,"Correspondence E-mail to Gullah/Geechee Sea Island Coalition," July 2, 2019. I refer to this person often, because some of the scholars I mention have conducted interviews with her for information on the Gullah/Geechee; Geneaology Adventures Live, S03 E02 Genealogy Adventures Live Gullah Geechee Genealogy with Althea Sumpter" *YouTube* (September 16, 2019), https://www.youtube.com/watch?v=qV-RxvDv4eo (accessed February 8, 2020). Sumpter clarifies the representation of the Gullah name in the opening minutes of the episode.

[6] Sherbro Foundation, "Connecting the Dots: Sierra Leone—US Shared History," 2013 (?). https://sherbrofoundation.org/2014/02/17/connecting-the-dots-sierra-leone-us-

frequently describe the Gullah/Geechee language as a Creolization of African and English, often as a refutation of its connection to African American Vernacular English (AAVE). Scholarship on the Gullah/Geechee and West African connections often reveal direct cultural and ancestral links via DNA testing and commonalities in customs.[7]

"Geechee" primarily consists of two meanings. First, it refers to the community of people of West African descent based in the southeastern coast of the United States in Georgia and North Florida (Jacksonville and parts of St. Augustine). The name often functions as a geographical signifier to distinguish people from the Gullah of South Carolina. The second, and more problematic, definition applies the name "Geechee" as an insult that implies a person who is socially and culturally ignorant. To put it in more direct terms, "Geechee" has often been used by society as a derogatory name for referring to someone from the community as "backwards." In more recent years, members of the Gullah/Geechee community have raised awareness against using the demeaning definition of "Geechee" and against the constant devaluation of the Gullah/Geechee linguistic culture. This activism partially serves as a reaction against the generational suppression of the Gullah/Geechee language in the twentieth century, which had frequently been misinterpreted by the rest of society (including African Americans not raised in Gullah/Geechee culture) as a form of "broken" English.[8] As I discuss in detail later, the application of

---

shared-history/amp/?fbclid=IwAR2GP7RmqS_AeK3eq1Vd9eXvQv1WxI57o7Hs-5sO39IZWenIisGiuo7xiEM (accessed November 1, 2019). As of 2019, some of the links to related media in this article are longer available to viewers and researchers: mainly, because of issues concerning copyright.

[7] Sherbro Foundation, 2013 (?).

[8] Pablo Correa and Brian Graves, "Articulating Cultural Belonging at the Border of the Heritage Corridor: Public Communication and the Preservation of North Florida's Gullah/Geechee Culture." *Florida Communication Journal* 43, No. 1 (2015), https://s3.amazonaws.com/academia.edu.documents/40858091/Florida_Gullah_Geechee_FSU.pdf?response-content-disposition=inline%3B%20filename%3DArticulating_Cultural_Belonging_at_the_B.pdf&X-Amz-Algorithm=AWS4-HMAC-SHA256&X-Amz-Credential=AKIAIWOWYYGZ2Y53UL3A%2F20191205%2Fus-east-1%2Fs3%2Faws4_request&X-Amz-Date=20191205T163040Z&X-Amz-Expires=3600&X-Amz-SignedHeaders=host&X-Amz-Signature=377f6e41737c86ebf76b75f9f02ac2fa2a0d4fb55ada1205f9003b682863c8cd (accessed September 23, 2019).

"Geechee" to popular music genres can often produce convoluted messages about the culture.

The Gullah/Geechee Cultural Heritage Corridor Commission

Since October 12, 2006, The United States Government has recognized the presence of the Gullah/Geechee people and lands through the "Gullah/Geechee Cultural Heritage Act" via the Committee on Energy and Natural Resources. This congressional act established a commission comprised of people from within the Gullah/Geechee communities from all representative states in the Corridor: from Wilmington, North Carolina to Jacksonville, Florida. Under "Section 2" of the Gullah/Geechee Cultural Heritage Act (Lines 5 through 19), which I quote in full:

> The purposes of this Act are to—
> 6 (1) recognize the important contributions made
> 7 to American culture and history by African Ameri
> 8 cans known as the Gullah/Geechee who settled in the
> 9 coastal counties of South Carolina, Georgia, North
> 10 Carolina, and Florida;
> 11 (2) assist State and local governments and pub
> 12 lic and private entities in South Carolina, Georgia,
> 13 North Carolina, and Florida in interpreting the
> 14 story of the Gullah/Geechee and preserving Gullah/
> 15 Geechee folklore, arts, crafts, and music; and
> 16 (3) assist in identifying and preserving sites,
> 17 historical data, artifacts, and objects associated with
> 18 the Gullah/Geechee for the benefit and education of
> 19 the public.[9]

Reading through the Gullah/Geechee Cultural Heritage Act, one can see the strict nature of the rules for the Gullah/Geechee Cultural Heritage Corridor Commission. Appointed members must have experts in Gullah/Geechee culture and history, as well as work together to plan activities related to Gullah/Geechee culture based on the "Purposes" mentioned in "Section 2." They also must provide credible evidence of proper documentation and funding for tax

---

[9] House of Representatives, "H.R. 694 Gullah/Geechee Cultural Heritage Act," *Congress,* 2005-2006, https://www.congress.gov/bill/109th-congress/house-bill/694 (accessed February 14, 2020), Public Domain. The numbers on the left side, which are included in the original document, serve as a place marker for each respective line of text to avoid confusion.

reasons and to demonstrate the legitimacy of the commission. Planning for projects, which cannot take longer than five years, must be initially completed and submitted to the Secretary of the Gullah/Geechee Cultural Heritage Corridor for approval. They must do this under the constraints of a limited budget (no more than $1,000,000—which they must divide evenly to cover expenses and utilities—and no more than $10,000,000 for legitimate external funds).[10]

The text for the Gullah/Geechee Cultural Heritage Act additionally indicates that the Gullah/Geechee Cultural Heritage Corridor Commission is not a permanent organization. Besides periodically appointing new members over time, the commission must be renewed and approved by the Committee on Energy and Natural Resources in Congress. That committee must, then, legislate a proposed extension to the commission for approval in the House of Representatives and the Senate. "Section 13" of the Gullah/Geechee Cultural Heritage Act originally placed the timeframe and termination for the Gullah/Geechee Cultural Heritage Corridor Commission at ten years. In 2016, through a revision of this act, the commission received an extension of five more years of activity. It is set to expire on October 12, 2021 and must be renewed again to stay active.[11]

It can be tempting for some readers to interpret the congressional legislation that I have just described as positive and to perceive the Gullah/Geechee Heritage Corridor as a new concept. This is only partially true. The Gullah/Geechee people and their land have been around for centuries. The Gullah/Geechee Cultural Heritage Act merely demonstrates that more people have been paying attention to this cultural and historical presence in the twenty-first century on a national level. Scholars and musicians outside the Gullah/Geechee community in the twentieth century *did* investigate the Corridor through other governmental projects, and I discuss their efforts at length in my research. However, readers should also understand that some of these scholars and researchers often perceived this coastal region and its people as isolated from the rest of the United States and (in extreme cases) exhibited observational biases.

---

[10] House of Representatives, 2005-2006.

[11] House of Representatives, "H.R.3004 - To amend the Gullah/Geechee Cultural Heritage Act to extend the authorization for the Gullah/Geechee Cultural Heritage Corridor Commission," *Congress*, 2015-2016, https://www.congress.gov/bill/114th-congress/house-bill/3004 (accessed February 14, 2020), Public Domain. As of February 2021, another extension had been introduced in Congress.

Such attitudes continued well after the construction of bridges connecting the Corridor in the 1950s. Additionally, the Gullah/Geechee Cultural Heritage Act exists today because members of the Gullah/Geechee community petitioned Congress for proper cultural representation and preservation.

It also deserves mention that the Gullah Geechee Cultural Heritage Corridor Commission did not just appear from nothing. The process in enabling the public to understand the Gullah/Geechee and who they are as a community required much planning in advance. The National Parks Service indicates that they began planning this process back in the late 1990s via the Low Country Gullah Culture Special Resource Study:

> The Low Country Gullah Culture Special Resource Study (SRS) was authorized by Congress to determine whether or not the National Park Service (NPS) should have a role in preserving Gullah culture and if so, what that role might be. The enabling legislation for the SRS was introduced in 1999 by United States Congressman James Clyburn (D- South Carolina) and was authorized in the Interior Appropriations Act of 2000... This act directed the NPS to determine the national significance of Gullah culture, as well as the suitability and feasibility of adding various elements of Gullah culture to the National Park System… Under the guidelines of this study, the NPS was directed:
> - to analyze the multi- faceted components of Gullah culture (known as Geechee in Georgia and Florida) using the established criteria for the study of areas for potential inclusion in the National Park System and;
> - to evaluate the resources of the Gullah/Geechee people and cultural landscape for potential national significance and;
> - to determine how these resources could be protected, interpreted, and used for the benefit of the Gullah/Geechee people and the general public and;
> - to make recommendations to Congress based on those criteria.[12]

---

[12] National Park Service, "1. Purpose and Need for the Study," in *Low Country Gullah Culture Special Resource Study and Final Environmental Impact Statement* (Atlanta, GA: NPS Southeast Regional Office, 2005), 1.

The criteria presented form the basis for the lengthy booklet issued in 2005 by the National Parks Service. It details the planning process for how to properly interpret Gullah/Geechee history, cultural customs, and geography while simultaneously maintaining respect and avoiding exploitation. It does these tasks by also informing audiences about the Gullah/Geechee through extant research materials on the community and segments from ethnographic interviews.[13]

Avoiding Questionable Approaches to Research

Part of this current study involves analyzing archival audio materials and sources predominantly related to music and culture theories. I discuss the impact of scholars who have sought to understand and collaborate with members of the Gullah/Geechee, Latin American, and Caribbean communities through documented research and audio recording preservation. With that said, one must try to avoid portraying these scholars or investigators via "White Savior" descriptions. How and why does that approach become a problem? That denotes covert racism because it attempts to represent another group or foreign culture while also denying input and feedback from the community being studied. The "White Savior" narrative frequently manifests itself in popular culture media and (sometimes) in academia as forms of revisionist history or culturally selective language.

As a researcher who is not affiliated with the Gullah/Geechee and Afro-Latin communities, I *do* have indigenous (Taino) and African ancestry. Part of this research stemmed from my curiosity in understanding more about the global African cultural connections. I also realize that ethnography should focus more on comprehending and respecting cultural communities instead of expressing ignorance by trying to speak for and "save" people. That latter approach has been the common mistake in older ethnographic research from the early twentieth century. The information that I present in this book demonstrates the importance of non-invasive research by gaining trust and learning to accurately document details about communities.

Other key misconceptions throughout some historiographies that I have encountered about Afro-Latin and Gullah/Geechee cultures stems from the assumptions about slavery: more specifically, that enslaved Africans accepted their situations and did not find ways

---

[13] National Park Service, "1. Purpose and Need for the Study," in *Low Country Gullah Culture Special Resource Study and Final Environmental Impact Statement* (Atlanta, GA: NPS Southeast Regional Office, 2005), 1-12.

to fight back against their oppressors. This is both incorrect and misleading. I have found documented evidence where the Gullah/Geechee and Afro-Latin communities *did* revolt against slavery through instances like the Stono Rebellion in the 1730s and multiple insurrections across Latin America and the Caribbean in the nineteenth century. Consider, too, the emergence of autonomous freedmen and freedwomen colonies and their economic stability in these time periods. The Gullah/Geechee had places like Mitchelville, South Carolina and Cosmo in Jacksonville, Florida, among many other areas. Parts of Latin America and the Caribbean had places like San Mateo de Cangrejos in Puerto Rico.

Concerning the written narratives by enslaved Africans in the United States, many refer to the ethnographic fieldwork from the Federal Writers' Project: a part of the Works Progress Administration (WPA) from the New Deal in the 1930s and 40s. These documents, which span multiple volumes, consist of written recollections and testimonies from formerly enslaved African Americans from across the southern and midwestern regions of the United States. Digital versions of the project transcripts are currently available via the Library of Congress website.[14] Many of the interviews with informants derive from people born in the nineteenth century in or around the Civil War (1861-1865). In this respect, the compilation of Slave Narratives from the WPA provides readers with a glimpse into the past from the people who experienced enslavement. At least, that is the original intention of the project.

Readers should consider the following questions when examining the former enslavement narratives compiled by the WPA (or any other ethnographic interviews or testimonies). Who controls the information: the informant, or the field researcher? How does the information get presented to audiences? How reliable is the information? Does the field researcher strive to maintain accuracy, or does he or she mess with the data through exaggeration or inserting personal biases about the topic? Does the informant have a choice in their representation as an interviewee?

---

[14] Library of Congress, *Born in Slavery: Slave Narratives from the Federal Writers Project, 1936-1938*, https://www.loc.gov/collections/slave-narratives-from-the-federal-writers-project-1936-to-1938/about-this-collection/?&loclr=reclnk, (accessed July 20, 2021), Archival Resource.

One could argue that, because the narratives provided by the WPA came from people who lived through slavery and Emancipation, their insight should reveal accurate details. While that would present the most logical approach, readers and scholars get left with questionable results instead. Consider that predominantly White ethnographers collected and transcribed these narratives in the early twentieth century in the "Jim Crow" era.[15] This aspect of the research matters because it challenges the authenticity of the transcripts.

Upon closer inspection, one notices another problem with the narratives: the "voices" of the informants shown in the transcripts. While the names of the informants and their locations appear in the transcribed interviews, the ethnographers take too many liberties with how to present the details. They display the texts from the African American informants as stereotypical "Black voices" that use a "broken" English dialect. This is best exemplified in a selection of former slave narratives based in Georgia. Not only do readers get exposed to the culturally offensive dialectical interpretations. Interviews are littered with racial epithets (eg., frequent uses of the "n-word" or similar slurs: sometimes presented as coming from the informants themselves) and descriptions that insult the intelligence of the people under scrutiny.[16] These ethnographic efforts, while beneficial on the surface, do more harm than good by presenting the materials from etic perspectives. They do not give the opportunity for the formerly enslaved people to speak about their previous experiences *in their own words*. Audio recording preservations of these narratives have attempted to remedy these mistakes. I will discuss that aspect of ethnographic research later in this book.

Certain other methodologies applied by some ethnomusicologists and researchers in the early twentieth century could also be interpreted as suspicious or inaccurate. Some of these studies from that period would often base arguments on assumptions rather than on facts—especially when the process meant tampering with evidence. Concerning the Gullah/Geechee and Afro-Latin communities, contemporary discussions and critiques eschew from portraying the culture as "dying" or struggling for survival due to

---

[15] Library of Congress, *Slave Narratives from the Federal Writers' Project, 1936-1938: Georgia*, (Bedford, MA; Washington, D.C.: Applewood Books, Library of Congress, 2005), 1-159.

[16] Library of Congress, 1-159.

modernization in the twentieth and twenty-first centuries.[17] Those that do address cultural facets in that way, such as with the Afro-Latin *Bozal* language, attempt to address cultural preservation tactfully without indirectly expressing absolutist ideas or ethnocentricities (eg., claiming that one culture is better or "superior" to another, usually marginalized, culture).

Religion, Geography, and African Connections to Musical Genres

It is also important to frame religion as a form of resistance when discussing the Gullah/Geechee and Afro-Latin applications of Christianity and syncretic practices. In every case (United States, Puerto Rico, Brazil, and Cuba), the forms of resistance would fuse religious rituals from Africa with European (Spanish and Portuguese) belief systems. One should not assume, however, that the African communities in these areas completely abdicated their original cultural identities. Miguel Ramos points out in his study of the Lucumí (Yoruba) in Cuba, for instance, that the Lucumí have been able to retain their African religious and cultural identities under the guise of assimilating to Catholicism by repurposing Catholic icons as African *orishas*, or deities.[18] Similar practices manifest themselves in Puerto Rico and Brazil under different names: Espiritismo and Candomblé. It is additionally important that I address the following disclaimers

---

[17] J. Lorand Matory, "The Illusion of Isolation: The Gullah/Geechees and the Political Economy of African Culture in the Americas." *Comparative Studies in Society and History* 50, No. 4 (2008). www.jstor.org/stable/27563714 (accessed December 5, 2019); Kendra Hamilton, "Mother Tongues and Captive Identities: Celebrating and 'Disapearing' the Gullah/Geechee Coast," *Mississippi Quarterly* 65, No. 1 (2012), https://www.jstor.org/stable/26467170?Search=yes&resultItemClick=true&searchText=gullah&searchText=geechee&searchText=music&searchUri=%2Faction%2FdoBasicSearch%3FsearchType%3DfacetSearch%26amp%3Bcty_journal_facet%3Dam91cm5hbA%253D%253D%26amp%3Bsd%3D%26amp%3Bed%3D%26amp%3BQuery%3Dgullah%2Bgeechee%2Bmusic&ab_segments=0%2Fdefault-2%2Fcontrol&refreqid=search%3A42dff46f866b6678b1dd5f90ccec0f74&seq=1#page_scan_tab_contents. (accessed July 8, 2019); Zachary Hansen, "Rescue of St. Simons schoolhouse also protects Gullah-Geechee culture," *Atlanta Journal Constitution* (January 23, 2017), https://www.ajc.com/lifestyles/rescue-simons-schoolhouse-also-protects-gullah-geechee-culture/JHh6FtuyQiQXDKiWzSOCPM/ (accessed April 28, 2019).

[18] Miguel Ramos, "I. Introduction," in *Lucumí (Yoruba) Culture in Cuba: A Reevaluation (1830s-1840s)* (Miami: Florida International University FIU Digital Commons, 2013), 1-37, https://digitalcommons.fiu.edu/cgi/viewcontent.cgi?article=2083&context=etd (accessed February 11, 2021).

immediately, both to avoid confusion among readers and to refute previous assumptions based on what I have found throughout this investigation.

I talk about religions from historical and cultural perspectives. While I do mention the effects of Christianity on the Gullah/Geechee and Afro-Latin communities via colonization, this book primarily focuses on how and (especially) *why* religious conversions occurred. I do not use these sections to openly attack different religious belief systems. It also deserves mention that syncretic religions have faced persecution from both Catholic and Protestant Christianity.[19] Whether some denominations wish to admit it or not, Christianity and syncretic religions derived from Africa coexist in the United States, Latin America, and the Caribbean. Both academic resources and Christianity tend to interpret syncretic religions as "cults." This interpretation can present the possibility for observational biases, meaning that the research on the topic must be scrutinized for inaccuracies.

Another necessary clarification is that *Spiritualism* and *Spiritism* do not mean the same concept. Spiritualism originated in the United States in the 1840s from Kate and Margaret Fox and involved communicating with the deceased for money.[20] The philosophical components behind Spiritism date from the 1850s in France (and popularized in Latin America and the Caribbean) from Allan Kardec (real name Hyppolyte Leon Denizard Rivail). Even though Spiritism also involves interacting with the dead, the practice is not meant for profit. Instead, it is based more on interpretations of morality not attached to Christianity.[21] This important distinction becomes necessary because contemporary scholars show that Allan Kardec did not "create" Spiritism. Spiritism also exists globally as different subsets of the syncretic religion across different Latin American and Caribbean

---

[19] Bettina E. Schmidt, "The Power of the Spirits: The Formation of Identity based on Puerto Rican Spiritism," *Revista de Estudos da Religiao* No. 2 (2006), 127-154, https://www.pucsp.br/rever/rv2_2006/p_schmidt.pdf (accessed February 25, 2021).

[20] Melissa Cooper, "Chapter 3: The Voodoo Craze: Popular Media Interprets African Survivals During the 1920s and 30s," in *"They Made Gullah": Modernist Primitivist and the Discovery and Creation of Sapelo Island, Georgia's Gullah Community, 1915-1991* (New Brunswick, NJ: Rutgers University, 2012), 107-145. PhD Dissertation.

[21] Bettina E. Schmidt, "The Power of the Spirits: The Formation of Identity based on Puerto Rican Spiritism," *Revista de Estudos da Religiao* No. 2 (2006), 127-154, https://www.pucsp.br/rever/rv2_2006/p_schmidt.pdf (accessed February 25, 2021).

regions, which I mention in this book. These are found and practiced in Cuba and Brazil *in addition to* Puerto Rico.

This does not suggest that academic sources from the twenty-first century do not feature problems. For instance, some journal articles from the 2010s discuss Candomblé in Brazil and the application of spirit possession, such as the ethnographic work from Bettina Schmidt.[22] It is understandable that concentrating on that aspect would be considered offensive to some audiences. At the same time, though, scholars in the twenty-first century address spirit possession as a key component of syncretic religious practices to demonstrate forms of communication between the living and the dead. They try to avoid explaining it in ethnocentric terms.

According to Miguel Ramos in his research on Cuba, the Lucumí (Yoruba) people were not the only group of Afro-Cubans who practiced syncretic religion. He also mentions the Congo (Kongo) and Carabali (Calabari) people. Ramos posits that the Lucumí receive more attention (despite having a small representation in Cuba) because Cuban society in the twentieth century often demonized and criminalized the Congo and Carabali people. Of course, he also says that the Lucumí faced similar persecution.[23]

Discussing musical genres according to "race" denotes a form of racialization. Despite this problem, it is also unavoidable due to the sociocultural perceptions of music. Concerning slavery and anti-Black racism, these topics are not strictly limited to the United States, nor should they be understood as such. These social problems have had global effects and approaches to implementation, such as visual caste systems, forms of denial, and deflection through scapegoating and persecution. Regarding discussions about colonialism, I do not use an apologist perspective that tries to excuse the dangerous historical effects on Africa, Latin America, and the United States. European colonizers were *not* benevolent people. Most who arrived in the New World (North and South America) treated enslaved Africans and Blacks harshly or viewed them as inferior.

---

[22] Bettina Schmidt, "Spirit Possession in Brazil: The Perception of the (Possessed) Body," *Anthropos* 109, H1 (2014), https://www.jstor.org/stable/43861689 (accessed February 17, 2021).

[23] Miguel Ramos, "I. Introduction," in "Lucumí (Yoruba) Culture in Cuba: A Reevaluation (1830S -1940s)" (2013). *FIU Electronic Theses and Dissertations*. 1-37. https://digitalcommons.fiu.edu/etd/966 (accessed February 11, 2021).

Many Western studies concerning African history and culture tend to begin with slavery. While this topic is clearly important, it also presents the problem of ignoring or dismissing what occurred in parts of Africa *before* European involvement and the ransatlantic Slave Trade. Readers should realize that contemporary culture studies about Africa have been trying to fix this problem.[24] Discussions about the Gullah/Geechee and Afro-Latin communities presented here address national and international comparisons in terms of oppression, resistance, and cultural preservation. Even though African historical and cultural memories serve as the main connections among these regions, readers should not assume exact similarities. It additionally helps to consider the African diasporic impact of Latin American cultures in the United States, although that topic exceeds the scope of this investigation.

Just as Africanized syncretic religions in Latin America and the Caribbean cannot (and should not) get lumped together as one practice, the African-based musical genres in these regions should not be misinterpreted as homogeneous. They do not all sound the same across all regions. A Brazilian *samba* is not the same as a Cuban *rumba*, which is not the same as a Puerto Rican *bomba* or *plena*.[25] I had previously written about the *habanera* rhythm (or the "café con pan") as an underlying rhythmic pattern across many of Latin American and Caribbean musical genres and regions (See Figure 1). However, people must avoid assuming musical homogeneity across these areas. For example, when I discuss the Afro-Puerto Rican *bomba* in this investigation, music that uses rhythms in duple meter ("in two") with dancing and "call and response" chants, that music should be thought of as consisting of different *types* of bomba based on different types of rhythmic drumming patterns: patterns like the *bomba sica*: one of the

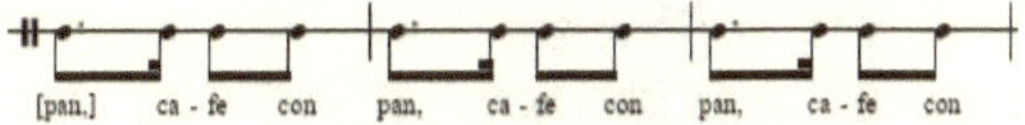

Figure 1: Habanera Rhythm ("café con pan")

<hr>

24 Errol L. Montes Pizarro, *Mas ramas que raices: Dialogos musicales entre el Caribe y el continente africano* (San Juan Ediciones Callejon, 2018).

25 Kaito Nagashima, Matthew Bellury and Trevon Johson, "Plena: A Music of the Puerto Rican People," *The Classic Journal* (April 10, 2017), http://theclassicjournal.uga.edu/index.php/2017/04/10/plena-a-music-of-the-puerto-rican-people/ (accessed April 28, 2019).

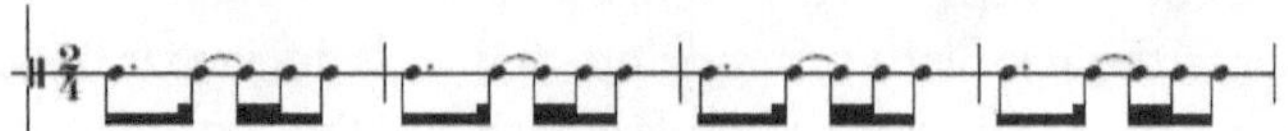

Figure 2: Bomba Sica Rhythm

Figure 3: (Stylized) Bomba Dance

Figure 4: (Stylized) Bomba Dance with Drumming

most basic syncopated rhythms in bomba music (See Figure 2). I should also add that Latin American and Caribbean musical genres are not exclusive to these areas and the U.S. They have also maintained an expansive global presence and popularity in parts of Africa through genres like *salsa*.[26] In other words, it is both insufficient and inaccurate to try and categorize these musical genres and audience demographics solely by region.

Even though "bomba" signifies the Spanish word for "bomb," that is not what the *musical* context means. Some speculate that the Spanish term "bomba" is a mistranslation of the French musical term *bamboula*. How is that linked to France? Some point to the writings from André Pierre Ledru, who visited Puerto Rico in 1797 to document the geography and people. He refers to the bamboula (the drum, song, and dance processes) in a description of his visit to Loiza. The Spanish mistranslation (as "bomba") appears in the 1860s via the Puerto Rican author Julio Vizcarrondo, on the grounds that people on the island had been using that term decades earlier. Those who want more information about the theoretical aspects of bomba should consult the ethnographic study from Salvador Ferreras.[27]

Concerning the geographical regions covered for this study, there have been instances where governments and news media outlets in the nineteenth and twentieth centuries attempted to suppress or devalue African cultures, syncretic religions, and practices: often through fearmongering and racism by intentionally presenting false information. One must also take into consideration that many of the respective ethnographic and anthropological studies about the Gullah/Geechee and Afro-Latin communities in relation to religion and other customs derive from cultural outsiders. A more tactful approach to avoiding biases in ethnographic work is to try and maintain cultural respect instead of hastily jumping to conclusions and creating false assumptions about people.

---

[26] Errol L. Montes Pizarro, *Mas ramas que raices: Dialogos musicales entre el Caribe y el continente africano* (San Juan Ediciones Callejón, 2018).

[27] tucidides, "Andre Pierre Ledru en Puerto Rico 1797," *Asociación Estudiantil de Historia: Recinto de Rio Piedras, Universidad de Puerto Rico* (2 abril 2010) https://aehuprrp.wordpress.com/2010/04/02/andre-pierre-ledru-en-puerto-rico-1797/ (accessed August 18, 2021); Salvador E. Ferreras, *Solo Drumming in the Puerto Rican Bomba: An Analysis of Musical Processes and Improvisational Strategies* (Vancouver, BC, CA: University of British Columbia), 2005, PhD. Dissertation, https://open.library.ubc.ca/cIRcle/collections/ubctheses/831/items/1.0092337#downloadfiles (accessed August 28, 2019).

While establishing cultural respect forms a significant part of ethnography and musicological research, early attempts at understanding Gullah/Geechee and Afro-Latin communities would demonstrate racism and cultural exploitation to attract and motivate readers. Such unscientific approaches proved that some scholars did not know enough about the cultures that they were studying. That is why I address these past attempts at ethnographic fieldwork to demonstrate the incorrect and unethical nature of some of the approaches at the time.

Details About the Gullah/Geechee and Afro-Latin Communities

One important point to understand at the outset of this investigation is that the existing scholarship about Gullah/Geechee and Afro-Latin people demonstrates an imbalance in terms of resources. Myriad articles and books have been written about Cuban and Brazilian history and culture: too many. Concerning resources that focus on Puerto Rico, consider that many academic materials that discuss "Puerto Ricanness" combine or compare historiographies of life and customs on the island under Spanish and U.S. colonial rule with transnational migration and adaptation to the mainland U.S. Although most of that latter information addresses the effects of migration to New York City, it is a mistake to assume that Puerto Rican migration to the mainland United States is restricted to New York. Some information clearly refutes that assumption and demonstrates the significance of other states in relation to Puerto Rican migration, like Florida.[28]

What about the Gullah/Geechee? Credible information about that community presents sporadic resources. One possible reason for this is that some previous research on specific states within the Gullah/Geechee Cultural Heritage Corridor present scant or uneven details. Most primary and secondary sources about the Gullah/Geechee that I have encountered throughout this investigation concentrate more on South Carolina and Georgia than on Florida and North Carolina, with South Carolina receiving the bulk of academic

---

[28] Jorge Duany, "Mickey Ricans? The Recent Puerto Rican Diaspora to Florida," (Miami, Florida International University, 2012), 1-43, https://scholarcommons.usf.edu/cgi/viewcontent.cgi?article=1019&context=las hhfc (accessed February 17, 2021). Conference Paper; Jorge Duany and Patricia Silver, "The 'Puerto Ricanization' of Florida: Historical Background and Current Status," *Centro Journal* XXII, No. 1 (2010). https://www.redalyc.org/html/377/37721077001/ (accessed March 25, 2019).

attention. Research about the Gullah/Geechee in Florida demonstrates good, albeit preliminary, efforts. In terms of the scholarship about the Gullah/Geechee in coastal Georgia, the state features the Geechee Kunda Center in Riceboro, complete with relevant artifacts collected by the late Jim Bacote. Since the 2020s, it currently operates as a nonprofit (501c3) organization under the name *Geechee Kunda Cultural Arts Center & Museum*.[29] Riceboro also hosts the annual RiceFest, where visitors can sample different West African-based rice dishes, learn about rice cultivation, and experience Gullah Geechee music. Amy Lotson Roberts and Patrick J. Holladay have also published their findings on Gullah/Geechee culture in Georgia in 2019. Their research functions mainly as a hybrid travel and historical narrative. Roberts and Holladay attempt to educate tourists about important Gullah/Geechee communities, landmarks, people, and key historical events: presented in a manner that does not exploit the culture.[30] Resources on the Gullah/Geechee presence in North Carolina have started to accumulate over the past few years. Poplar Grove Plantation near Wilmington, North Carolina has been documenting the history of the Gullah/Geechee people in that area by uncovering details about slavery and agriculture: with specific focus on the significance of the peanut crop.[31]

Much has been written about the British link to the Gullah/Geechee in relation to slavery in the United States and the significance of 1619. However, contemporary research reveals that some scholars have tried to encourage audiences to expand their understanding of enslavement in the American colonies beyond this date. To clarify, such researchers do *not* suggest that people forget

---

[29] Geechee Kunda Cultural Arts Center & Museum, "Home," *Geechee Kunda Cultural Arts Center & Museum*, https://www.geecheekunda.org/home (accessed January 19, 2022).

[30] Kim Gusby, "Geechee Kunda: Preserving, celebrating Gullah-Geechee culture." *WSAV 3* (February 14, 2019). https://www.wsav.com/events/celebrating-black-history/geechee-kunda-preserving-celebrating-gullah-geechee-culture/1783268009 (accessed March 13. 2019); Orlando Montoya, "Remembering Jim Bacote." *Connect Savannah* (June 6, 2018). https://www.connectsavannah.com/savannah/remembering-jim-bacote/Content?oid=8618900 (accessed March 13, 2019); Amy Lotson Roberts and Patrick J. Holladay, PhD. *Gullah Geechee Heritage in the Golden Isles*. Stroud, UK (?): HISTORY Press, 2019.

[31] Poplar Grove Plantation, "Gullah Geechee Corridor," http://poplargrove.org/discover/gullah-geechee-2/ (accessed August 16, 2021).

about 1619. They urge the public to rethink slavery in colonial America as occurring *earlier* in time and involving multiple colonizers.

Michael Guasco finds the constant use of 1619 as a troubling historical marker because of its English revisionist implications. He warns readers that the frequent acceptance of that year promotes a dangerously selective memory by favoring British contributions to the formation of the United States over the much older colonial Spanish, who arrived earlier and imported enslaved Africans in the sixteenth century.[32] Guasco is not alone in expressing alarm over such historical inaccuracy. Rick Springston addresses similar concerns over the frequent neglect of the Spanish involvement in the transatlantic slave trade. He also stresses that American colonization began in St. Augustine, Florida in 1565: *not* in Jamestown, Virginia in 1607. Despite efforts to mention these problems and persuade readers to think more critically, the anglicized narrative behind 1619 remains for many the "initial" year for the painful chapter in United States history.[33] In relation to the Gullah/Geechee, areas like St. Helena Island, South Carolina candidly acknowledge the historical impact of Latin American cultures on the community. This is best evidenced in the exterior flag displays at the annual Gullah Heritage Fest at the Penn Center , which feature representations of countries like Cuba and Brazil.

Readers should not misinterpret the information that I present as revisionist history. Revisionist narratives, like "White Savior" interpretations, attempt to either erase or minimize crucial historical moments (often in relation to marginalized cultures and groups) and replace them with romanticized versions of what occurred in the past. Although this tactic has become more prominent in the 2020s as a political device for cultural suppression in the United States[34], I

---

[32] Michael Guasco, "The Misguided Focus on 1619 as the Beginning of Slavery in the U.S. Damages Our Understanding of American History." Smithsonian (September 13, 2017), https://www.smithsonianmag.com/history/misguided-focus-1619-beginning-slavery-us-damages-our-understanding-american-history-180964873/ (accessed June 19, 2019).

[33] Rick Springston, "Much of what we've been told about Virginia's 1619 first Africans is wrong." *Virginia Mercury* (August 11, 2019). https://www.virginiamercury.com/2019/08/11/what-are-we-commemorating-much-of-what-weve-been-told-about-virginias-1619-first-africans-is-wrong/ (accessed December 30, 2019)

[34] Sarah Ellison, "How the 1619 Project Took Over 2020," *Washington Post* (October 13, 2020), https://www.washingtonpost.com/lifestyle/style/1619-project-took-over-2020-inside-story/2020/10/13/af537092-00df-11eb-897d-3a6201d6643f_story.html (accessed June 28, 2021).

encourage readers to *expand upon* what they know about the colonization of the U.S. and demonstrate that other foreign colonizing powers also participated in the process: colonizers who were equally as cruel as the British settlers and who also promoted the enslavement of Africans.

Discussions concerning musical aspects of Gullah/Geechee culture present mixed results. Gullah/Geechee music serves primarily as an oral and aural cultural tradition. Except for some spirituals, songs within the Gullah/Geechee culture are mostly not notated. Most of the related sources available stem from audio recordings (either as field or commercial recordings) and textual transcriptions, which apply to both recorded music and speech. I have found it best to avoid the pitfall of cultural homogeneity: in this case, that the instruments involved in Gullah/Geechee music remain the same across the Gullah/Geechee Heritage Corridor. While it is true that singing and clapping serve as the common instrumentation in South Carolina, it is not the same in places like coastal Georgia. Areas like Riceboro, Georgia apply extra instruments to reinforce the percussive elements of music like Ring Shouts. It is also incorrect to assume that religious music and the Ring Shout serve as the *only* notable forms of Gullah/Geechee music just because they receive the most attention in academia. One must additionally consider other types of music within the Gullah/Geechee culture, like "play songs" directed towards children and protest songs that stress civil and socioeconomic equal rights.[35]

This research mentions perceptions of "race" and African identity in Latin America and the Caribbean in relation to music, history, religion, and culture. My discussions serve as more than just a comparison among Latin America, the Caribbean, and the United States. They refer to the contemporary scholarship on this topic (of which, sources abound) and explore the historical and sociocultural effects and of acceptance versus denial of Blackness and African identity in Latin America and the Caribbean. In doing this, I demonstrate the polarizing effects of acknowledging this identity: mainly, that some people in the United States accept this identity more candidly than in parts of Latin America and the Caribbean.

---

[35] Ranky Tanky, *Good Time*, Resilience Music, LLC., 2019 (accessed November 1, 2019). https://open.spotify.com/album/00U3tf4nUq23aULqpiBbZt.

Accessing credible resources about the Gullah/Geechee or Afro-Latin communities can often prove complicated. At times, it may be tempting for some readers or scholars to jump to conclusions and assume that certain crucial pieces of information do not exist merely because nobody wrote about it. This logic presents an egregious error in terms of research. One should never assume that credible information on a given topic is nonexistent simply because the resources are inaccessible or difficult to locate.

Parts of the current study incorporate research from my previous investigation on the Gullah/Geechee community and audio recording preservation entitled "Your Voice is My Sound: Audio Recording Technology, Identity and Re-Creating the Gullah/Geechee Diaspora." In this respect, this serves as an extension of these academic materials by including information not previously addressed. These can be found in instances like Chapter 6, where I provide details regarding the ethnomusicological efforts of the Society for the Preservation of Spirituals.

Archival Materials

Locating audio recordings related to the Gullah/Geechee and Afro-Latin cultures serves as both a beneficial and complex experience. To comprehend the reason for this conflict, one must think about several aspects. This process involves factoring the impact of modernity on the Gullah/Geechee and Afro-Latin people through these recordings and the accessibility of these recordings to audiences in the twenty-first century. Devices like the phonograph and gramophone, developed in the 1870s and 90s by Thomas Edison and Emile Berliner respectively, functioned as devices for both dictation *and* music. This is known because Edison wrote extensively about his perceptions of the phonograph in 1878 and 1888[36]: information which is currently accessible to researchers in the twenty-first century. The patents for the phonograph and gramophone can also be accessed and downloaded online. Researchers can easily view the blueprints and

---

[36] Thomas A. Edison, "The Phonograph and its Future." *North American Review* 126, No. 262 (1878). https://www.jstor.org/stable/pdf/25110210.pdf (accessed January 4, 2020); "The Perfected Phonograph." 146, No. 379 (1888). https://www.jstor.org/stable/pdf/25101531.pdf (accessed January 4, 2020).

textual descriptions regarding the functionality of each machine and their respective parts.[37]

Most of the early Gullah/Geechee audio recordings date from the early twentieth century, beginning roughly in the 1920s. Given this information, researchers should also think critically about how modernization positively and negatively affected the Gullah/Geechee people via the construction of bridges linking the Corridor to the rest of the southern regions of the United States in the 1950s. Consider that this event presented a dichotomy. It allowed for cultural visibility through preservation activities, tourism, and Gullah/Geechee heritage festivals for the public to experience. At the same time, it also promoted *invisibility* through external developments on Gullah/Geechee land and cultural exploitation.[38] The available audio recordings also apply the advancements in sound technology throughout the decades: from wax cylinders and acetate discs to magnetic tape and digital restorations. Further research also indicates that many of these audio recordings from the early twentieth century, usually in the form of ethnographic field recordings, devote equal attention to music and speech.

Audio recordings of Latin American music (and, in some cases, speech) also date from the early twentieth century, albeit several decades prior in the 1900s and 1910s. The type of music varies. In the case of Puerto Rico, for instance, some recordings tend to focus on the *música típica* (folk music) from the mountainous regions of the island. While I have mentioned that aspect in previous musicological

---

[37] Thomas A. Edison, "Improvement in phonograph or speaking machines," US Patent 200,521 (February 19, 1878), *Google Patents*, https://patents.google.com/patent/US200521A/en (accessed January 4, 2020); Emile Berliner, "Gramophone, &c." US Patent 637,197 (January 25, 1899), *Google Patents*, https://patents.google.com/patent/US637197A/en (accessed January 3, 2020).

[38] Bynum Boley and Cassandra Johnson Gaither, "Exploring empowerment within the Gullah Geechee cultural heritage corridor: implications for heritage tourism development in the Lowcountry." *Journal of Heritage Tourism* (2015), http://dx.doi.org/10.1080/1743873X.2015.1080712 (accessed September 10, 2019); Ken Otterbourg, "Being Gullah or Geechee, Once Looked Down On, Now a Treasured Heritage," *National Geographic* (October 16, 2014), https://www.nationalgeographic.com/news/2014/10/141017-gullah-geechee-heritage-corridor-lowcountry-coast-sea-islands-sweetgrass/ (accessed January 4, 2020).

research[39], this current research expands that information with the availability of more digital resources. I also include discussions about audio recordings and audio archiving resources from both Puerto Rico and stateside areas.

Archived recordings pertaining to the Gullah/Geechee and Latin American cultures have recently undergone digitalization in efforts to restore and disseminate the available information for future generations. Based on this detail, readers and researchers must consider the following questions: some of which do not have immediate or definitive answers. Which archival centers in the United States and abroad control the distribution of these audio recordings? What purposes do these recordings serve: educational, artistic or both? If this music has been digitized in contemporary times, then how can people access these materials? In terms of Gullah/Geechee audio recordings as archival artifacts, what can people discern from their contents? What about the emic (insider) and etic (outsider) perspectives of these recordings (or, to briefly borrow the Gullah/Geechee language, *Binya* versus *Comya*)? Does the act of recording and preserving music from the Gullah/Geechee culture constitute a form of respect? Or, does it promote cultural exploitation and assimilation? Early investigations into these questions reveal that people have used Gullah/Geechee and Latin American audio recordings both to teach listeners and as inspiration for musicians. Their overall impacts vary by approach based on the comprehension of the cultures, or lack thereof. I refer to several audio archival centers and digital resources in this book:

1) American Folklife Center
2) Library of Congress
3) *Voices in Time* (YouTube channel)
4) Association for Cultural Equity (ACE)
5) the "Grabaciones" ("Audio Recordings") section of the Archivo Virtual Instituto de Cultura Puertorriqueña (ICP).[40]
6) The Colección Gladys Palmera (Gladys Palmera Collection)

---

[39] Anthony L. Sanchez Cruz, *The Jíbaro and the Gaucho United in Music and Song* (English Translation), Vancouver, BC: Ditrie Marie Bowie, 2019.

[40] Virtual Archive Institute for Puerto Rican Culture.

About the Author

Robyn Mitchell left the comforts of teaching in a classroom to explore the open road in an 18-wheel sandhauler. Her experiences and time on the road birthed Mother Trucker, a series of suspenseful thrillers based on the trouble and happiness Shelby Mathews—a well-educated, gorgeous blonde, wife, and mother of three grown men—finds while trucking.

<u>**Read More**</u>
<u>**Mother Trucker Book Series**</u>
Mother Trucker
Trucktress
Outlaws
Jumpers
Terror West

7) *Memórias Afro-Atlânticas: as gravações de Lorenzo Dow Turner na Bahia (1940-1941)*[41] (Vagner Soares' YouTube Channel)

Some people will notice throughout this study that I include several social media links and documentary films as part of the research. My reasoning behind this choice is not to take shortcuts with academia. I realize that most social media outlets have a bad reputation for posting commercial, misleading, or irrelevant content on their platforms. At the same time, however, organizations and academic institutions have also embraced these platforms to educate audiences through virtual lectures, colloquia, and other valuable resources. This process has especially become crucial in the era of the Coronavirus pandemic.[42] At times, these resources include information that cannot be found elsewhere. I also realize that documentary films can also contain inaccuracies or biases due to some mistakes or shoddy reporting. Nevertheless, the documentaries that I refer to come from scholars who have thoroughly researched their topics, The documentaries that I found concerning Africanized syncretic religions also feature interviews with the people who practice these religions. It is for these reasons that I treat such intangible material as supplemental to this discussion.

Interviews and Correspondence Letters with Members of the Gullah/Geechee

Uncovering information about the Gullah/Geechee culture requires a lot more than citing printed and electronic materials through books and articles. Researching a given culture means that the researcher must also participate in the community in some form or another. This involves either physically visiting the people or communicating with specialists from the respective cultural communities for guidance. These processes frequently require travelling and remote communication via e-mail. Recording interviews for this research also means expressing tact and respect for the cultures in question.

Bruno Nettl and Bonnie C. Wade attest in their guidance about musical ethnographic field research that the process must involve an approach that avoids invasiveness. Informants must be notified of

---

[41] *Afro-Atlantic Memories: The Recordings of Lorenzo Dow Turner in Bahia (1940-1941)*

[42] Gullah Geechee Chamber of Commerce, "Covid-19," (2020), *Gullah Geechee Chamber of Commerce,* https://www.gullahgeecheechamber.org/corona-virus-covid-19/ (accessed July 23, 2021).

interviews in advance so that they know what to expect. Depending on the academic environment, such as in a university setting, ethnographers must also comply with the regulations established by the Internal Review Board (IRB) beforehand to avoid violating ethical codes.[43] Independent researchers working outside the scope of a university often do not need to worry about such restrictions and obstacles. In my case, I had to ask for permission and consent from the informants verbally and in writing through e-mail before I sent them my interview questions or corresponded with them.

Transcribing ethnographic interviews can frequently come off as tedious work (because it is). It is also a necessary and effective process for gathering information from people within communities. Documenting recorded field interviews through written transcriptions also involves listening to what the informants said: *not* assuming what they said. Ethnography, in this sense, involves striving for as much accuracy as possible and carefully exercising judgement about what information to keep, what to remove that could be deemed trivial, and how to describe mannerisms. "Appendix D" features a transcription excerpt of an ethnographic interview that I conducted in January 2020 with the head of a local radio station manager in Beaufort, South Carolina. I made sure to concentrate on what the informant said and take out redundancies in the (excessive uses of "um," and "uh.") In certain sections in the transcription, I present words or phrases in parentheses that try to clarify what is being discussed. I use question marks or educated guesses for parts that are difficult to hear or interpret.

Demonstrating respect for another culture is key because it attempts to avoid personal assumptions and observational biases. As I will discuss later, and like I demonstrated with the WPA Slave Narratives, some ethnographers and scholars in the past would either directly or indirectly allow their prejudices to mar the credibility of their research. At the same time, though, it can prove difficult to maintain respect for all cultures all the time. Ethnographic field research will almost always include moments of resentment toward cultural

---

[43] Bruno Nettl, "10. Come Back and See Me Next Tuesday: Essentials of the Fieldwork Tradition," in *The Study of Ethnomusicology: Thirty-Three Discussions*, Urbana, IL: University of Illinois Press, 2015, 141-156; Bonnie C. Wade, "Chapter 7. Thinking About Fieldwork," in *Thinking Musically: Experiencing Music, Expressing Culture*, New York: Oxford University Press, 2013, 195-204.

outsiders from a group under study.[44] In the case of learning about the Gullah/Geechee, researchers must try to gain trust and respect from the people within the community to demonstrate that the work in question will not exploit the culture. Throughout the research, I carefully explained the purpose for each interview or correspondence e-mail, wrote several relevant questions beforehand and asked the informants for permission to include their words in this current research.

---

[44] Bruno Nettl, "11. You Will Never Understand This Music: Insiders and Outsiders," in *The Study of Ethnomusicology: Thirty-Three Discussions*, Urbana, IL: University of Illinois Press, 2015, 157-168.

Selected Culture Theories (and Their Problems)

"… that complex whole which includes knowledge, belief, art, law, morals, custom, and any other capabilities and habits acquired by man as a member of society."

~Edward B. Tylor on Defining Culture

The following sections provide an overview of the significance and practicability of certain culture theories and concepts, in addition to critiquing their problems. I cover this information, specifically transculturation theory, in greater detail in my previous investigations on Latin American and Caribbean music.[45] Readers should not assume, though, that all scholars concur with the definitions and applications of transculturation and cultural appropriation. In certain instances, some academics expand upon or refute previous research. While some researchers write about transculturation from a positive standpoint, like Fernando Ortiz, other scholars cannot ignore the negative consequences of the theory on the identities of different cultures under study. Fabienne Viala, for instance, suggests that transculturation can promote selective memory by focusing too much on the actions of cultural outsiders and oppressors.[46] Discussions about cultural appropriation, while plentiful, also reveal glaring problems. Some scholars who talk about the concept do not come to a consensus regarding how to properly define it. What is more, its contemporary application to culture studies often serves to denote politicized arguments in both academia and society via unscientific information.

Contemporary research from the 1990s and beyond also applies different or archaic terminology when discussing the processes

---

[45] Anthony L. Sanchez, *The Puerto Rican Cuatro as a Device for Transculturation: A Contemporary Compositional Approach in Estampas de La Isla del Encanto.* University of Georgia, D.M.A. Dissertation. http://dbs.galib.uga.edu/cgi-bin/getd.cgi?userid=galileo&serverno=18&instcode=publ&_cc=1 (accessed December 30, 2019); *The Jíbaro and the Gaucho United in Music and Song* (English Translation), Vancouver, BC: Ditrie Marie Bowie, 2019.

[46] Fernando Ortiz and Harriet de Onís (English Trans.). "II. The Ethnography and Transculturation of Havanna Tobacco and the Beginnings of Sugar in America. 2: The Social Phenomenon of Transculturation and its Importance," in *Cuban Counterpoint, Tobacco and Sugar* (Durham, NC: Duke University Press, 1995). 97-103; Fabienne Viala, "Chapter 1: Transculturation as Commemoration: Fernando Ortiz, The Cuban *longue duree*, and the Role of Columbus," in *The Post-Columbus Syndrome: Identities, Cultural Nationalism, and Commemorations in the Caribbean.* (New York: Palgrave Macmillan, 2014), 21-39.

behind cultural contact and transformation. Throughout this project, I have found uses of the terms *cross culturation*, *syncretism*, and *acculturation*. I find this last part strange, considering that acculturation functioned as an anthropological theory as early as the 1930s. Some scholars in the 1980s, like Margaret J. Kartomi, have no longer accepted acculturation as a practical theory when discussing aspects of cultural contact.[47]

The Convoluted Meanings of "Race," "Ethnicity," "Diaspora," and "Racialization"

Peter Wade defines "race" according to its European contexts. He accomplishes this by tracing the historical applications of this word: from the Bible and forms of ethnocentric pseudo-sciences up to the nineteenth century, to eugenics and anthropology in the twentieth century. Wade concludes that some interpretations of race as a term involve focusing on categories and phenotypes of people.[48] He also mentions that the word "ethnicity" contains a European connection. However, it features a slightly more contemporary origin via the nineteenth and twentieth centuries. To contrast with race, Wade focuses on the problem associated with defining ethnicity: that the concept concentrates too much on understanding groups of people via their points of origin (meaning, the country in which they were born or their family heritage through generations).[49]

More contemporary scholarship on "race" and "ethnicity" from the twenty-first century attempts to both expand and re-evaluate public and academic perceptions of these concepts. Such research often involves addressing the application of racialization and culturally essentialist ideas. Scholars who succumb to these errors often rely on assumptions and groundless data about "race" to support their claims. Research in modern genetics often encourages the public to think about "race" more as a social construction and the dangers of racial discrimination rather than focusing on phenotypical biology via categorization as defining factors for humanity (eg., "White" and "Black" people). While there technically is no such thing as "race,"

---

[47] Margaret J. Kartomi, "The Processes and Result of Musical Culture Contact: A Discussion of Terminology and Concepts." *Ethnomusicology* 25, No. 2 (1981), 227-249, http://www.jstor.org/stable/851273 (accessed December 1, 2019).

[48] Peter Wade, "The Meaning of 'Race' and 'Ethnicity,'" in *Race and Ethnicity in Latin America.* Sterling, VA: Pluto Press, 1997, 5-24.

[49] Peter Wade, 1997.

such research also encourages deeper understandings of racism and its social effects.[50]

The term "diaspora" has also sparked intriguing debate in terms of its historical, anthropological, and sociological uses. Janna Evans Braziel and Anita Mannur try to define diaspora in relation to migration and immigration to the United States. Based on their research, they explain that diaspora serves two main purposes. The first highlights a common mistake behind comprehending this term, which stems from the fact that people confuse it with the deceptively similar term "transnationalism." To clarify their differences in meaning, Braziel and Mannur define "transnationalism" in terms of the effects of globalization. "Disapora," by contrast, denotes the *physical* process of groups travelling from place to place.[51].

The second function of diaspora stresses that people also consider the *economic* impacts of this concept within a global context. While both functions can apply to Latin Americans who move to the United States, Braziel and Mannur indicate that diaspora includes migrants and immigrants from *all* groups. Oftentimes, these groups move to the United States to escape physical or economic conflicts in their native countries. Depending on the generation of migrants or immigrants, many choose to adapt to United States customs and lifestyles while simultaneously maintaining traditions established in their previous homelands.[52]

More Contemporary Perceptions of "Race" and "Ethnicity"

Given what I just discussed, I must add that there exist multiple interpretations of "race" and "ethnicity." These interpretations often depend on the scientific or social perceptions of these terms and their conceptual variants. Contemporary debates often argue that, from the scientific perspectives of biology and genetics, "race" technically does not exist.[53] The reason why "race" persists as a point of discussion,

---

[50] Andrew Smart et al, "1. 'Race' as Social Construction in Genetics," in *Identity Politics and the New Genetics Re/Creating Categories of Difference and Belonging*, edited by Katharina Schramm, David Skinner, and Richard Rottenburg (New York: Berghahn, 2015), 30-52.

[51] Jana Evans Braziel and Anita Mannur, "Nation, Migration, Globalization: Points of Contention in Diaspora Studies," in *Theorizing Diaspora: A Reader*. Malden, MA: Blackwell Publishing Ltd, 2003, 1-21.

[52] Jana Evans Braziel and Anita Mannur, 2003.

[53] Andrew Smart et al, "1. 'Race' as Social Construction in Genetics," in *Identity Politics and the New Genetics Re/Creating Categories of Difference and Belonging*, edited by Katharina

according to Smart et al and Miles and Brown, stems from the social (mis)understanding of visible, physical differences in human beings and groups as "definitive" attributes. While these scholars also discuss the historical impact of "race," they do so primarily to illustrate the flawed (and alarmingly unscientific) approaches from the past. They point out that uncritical social (and academic) discussions about "race" can often give way to aspects of racism, which destroy the credibility about research about cultures.[54]

"Ethnicity" proves equally problematic in terms of culture studies. Miles and Brown indicate that the term has frequently been applied as an alternative to "race." The issue concerning its potential for spreading racism stems from the social application of "ethnicity" as a designation for groups of people. Within that context, the misinterpretations of "ethnicity" concentrate on the physical differences via categorization. This can denote racist tendencies through ethnicization, which often can give way to internal social class conflicts.[55]

Transculturation: A Cultural Fusion?

What about transculturation? How does *that* theory relate to everything that I just said? Transculturation theory encompasses multiple academic disciplines. I have previously examined transculturation from the musical perspective within the contexts of music composition and Latin American cultures from Puerto Rico and Argentina.[56] It also deserves mention that, despite its initial emphasis on Latin American cultures, transculturation is not limited to these regions and should be understood on a global scale.

I had talked about Fernando Ortiz (1881-1969) in previous research regarding transculturation theory and his publication, *Cuban Counterpoint: Tobacco and Sugar* from 1940. As a cultural anthropologist, his research at that time initially refuted the effectiveness of *acculturation* and examined the sociocultural and economic conditions in his native Cuba throughout history by using tobacco and sugar cultivation as

---

Schramm, David Skinner, and Richard Rottenburg (New York: Berghann, 2015), 30-52.

[54] Andrew Smart et al, 30-52; Robert Miles and Malcolm Brown, "4. On signification," in *Racism (Second Edition)* (London: Routledge, 2003), 87-114.

[55] Robert Miles and Malcolm Brown, 87-114.

[56] Anthony L. Sanchez, *The Jíbaro and the Gaucho United in Music and Song* (English Translation), Vancouver, BC: Ditrie Marie Bowie, 2019.

comparative metaphors. Transculturation theory constitutes a process between two cultures and involves three crucial steps: the loss of the old culture (in the case of Fernando Ortiz and his research, the indigenous and African populations in Cuba), acquiring the new culture (the European Spanish) and the combination and coexistence of the two through a new identity.[57]

Just like with diaspora, transculturation theory does not mean the same thing as *transnationalism*. I have already hinted that that theory frequently presents confusing meanings with no clear agreement on the subject from scholars. Research in the 2000s from Laura Briggs, Gladys McCormick and J.T. Way complement or expand upon what Janna Evans Braziel and Anita Mannur uncover in their research. Briggs, McCormick and Way encourage perceiving transnationalism as a form of globalization and imperialism through United States commercial and cultural intervention and influences.[58]

Transculturation theory, as Fernando Ortiz uses it in his research, functions as a tool for explaining the effects of immigration and cultural contact in Cuba. Although Ortiz does briefly discuss the early Spanish colonization on the island, he concentrates more on the influx and impact of foreigners from other areas of Europe and Asia on the Caribbean country. According to Ortiz, these cultures who arrived and established themselves in Cuba all had to sacrifice part of the cultural customs from their homeland and adjust to their current environment.[59] As a result of their sacrifices and adaptations, they created new and fused cultures. In the case of the African populations, Ortiz acknowledges that immigration carried a different connotation for the varied groups (which he does not explicitly specify) who arrived

---

[57] Fernando Ortiz and Harriet de Onís (English Trans.). "II. The Ethnography and Transculturation of Havanna Tobacco and the Beginnings of Sugar in America. 2: The Social Phenomenon of Transculturation and its Importance," in *Cuban Counterpoint, Tobacco and Sugar* (Durham, NC: Duke University Press, 1995). 97 103.

[58] Laura Briggs, Gladys McCormick and J.T. Way, "Transnationalism: A Category of Analysis" *American Quarterly* 60. 3 (2008), https://pages.ucsd.edu/~rfrank/class_web/ES-200A/Week%207/60.3.briggs.pdf (accessed February 5, 2020).

[59] Fernando Ortiz and Harriet de Onís (English Trans.), "II. The Ethnography and Transculturation of Havanna Tobacco and the Beginnings of Sugar in America. 2: The Social Phenomenon of Transculturation and its Importance," in *Cuban Counterpoint, Tobacco and Sugar* (Durham, NC: Duke University Press, 1995). 97-103.

ACKNOWLEDGMENTS

I would like to thank Danielle H. Acee, Mindy Reed, Douglas Brown, and all those involved in editing and perfecting the text. Their guidance made the book release possible.

I also can't forget all of the individuals who supported me with their encouragement—my daughter-in-law, Cydney and my friends, Tina, Tamra, and Tammy. To so many others (truckers, friends, family members) who helped me in this endeavor, sometimes without even knowing it, thank you.

I will always remember all those who helped make this dream a reality.

With all my heart forever.
—Robyn Mitchell
robynmitchellauthor.com

in Cuba under enslavement.[60] As I will discuss in a later section concerning Afro-Latin religious practices, the way in which Ortiz understood the Afro-Cuban population evolved over the long span of his career in Criminology, Law, Spiritism, and Anthropology: from candidly racist assumptions in the 1900s to a more Positivist outlook in later decades.

This does not suggest that the theoretical work behind transculturation does not contain errors. Ortiz perceives transculturation as a "solution" to racial discrimination. At the same time, he also promotes cultural mixing (*mestizaje*) as part of that solution. His theory also stresses the dominance of the new, foreign culture: in this instance, Spain, over the indigenous and African influences. Transculturation also leads to the loss of cultural identity by partially abdicating the older culture and customs.[61] Thinking within these contexts, one can see that the racialized ideas about Cuba and Afro-Cubans espoused by Ortiz shift from overt to covert. I say "covert" because cultural miscegenation remains a debatable topic in the twenty-first century: not just in Cuba, but throughout Latin America and the Caribbean.

Cultural Appropriation: Cultural Theft, or Unscientific Nonsense?

Studies concerning cultural appropriation, which frequently gets used interchangeably with "appropriation," suggest difficulties in theorizing the concept due to multiple (mis)interpretations depending on a given topic. Many scholars in the 2000s, like John O. Young, Emanuel Melissaris and Marcus Boon, write about cultural appropriation as it pertains to law and branches of the arts.[62] Music is not exempt from

---

[60] Fernando Ortiz and Harriet de Onís, 97-103.

[61] Fernando Ortiz, 97-103.

[62] James O Young, "Art, Authenticity and Appropriation." *Frontiers of Philosophy in China.* 1, No. 3 (2006). https://www.jstor.org/stable/30209982?Search=yes&resultItemClick=true&searchText=%22Authenticity+and+Appropriation.%22&searchUri=%2Faction%2Fdo BasicSearch%3FQuery%3D%25E2%2580%259CAuthenticity%2Band%2BAppro priation.%25E2%2580%259D%26amp%3Bfilter%3D&ab_segments=0%2Fbasic_ SYC-4929%2Ftest&seq=1 (accessed December 30, 2019); Emmanuel Melissaris, "The Concept of Appropriation and the Offence of Theft." *Modern Law Review.* 70, No. 1 (2007). https://www.jstor.org/stable/4543155 (accessed December 30, 2019); Marcus Boon, "On Appropriation." *CR: The New Centennial Review*, 7, No. 1 (2007). https://www.jstor.org/stable/41942891?Search=yes&resultItemClick=true&searc hText=On&searchText=Appropriation&searchUri=%2Faction%2FdoBasicSearch

these discussions of the concept. In the 2010s, scholars and critics wrote extensively about appropriating African American popular music by artists outside of the culture. This topic has frequently surfaced and resurfaced via debates online and through social media platforms, often with polarizing reception.[63]

Critiques of cultural appropriation in music or other subjects usually perceive the process on a basic level as stealing from another culture. More specifically, appropriation involves taking and applying materials from another, foreign culture and claiming it as original or individual artistic inspiration. Although many discussions address intent as a factor of appropriation, the process can function both in a direct and indirect manner. Given the staggering amount of scholarship concerning cultural appropriation, it can come as a surprise to readers that many who explain the concept do not explore it well enough as a theory. They mostly imply what the process signifies in simple terms and assume that readers will comprehend it.

Richard A. Rogers has attempted to provide a concrete theory about cultural appropriation in his research from 2006. Rogers examines cultural appropriation as a process that incorporates four types of cultural contact: the exchange of cultures, the dominance of one culture over the other, the exploitation of a foreign culture (usually due to cultural dominance), and the transculturation process.[64] I find the inclusion of transculturation unusual because, as I demonstrated earlier, much of the previous research on transculturation does not describe the concept as a type of cultural theft. Based on the information presented by Rogers, cultural appropriation involves some form of power acquisition and struggle between two cultures. This struggle usually stems from an external culture or group claiming

%3FQuery%3DOn%2BAppropriation&ab_segments=0%2Fbasic_SYC-4929%2Ftest&refreqid=search%3A4dee5fd0e07c5c151414979b56b5c922&seq=1 (accessed December 30, 2019).

[63] Tom Connick, "Bruno Mars accused of cultural appropriation." *NME* (March 13, 2018). https://www.nme.com/news/music/bruno-mars-accused-cultural-appropriation-2261789 (accessed December 30, 2019).

[64] Richard A. Rogers. "From Cultural Exchange to Transculturation: A Review and Reconceptualization of Cultural Appropriation." *Communication Theory* 16 (2006). http://jan.ucc.nau.edu/~rar/papers/RogersCT2006.pdf (accessed October 8, 2019).

resources from another foreign culture for creative or commercial purposes without crediting the original culture.[65]

Cultural appropriation *could* appear obvious on the surface in terms of the first three processes outlined by Rogers, especially with the effects of dominance and exploitation. However, Rogers views transculturation as a conflicting component of cultural appropriation. Transculturation signifies the fusion that results from cultural contact. Recall that transculturation involves combining old and new cultures and customs to create a distinct identity or society.[66] As Rogers indicates in his research, this result also proves problematic. *Both* cultures involved (the old and the new) partake in cultural theft, because they *both* absorb and learn customs from each other. Some people might not initially recognize transculturation as "theft," though, because the process also stresses the partial retention of the older culture.[67]

More recent research on cultural appropriation highlights several other problems that readers must consider. Erich Hatala Matthes reveals that cultural appropriation presents a dilemma in terms of the ethical and moral implications of the act through speech and cultural subjugation. However, he also takes issue with how the current scholarship addresses cultural appropriation. Matthes criticizes academics like John O. Young and Richard A. Rogers for not truly condemning cultural appropriation and its pernicious effects on society.[68]

Equally troublesome to Matthes is the methodology that most scholars apply to their work to describe (or, more commonly, to avoid) the concept. He does not perceive the opposite of cultural appropriation, *cultural essentialism*, as an effective enough tool. He indicates that cultural essentialism can also produce problems, because it inadvertently stresses cultural and societal differences through stereotyping and marginalization. This means that cultural essentialism can produce nearly the same effects as cultural appropriation.[69] Matthes primarily focuses on the overreliance on "insider" versus

---

[65] Richard A. Rogers, 2006.

[66] Richard A. Rogers, 2006.

[67] Richard A. Rogers, 2006.

[68] Erich Hatala Matthes, "Cultural Appropriation Without Cultural Essentialism?" *Social Theory and Practice* 42, No. 2 (2016), https://www.jstor.org/stable/24871347 (accessed September 24, 2020).

[69] Erich Hatala Matthes, 2016.

"outsider" distinctions, "oppressor" versus "oppressed" cultural relations, and the tendency to "speak for" another culture or community. He also highlights that addressing cultural appropriation by avoiding essentialist language, while possible, also does not really fix the problem.[70]

I also partially frame my investigation in the format that Matthes would describe as "essentialist." However, the goal for my research is neither to stereotype nor to "speak for" the respective Gullah/Geechee and Afro-Latin populations. My goal is to present and critique the data on these communities. Wherever possible, I also strive to get their perspectives in their own words.

In relation to the Gullah/Geechee, not everyone in these communities agrees with each other on how to accurately represent themselves. I refer to organizations like the Gullah/Geechee Nation and Gullah Geechee Cultural Heritage Corridor Commission. These organizations present opposing views on what defines Gullah/Geechee culture, and they often do not acknowledge each other. Readers must additionally consider that the Gullah/Geechee Nation and Gullah Geechee Cultural Heritage Corridor Commission promote Gullah/Geechee history and culture, but they do not "speak for" all Gullah/Geechee people. Take, for instance, the problem with commercially applying the names "Gullah" and "Geechee" to food and drink products. Over the past few years, manufacturers who have used these names would initially encounter backlash on social media from members of the Gullah/Geechee community on the grounds of cultural appropriation. Attempts to resolve the problem with the GGCHCC have caused more outrage from the Gullah/Geechee people, because many perceive that organization as not fully representative of the culture. Manufacturers have since agreed to rebrand their products due to mounting pressure from the Gullah/Geechee.[71]

One way that members of the Gullah/Geechee have sought to avoid cultural theft is by establishing their own businesses. This approach has become significant in the era of the Coronavirus

---

[70] Erich Hatala Matthes, 2016.

[71] Emily Williams, "Charleston businesses using 'Gullah' and 'Geechee' in brands say they'll change names," Charleston, SC: *Post and Courier* (July 20-September 14, 2020), https://www.postandcourier.com/business/charleston-businesses-using-gullah-and-geechee-in-brands-say-theyll-change-names/article_6854de70-c051-11ea-9dd9-eb93b822e43c.html (accessed September 24, 2020).

pandemic, where many companies have struggled to survive and reopen. In February 2021, I corresponded with a young entrepreneur named Sonya Grant (See photograph in Appendix F). Grant, whom I initially met that month at a Gullah Geechee food festival in South Carolina, manages an online clothing company called *Gullah Ts N' Tings*. I asked her the following questions via email as part of this study to get the perspective from the Gullah/Geechee youth about maintaining a business in times of uncertainty while still respecting the culture:

1) As a Gullah/Geechee business owner, what is your role in interpreting and disseminating information about the Gullah/Geechee community?

2) How did you start your company, and what were your goals in relation to the Gullah/Geechee?

3) How does your work aim to incorporate the entire Gullah/Geechee Heritage Corridor?

4) Realizing that cultural exploitation of the Gullah/Geechee has become a growing problem in recent years, how do you respond to possible negative criticisms from within the Gullah/Geechee community regarding your company?

5) What approaches do you use to educate the general public and younger generations of people about the Gullah/Geechee through your company?

6) How do you think that the Gullah/Geechee maintain relevance in the twenty-first century through social media platforms or collaborations with organizations related to Gullah/Geechee culture?

7) Given the impact of COVID-19, how would you say that the effects of the virus and Social Distancing have impacted the Gullah/Geechee community: either via your business, or other means?

8) Given the recent peaceful protests in solidarity for Black Lives Matter, how would you say that the Gullah/Geechee community

have reacted and responded to the events that have unfolded in the United States?[72]

The responses from Grant proved beneficial, in that they illustrate a dual purpose. She uses her clothing business to teach people about Gullah/Geechee culture. On the other end, as someone raised in Gullah/Geechee culture, she ensures that her work does not use exploitative material. Her answers also demonstrate how the Gullah/Geechee have adapted to the restrictions imposed by COVID-19 and the contemporary struggles that Black Americans face every day:

1) As a Gullah/ Geechee business owner my role is to bring awareness and create a greater sense of pride throughout the Gullah community and beyond through clothing and apparel.

2) I started my company during the Covid-19 pandemic, my original goal was to design something that I liked to share my culture with others and it has now turned into creating designs that my people will love and cherish and to make a mark in our history.

3) I incorporate the Gullah/ Geechee corridor in my work by highlighting each island and areas in my designs and hope to eventually sell locally in those areas.

4) I have yet to receive negative criticisms about my work.

5) I use my designs to educate the culture, for example, the "Crossword Tee" comes in several variation. Each variation highlights the communities where Gullah people reside. It gives others awareness about where they can still find rich culture traditions in this modern society.

6) That is exactly how we maintain relevancy, through social media, especially in a pandemic. Promoting the culture through art, virtual story tellings and even foods.

7) Although my business was started during the pandemic, the virus has heavily impacted Gullah tours that would usually be given and even

---

[72] Sonya Grant, "Correspondence E-mail to Sonya Grant," February 23, 2021.

classes taken by culture enthusiasts. My business would not exist had I not had the time to slow down and start it, but it would thrive even more if people had the chance to be educated first hand about the culture through the Gullah Tours here on Hilton Head Island.

8) The Gullah community has only become stronger despite the racial climate in the United States. Although always cherished by the elders, it has given the younger generations an even bigger reason to cling tighter to our roots and gain a deeper understanding on what it truly means to be Gullah.[73]

Similar problems concerning representation and cultural appropriation arise for Afro-Latin communities, like Puerto Rico in relation to the island and stateside communities. Both areas demonstrate pride and concern for Puerto Rican identity and heritage, and both feature Afro-Puerto Rican communities. However, their approaches to such matters can produce polarizing effects: often via Spanish and English language barriers, social causes, and musical appropriation of Blackness through genres like hip hop. The problem stems from when island or stateside Puerto Rican artists are publicly accused of appropriating from Black hip-hop musicians and genres. Such has been the case for artists like Bad Bunny, where public criticism online has produced polarization.[74]

Cultural appropriation not only affects the realm of popular music culture. The concept also illustrates problems with cultural representation in classical music by applying jazz elements (like the classical pieces by George Gershwin)[75], exoticism (music that evokes the culture from another country, albeit through a Westernized frame), and using non-Western[76] instruments by composers not from the culture. Alex Temple writes about cultural appropriation in contemporary classical music from the perspective of a composer. As

---

[73] Sonya Grant, February 23, 2021.

[74] Cristina Jerome, "Bad Bunny's Latin Trap is Cultural Appreciation, Not Appropriation," Miami: *Miami New Times* (March 7, 2019), https://www.miaminewtimes.com/music/things-to-do-miami-bad-bunny-at-american-airlines-arena-march-16-11103116 (accessed September 24, 2020).

[75] Ray Allen, "An American Folk Opera? Triangulating Folkness, Blackness and Africaness in Gershwin and Heyward's 'Porgy and Bess,'" *Journal of American Folklore* 117, No. 465 (2004), http://www-5.unipv.it/girardi/2020_DM/2004_Allen.pdf (accessed January 16, 2020).

[76] In many respects, the term "non-Western" could also prove problematic for some people, given its use to distinguish cultures outside of Europe and North America.

a White Jewish person from the LGBTQIA+ community, they[77] initially do not claim expertise on the topic. What concerns them more is not defining cultural appropriation, but how to apply music from another culture without exploitation or "Westernization." Temple stresses that composers need to exercise tact and respect when borrowing materials from another culture that is not theirs. It requires understanding the power dynamics and hierarchies involved in the cultural borrowing, in addition to thoroughly researching the foreign culture *before* applying the music to a new piece.[78]

This cautious approach to music composition and cultural appropriation persists in the 2020s. Like Alex Temple, Nicolas Lell Benavides addresses many of the same points on the concept as a composer and music educator. The key difference is that he mentions the problem in relation to "White Privilege" as a form of artistic power. To clarify, Benavides has no problems with musicians and composers expressing their creativity. His main concern stems from how artists can take their creativity to extremes by freely lifting materials from other cultures without expecting negative criticism for their efforts or not properly defending themselves against social backlash from marginalized communities.[79]

The musical contexts of cultural appropriation involve understanding the depth and significance of representation. Which musicians or composers get to display or depict foreign or non-Western cultures to audiences, and how should they do so? Do they wish to educate the public, or do they exploit foreign cultures for profit? Benavides suggests that musicians and composers, specifically White people, must develop more active social awareness about non-Western or marginalized cultures. They must not randomly take materials that sound "exotic" or "different" solely for their creative purposes and change the contexts of these materials. Apologizing by not intending to take materials from foreign cultures while still justifying the act is equally unacceptable in the twenty-first century. Taking that position serves to further anger marginalized communities

---

[77] I use the "they/them" gender pronouns out of respect for the Transgender community.

[78] Alex Temple. "The Appropriation Problem," *NewMusicBox*, January 23, 2014, https://nmbx.newmusicusa.org/the-appropriation-problem/ (accessed December 6, 2019).

[79] Nicolas Lell Benavides, "Out of Context #8: Privilege and Creative Consequence." New York: *I CARE IF YOU LISTEN* (August 26, 2020), https://www.icareifyoulisten.com/2020/08/out-of-context-8-privilege-and-creative-consequence/ (accessed September 24, 2020).

by giving the impression of not really demonstrating remorse. Understanding a different culture requires studying the language and customs well enough to the point of comprehension in addition to maintaining some form of respect.[80]

It is evident from what I have discussed that there is no clear definition of cultural appropriation: merely interpretations of the term as it *could* pertain to certain academic fields of study. If that is the case, then *why* do people continue to apply it to discussions about cultural studies and society when it is academically questionable? Convenience? Laziness? Besides not offering a clear understanding of what cultural appropriation means, social media debates from popular—that is, non-academic—entertainment outlets have amplified and aggravated the situation by weaponizing the term against people without offering proper justification or explanation. They accuse artists of "cultural appropriation" without defining the term.[81] Given all that information, I posit that cultural appropriation (and the other concepts that I have discussed) should be applied with extreme caution to prevent academic and social misuse through misinterpretation. I say that because discussions concerning "race" and cultural appropriation tend to elicit emotionally charged reactions and can detract from their academic potential. As I illustrate later in this book concerning the impact of popular music on the Gullah/Geechee culture, certain scholarly research via ethnography (like the efforts from the Society for the Preservation of Spirituals) has fallen prey to this approach via covert and overt forms of racialization. It is for these reasons that my work attempts to avoid committing the same critical mistakes.

---

[80] Nicolas Lell Benavides, 2020.

[81] Tom Connick, "Bruno Mars accused of cultural appropriation." *NME* (March 13, 2018). https://www.nme.com/news/music/bruno-mars-accused-cultural-appropriation-2261789 (accessed December 30, 2019).

Addressing Misconceptions About the Gullah/Geechee and Afro-Latin America

> "Until lions have their historians, tales of the hunt shall always glorify the hunters."
>
> -African Proverb

> "Our ignorance of history causes us to slander our own times."
>
> ~Gustave Flaubert

Scholars frequently consider the Gullah/Geechee people as one of the oldest African communities based in the United States. The Gullah and Geechee descend from areas of West Africa (primarily from Sierra Leone and Lybia among other countries) and have communities in the coastal southeastern region of the United States known today as the "Gullah/Geechee Cultural Heritage Corridor": extending from Jacksonville, Florida to Wilmington, North Carolina. As mentioned earlier, the duality associated with "Gullah/Geechee" stems from how people refer to these communities in certain areas: "Gullah" in South Carolina and "Geechee" in Georgia and Florida.

Available documentation about the Gullah/Geechee varies by topic. Scholarship presents credible, but uneven, sources about the community: some readily accessible to the public and many restricted to readers and researchers outside of academia. Throughout this investigation, I have noticed that certain topics and subtopics in question receive more attention than others. These often include discussions concerning land, language preservation, identity, food, basket making[82], and music. In specific instances, the research

---

[82] Brian Grabbatin, "Co-producing Space Along the Basket Makers' Highway in Mount Pleasant, South Carolina," *Southeastern Geographer* 52, No. 3 (2012), https://www.jstor.org/stable/26229016?Search=yes&resultItemClick=true&searchText=gullah&searchText=geechee&searchUri=%2Faction%2FdoBasicSearch%3FsearchType%3DfacetSearch%26amp%3Bsd%3D%26amp%3Bed%3D%26amp%3BQuery%3Dgullah%2Bgeechee%26amp%3Bpagemark%3DcGFnZU1hcms9Mw%253D%253D&ab_segments=0%2Fdefault-2%2Fcontrol&seq=1#page_scan_tab_contents (accessed July 8, 2019).

Figure 5: Boone Hall Plantation Slave Quarters—Mt. Pleasant, South Carolina

Figure 6: Hamilton Plantation Slave Quarters—St. Simons, Georgia

Figure 7: Kingsley Plantation (Ruins)—Jacksonville, Florida

concerning the Gullah/Geechee combines many of these topics to help readers understand multiple facets of the culture in relation to broader concepts, like cultural tourism.[83] One key component of scholarly research on the Gullah/Geechee derives from the importance of cultural preservation to try to prevent exploitation and assimilation from external, foreign influences. Concerning this current research, that involves instances like musicians or ethnographers outside the Gullah/Geechee community who take cultural materials for creative purposes without permission.

Much of the contemporary scholarship about Gullah/Geechee history and culture coincides with discussions about the American

---

[83] Ronald Daise, "Gullah Geechee Corridor's Management Plan is Meaningful to Many," *George Wright Forum* 32, No. 2 (2015), https://www.jstor.org/stable/43598416 (accessed September 24, 2020).

Colonial Era, Civil War (1861-1865), Reconstruction (1865-1876), and modernization in the twentieth century. Their inclusion in these historical periods matter because I have found that many studies concerning these topics either forget or diminish the impact of the Gullah/Geechee presence.[84] Locating these details requires finding resources that specialize in preserving Gullah/Geechee culture and reframing discussions about historical and social topics: most importantly, the Gullah/Geechee resistance to slavery in the United States. Perhaps, the best way to understand this is to approach these points by addressing and correcting the following misconceptions:

1) As enslaved Africans, the Gullah/Geechee in the United States accepted their condition and did not revolt against their oppressors.

Not only is that statement incorrect. Historical evidence from the 1990s to the 2020s[85] demonstrates the contrary. One of the most important topics linked to the Gullah/Geechee and slavery concerns the Stono Rebellion: a key event which occurred near Charleston, South Carolina. This specific moment in time proves significant because it shatters the stereotypes and assumptions about the Gullah/Geechee as an entirely peaceful people who did not fight. It is imperative to note that, while the extant account of the rebellion derives from a secondary description by the British colonizers, it has nevertheless served as a valuable document for analysis: both in terms of its tone and details.

John K. Thornton provides research on the Stono Rebellion by not only analyzing its historiography. He also argues for considering the impact of the African diasporic and religious motivations for the rebellion. Based on the existing anonymous account, historians know the following:

---

[84] Henry Louis Gates, Jr., *Stony the Road: Reconstruction, White Supremacy, and the Rise of Jim Crow* (New York: Penguin Press 2019).

[85] John K. Thornton, "African Dimensions of the Stono Rebellion," *American Historical Review* 96, No. 4 (1991), 1101-1113, https://www.jstor.org/stable/2164997 (accessed February 12, 2021); William Stanley, *Fear and Rebellion in South Carolina: The 1739 Stono Rebellion and Colonial Slave Society*, (Harrisonburg, VA: James Madison University, 2020), Master's Thesis, https://commons.lib.jmu.edu/cgi/viewcontent.cgi?article=1019&context=masters 202029 (accessed February 12, 2021).

1) The account reveals the date that the rebellion occurred (September 9, 1739).

2) It also provides the location of the rebellion (as a march to the Stono River on a Sunday: which, in those days, meant that enslaved Africans could rest).

3) The account mentions the person responsible for initiating the rebellion (an enslaved person named Jemmy).

4) The account explains why the enslaved Africans rebelled (because they wanted their freedom and would literally kill to get it).

5) Historians know the aftermath of the rebellion (that the British killed most of the enslaved people who incited the insurrection).[86]

It would be tempting to leave this discussion of the Stono Rebellion at such a basic description. However, there is clearly more information about what happened that demands attention. That is why Thornton and other scholars look beyond these details in their work by connecting the Stono Rebellion with aspects of geography and Theology: more specifically, Catholicism. Thornton notes that the available description of the enslaved Africans in the rebellion as Angolan people is inaccurate. He also points to how the same anonymous account tries to link the rebels to the Spanish and Portuguese colonizers.[87] What do the Spanish and Portuguese have to do with the Stono Rebellion? Looking at the situation from a surface perspective, the inclusion of these details appears illogical and unrelated.

Thinking more critically about the Stono Rebellion, however, reveals that these points *do* make sense in terms of colonial history. Why? John K. Thornton demonstrates that the account of the rebellion shows the distrust that the British exhibited towards foreign colonial powers… like the Spanish, who controlled Florida and whom they fought for more land and power at the time.[88] It also deserves mention that Fort Mose, the Spanish defense area near St. Augustine, Florida that was created one year before the Stono Rebellion, served as both a place of refuge and military recruitment for slaves who migrated to that colony. I go into more detail about the significance of Fort Mose and the Spanish perceptions of African slaves later in this chapter, keeping in mind that some sources do

---

[86] John K. Thornton, 1101-1113.
[87] John K. Thornton, 1101-1113.
[88] John K. Thornton, 1101-1113.

not fully accept accounts about Fort Mose[89] and that the Spanish also demonstrated distrust towards Africans.

What about the people who participated in the Stono Rebellion? Where are *their* accounts about what happened, and what do they have to do with Catholicism? As I said earlier, the account of the rebellion comes from a passive anonymous description. As the research on this historiography currently stands, there are no firsthand accounts from the enslaved Africans who took part in the insurrection. However, the scholarship on the topic suggests that the participants came from Kongo rather than Angola. Kongo has been linked to Catholicism because that was the predominant religion at the time of Portuguese colonization (hence, the reference to the Portuguese in the account: that, and the linguistic similarities to Spanish).[90] Other factors prove significant to understanding the Stono Rebellion according to Thornton. These include the incorporation of firearms in the 1700s and (from a musical perspective), the use of drumming and dance as protest.[91]

Another example of rebellion ancestrally connected to the Gullah/Geechee people occurred in coastal Georgia at Igbo Landing (pronounced "Eebo Landing.") This event took place in 1803 in St. Simons Island, GA and involved the insurrection from seventy-five West Africans from the Igbo tribe. They resisted enslavement while forcibly travelling from Savannah to St. Simons via the slave ship known as the *York*. In addition to commandeering the ship and killing the enslavers onboard, the members of the Igbo tribe who resisted also intentionally committed suicide by drowning in Dunbar Creek.[92] This solemn event in history matters in the twenty-first century because, like the Stono Rebellion, it not only demonstrates that enslaved Africans fought back against captivity. The rebellion at Igbo shows courage in that the enslaved did not fear death to obtain their freedom.

---

[89] History with No Chaser, "THE GULLAH WARS!!!" *YouTube* (August 17, 2020), https://www.youtube.com/watch?v=pUOf7Z0b6KE (accessed May 6, 2021). This video features profanity and graphically violent (but historically accurate) descriptions. It is also restricted to more mature audiences who do not easily take offense to the materials presented.

[90] John K. Thornton, "African Dimensions of the Stono Rebellion," *American Historical Review* 96, No. 4 (1991), 1101-1113, https://www.jstor.org/stable/2164997 (accessed February 12, 2021).

[91] John K. Thornton, 1101-1113.

[92] Samuel Momodu, "Igbo Landing Mass Suicide (1803)," *Black Past* (October 25, 2016), https://www.blackpast.org/african-american-history/events-african-american-history/igbo-landing-mass-suicide-1803/ (accessed October 19, 2021).

2) Because England enslaved Africans in the colonial American period, they continued the process in their home country throughout the nineteenth century.

No. While it *is* true that the British enforced the enslavement of Africans in the New World in the seventeenth and eighteenth centuries, England had established an abolitionist movement in the nineteenth century. *That* topic goes beyond the scope of this current research. What readers need to know is that this period leading to the abolition of the Transatlantic Slave Trade in England lasted from 1807 to 1833, partially because the abolitionists in the country understood slavery as an immoral act. As we have seen, though, Spain, Portugal, and the United States were still implementing slavery in the nineteenth century.[93]

3) Enslaved Gullah/Geechee people did not form their own autonomous colonies.

This statement is also wrong. In terms of physical spaces in the forms of colonies for freedmen and freedwomen, organizations like the Gullah Geechee Cultural Heritage Corridor Commission recognize historical markers like Mitchelville Freedom Park. This area of coastal South Carolina (near Hilton Head) initially served as one of the first colonies established by Free Blacks and escaped slaves in 1862: named after Union General Ormsby Mitchel. Mitchelville often functions as an important communal space for celebrating National Freedom Day (a holiday commemorating the signing of the Emancipation Proclamation on February 1, 1863 and officially recognized by President Harry S. Truman in 1948) as part of the Gullah-Geechee Festival, celebrated across coastal South Carolina.[94]

The reasons that areas like Mitchelville currently exist stem from excavations and the fact that people from within the Gullah/Geechee community promote the culture for educational purposes. Academic investigations about Mitchelville that I have found span from the 1980s and concentrate on archaeology, which refers to prior preliminary research from the 1960s.[95] Places like Mitchelville maintain relevance in the twenty-

---

[93] Thomas Clarkson, *History of the Rise, Progress, and Accomplishment of the Abolition of the African Slave Trade by the British Parliament* (London: John W. Parker, West Strand, 1839), 1-615.

[94] "About Us," *Historic Mitchelville Freedom Park* (No Date), https://exploremitchelville.org/about-us (accessed September 24, 2020).

[95] Michael Trinkley, "The Lifestyle of Freedmen at Mitchelville, Hilton Head Island: Evidence of a Changing Pattern of Afro-American Archaeological Visibility" (Columbia, SC: Chicora Foundation, 1987), 1-11,

first century because they expand upon and challenge previous perceptions about slavery in the United States beyond the Underground Railroad.

In addition to Mitchelville in South Carolina, recent evidence also reveals another Gullah/Geechee community in Jacksonville, Florida via the town of Cosmo in the southern area of the city along the St. John's River. While current resources about this area derive mainly from local news outlets and a blog about Florida archaeology, they nonetheless provide valuable information about the history of Cosmo. It was founded in the 1870s by formerly enslaved African Americans who migrated to Florida after the Civil War.[96] The reason why Cosmo has been shrouded in obscurity until recently is mainly due to modernization via land acquisition from private property contractors. Cosmo was renamed as the neighborhood "Fort Caroline," with houses and gated areas built on Gullah/Geechee land. How did this happen? Based on the available information, the Gullah/Geechee residents of Cosmo had been tricked into selling off their land to modern developers.[97] This process has, unfortunately, become a recurrent pattern in the struggle for Gullah/Geechee land preservation along the Corridor. It is because of that that the Gullah/Geechee in Jacksonville have recently found ways to try and honor the legacy of that community in Florida.[98]

The colonies described sound like a reflection of a Utopian concept where the enslaved Africans who escaped bondage found their path to freedom. There are many sides to history, however. Carefully interpretating these spaces for contemporary audiences also means understanding that these colonies did not just apply to the Gullah/Geechee. Some areas outside the Corridor, like Corinth, Mississippi, also had colonies for escaped enslaved African Americans in

---

https://dc.statelibrary.sc.gov/bitstream/handle/10827/33293/Chicora_Research_Contributions_021_1987.pdf?sequence=1 (accessed May 20, 2021).

[96] Florida Public Archaeology Network, "Where is Cosmo?" *Going Public* (December 9, 2019). https://fpangoingpublic.blogspot.com/2019/12/where-is-cosmo.html (accessed February 4, 2021).

[97] Cristin Wilson, "Remembering Cosmo: For about 100 Years, families of former slaves made a life on East Arlington Land," *Florida Times Union* (January 18, 2015), https://www.jacksonville.com/article/20150118/NEWS/801237613 (accessed February 4, 2021).

[98] David Jones, "Living History: Freedom Park will memorialize local Gullah Geechee people, veterans with PTSD in Jacksonville," *First Coast News* (March 14. 2020), https://www.firstcoastnews.com/article/news/local/living-history-freedom-park-will-memorialize-local-gullah-geechee-people-veterans-with-ptsd-in-jacksonville/77-9a2ad817-1c33-4967-9f77-e57d48d3b766 (accessed February 4, 2021).

the Civil War. Corinth lasted as a "contraband camp" from 1862 to 1863. People must also be aware that written historical records of these spaces from the era also present glaring pitfalls by applying "White Savior" narratives. Cam Walker demonstrates this problem in her 1974 research on Corinth by showing that the existing descriptions of that area come from White people, not from the perspectives of those who escaped enslavement and settled in the area.[99] It also must be said that the enslaved Africans who escaped to places like Mitchelville and Corinth also lived together with White people in these spaces: Union soldiers and Northern missionaries who tried to educate the formerly enslaved. Cam Walker demonstrates that situations like this could be interpreted as historically problematic because of how some Union troops viewed Blacks as needing guidance from White people to achieve freedom and survive. She also considers the growing fearmongering that some White Northern politicians expressed over the idea of an influx of freed Blacks living in the area.[100]

4) Gullah/Geechee colonial history is an exclusively English history because only the British impacted this community.

Much of the scholarship about the Gullah/Geechee and cultural contact stresses Great Britain as an underlying influence on that community through the application of the English language and colonization. This is best exemplified through the Gullah/Geechee presence in areas of the Anglophone Caribbean, like the Bahamas and Barbados[101], and in the

---

[99] Cam Walker, *Corinth: The Story of a Contraband Camp* (Fort Washington, PA: Eastern National, 2020), 8-36.

[100] Cam Walker, 8-36.

[101] Pablo Correa and Brian Graves, " Articulating Cultural Belonging at the Border of the Heritage Corridor: Communication and Preservation of North Florida's Gullah/Geechee Culture," *Florida Communication Journal* 43, No. 1 (2015), https://d1wqtxts1xzle7.cloudfront.net/40858091/Florida_Gullah_Geechee_FSU.pdf?1450934142=&response-content-disposition=inline%3B+filename%3DArticulating_Cultural_Belonging_at_the_B.pdf&Expires=1600981707&Signature=RLPzvz12xrSpjWjRnZ9zravBbuVPYmwK4n~naubmygOp6ZhQmVDOeriu0jEKrjRJC~~WTyr7mwWV0BlVarLzuyJN6ieCu6GDyc~4naBN~Y7IRJQjsHFDy261zQuXs2vm8VyW41F4CNDJFzbIwgyzQoy~havDZWxxpnuYx3BfdtfXt0bEn2Ihrx2q-lXeSIzfms7dIrzAc8pUolA1rqSfON9MahUHS6nhMPOwkpZu27TzM5S7BBa88SaIV0Qtfrp0IrZeaG0eVSV6SKl0OsvwP3HWgnl0L7T8o6EbyrTVzkb~C-jLpJC14CMJESypoWf5lDXv0uZ3lToz5wopmz7DTw__&Key-Pair-Id=APKAJLOHF5GGSLRBV4ZA (accessed September 24. 2020); Sanford Adams, *Beyond Barbados: The Carolina Connection*, etv, 2019, https://www.scetv.org/beyond-barbados-carolina-connection?fbclid=IwAR3W61J-

purposes behind West African enslavement by the British Crown in the seventeenth century. Stephanie Hackert and John A. Holm posit that the Gullah/Geechee use a partially Creolized African and English language, as opposed to what they refer to as African American Vernacular English (AAVE). They also suggest that this linguistic transculturation resulted from the forced migration of the Gullah/Geechee from West Africa to the American colonies.[102]

There is more to this story, however. Sandford Adams indicates that the main economic commodity in places like colonial Barbados, sugar, did *not* originate with the British. Dutch Sephardic Jews living in northern Brazil (to escape religious persecution from the Spanish Inquisition) immigrated to Barbados and brought windmill technology for sugar cultivation.[103] Additionally, the research presented by Adams demonstrates that Barbados began enslaving West Africans as early as 1627 as an alternative to Irish indentured servitude: partially based on the notion that West Africans could withstand the punishing tropical climate. Regarding the British colonization of South Carolina in the New World, Adams also indicates that this process partially resulted from immigration from Barbados due to greed and excessive deforestation of the island.[104] Many enslavers forcibly brought West Africans to the colonies for rice cultivation. British enslavers exploited the West African people for their knowledge of growing rice and applying the same agricultural techniques from their homeland to agriculture in the American colonies. Pablo Correa and Brian Graves also refer to the Bahamas as another key area for understanding Gullah/Geechee culture. They specifically refer to the Bahamian influence on the Gullah/Geechee in North Florida.[105]

NNcHyJ6__US5BOihBkY9AFlSjKOWruPbWApYXei-IhlXHnEGXr0 (accessed June 18, 2021).

[102] Stephanie Hackert and John A. Holm, "Southern Bahamian: Transported African American Vernacular English, Or Transplanted Gullah?" *College of the Bahamas Research Journal* (2009), https://pdfs.semanticscholar.org/b876/10aadbcfc9683dbdd6bd400c790703a05e67.pdf (accessed September 24, 2020).

[103] Sanford Adams, *Beyond Barbados: The Carolina Connection*, etv, 2019, https://www.scetv.org/beyond-barbados-carolina-connection?fbclid=IwAR3W61J-NNcHyJ6__US5BOihBkY9AFlSjKOWruPbWApYXei-IhlXHnEGXr0 (accessed June 18, 2021).

[104] Sanford Adams, 2019.

[105] Pablo Correa and Brian Graves, " Articulating Cultural Belonging at the Border of the Heritage Corridor: Communication and Preservation of North Florida's Gullah/Geechee Culture," *Florida Communication Journal* 43, No. 1 (2015),

These points all present some truths regarding the Gullah/Geechee people and language. However, the British and their respective colonies were not the only areas that influenced the Gullah/Geechee people. Recall what I said earlier about the dangers associated with anglicizing U.S. colonial history. One need only travel to Saint Helena Island, South Carolina to see why. For over the past thirty-five years every November, the Gullah/Geechee enclave hosts a "Heritage Fest" dedicated to educating people about Gullah/Geechee culture through entertainment, food and symposia addressing social issues affecting the community. Each festival begins with a parade of flags representing countries that form parts of the Gullah/Geechee Nation.

Despite the cultural diversity, most histories concerning the Gullah/Geechee focus too much on Great Britain. This anglicization inadvertently leads to a cultural erasure in terms of the *other* countries involved in affecting the Gullah/Geechee. One must understand that Spain and Portugal proved equally powerful colonial forces in shaping North and South America. Like Great Britain, Spain and Portugal implemented the enslavement and exploitation of West Africans to the New World… even though the process occurred *one century earlier* in the 1500s. Spain and Portugal also exhibited cruelty and used racist doctrines towards Africans under the guise of Christian (Catholic) dogma and proselytization. The Portuguese, according to Henry Louis Gates, Jr. in his ethnographic travels to Brazil, demonstrated extreme cruelty towards African slaves by seeing them as nothing more than replaceable property instead of as human beings. Gates posits that this attitude was largely due to the proximity of Brazil to Africa and forced marriages through rape and cultural mixing.[106]

---

https://d1wqtxts1xzle7.cloudfront.net/40858091/Florida_Gullah_Geechee_FSU.pdf?1450934142=&response-content-disposition=inline%3B+filename%3DArticulating_Cultural_Belonging_at_the_B.pdf&Expires=1600981707&Signature=RLPzvz12xrSpjWjRnZ9zravBbuVPYmwK4n~naubmygOp6ZhQmVDOeriu0jEKrjRJC~~WTyr7mwWV0BlVarLzuyJN6ieCu6GDyc~4naBN~Y7IRJQjsHFDy261zQuXs2vm8VyW41F4CNDJFzbIwgyzQoy~havDZWxxpnuYx3BfdtfXt0bEn2Ihrx2q-lXeSIzfms7dIrzAc8pUolA1rqSfON9MahUHS6nhMPOwkpZu27TzM5S7BBa88SalV0Qtfrp0IrZeaG0eVSV6SKl0OsvwP3HWgnl0L7T8o6EbyrTVzkb~C-jLpJC14CMJESypoWf5lDXv0uZ3lToz5wopmz7DTw_&Key-Pair-Id=APKAJLOHF5GGSLRBV4ZA (accessed September 24. 2020).

[106] Henry Louis Gates, Jr., "1. Brazil: 'May Exú Give Me the Power of Speech," in *Black in Latin America* (New York: New York University Press, 2011), 12-58.

Based on my findings, primary and secondary sources about the Gullah/Geechee additionally reveal uneven amounts of resources and data

Figure 8: Gullah/Geechee Rice in Basket

Figure 9: "Parade of Flags" at St. Helena Island, South Carolina

based on the given regions in which this community resides. Research focuses predominantly on the populations based in areas of coastal South Carolina: Hilton Head, St. Helena Island, Mitchellville, Charleston, and Mt. Pleasant to name a few. What about the other states that comprise the

Corridor, though? From what I have encountered, scholars *have* written about the Gullah/Geechee in Georgia and Florida. However, locating concrete details concerning their visibility in these areas of the Corridor depend on availability: primarily in parts of coastal Georgia (Savannah, Riceboro, St. Simons Island, Sapelo Island, Darien, etc.), North Florida (Jacksonville and near St. Augustine) and North Carolina. Areas like Riceboro, GA prove most valuable in terms of the availability of information about Geechee history, culture, and music. This is due to places like the Geechee Kunda Cultural Center and Museum, formerly operated by Gullah/Geechee historian Jim Bacote. Additionally, ethnomusicologists and folklorists, like Robert Winslow Gordon and Alan Lomax, travelled to areas of coastal Georgia in the twentieth century to preserve the legacy of Gullah/Geechee music: even though these scholars themselves were not part of the Gullah/Geechee culture.

Regardless of these efforts, some areas of Georgia (like Savannah) explain the Gullah/Geechee culture with reluctance. Much of the current information on Savannah and the connection to the Gullah/Geechee has focused on slavery. The city solemnly commemorates and has documented the auction of four hundred thirty-six enslaved Africans on March 3, 1859. This event is referred to historically as "The Weeping Time" because it rained that day, which gave the impression to many attendees that God was crying because of the atrocity.[107] Other areas of the Corridor, like North Florida and North Carolina, illustrate the error of cultural erasure due to suppression and lack of extant information. In the case of the Gullah/Geechee in Florida, this erasure has also affected their involvement in the colonial history of that state. While there is some valuable information on the Gullah/Geechee in Florida[108], this aspect of the research still requires more academic attention.

---

[107] Weeping Time Commemoration Primus, "The 162nd Commemoration of The Weeping Time," *YouTube* (March 6, 2021), https://www.youtube.com/watch?v=X-9k5fIdDdw (accessed March 18, 2021). Due to the lingering impact of COVID-19 in 2021, the commemoration for that year had to be adapted to a virtual setting. It consisted of lectures and prerecorded highlights of previous "Weeping Time" events over the years.

[108] J. Vern Cromartie, "Gullah Strata People: Historical Notes on the Geechees."in *Supporting Cultural Differences Through Research: 2011 Monograph Series* (Scarborough, ME: NAAAS & Affiliates, 2011), 1164-1197, https://d1wqtxts1xzle7.cloudfront.net/8268585/2011monograph2.pdf?1328290242=&response-content-disposition=inline%3B+filename%3DThe_Representation_of_Colonial_Africa_in.pdf&Expires=1601050706&Signature=eZDbgQTOT-XYVRHsAhpJ~C6B-uJmrH4pQwlygZx3~wg71xuikZoTgWQFF-

In terms of colonial American history, Fort Mose (in St. Augustine, Florida) served as both a military post and sanctuary for enslaved Africans escaping the British plantations in South Carolina in the eighteenth century. After establishing the area in 1738 (and again in 1752 in a different location) the Spanish promised to grant the escaped slaves their freedom, on several required conditions that they had to follow. The slaves had to agree that they convert to Catholicism and swear allegiance to the Spanish Monarchy. These conditions also meant enlisting in the Spanish Army to fight against the British.[109] Further evidence reveals more credible details about the Spanish perceptions of enslaved Africans in colonial Florida in St. Augustine. Christopher Beats illustrates why the Spanish used Catholicism to convert the enslaved Africans who arrived in La Florida by referring to colonial accounts about the founder of St. Augustine, Pedro Menendez de Aviles: some of which discuss his time in Europe and mention the 1500s, but still fit the research that Beats presents. From these accounts, readers get a glimpse into Menendez and his personality via his attitude toward foreign colonizers. They depict Menendez as a devout Catholic, but one who exhibited extreme religious intolerance towards Protestants: mainly, the British and French (Huguenots) who sought to seize Spanish territory. One of the accounts that Beats mentions refers to Aviles ordering the capture and execution of French Protestant men and women (but not children) who did not convert to Catholicism.[110]

How and why does this information relate to the current discussion? It demonstrates that Catholicism functioned as a driving factor for Spanish colonization in the New World. Hence, the Spanish tolerated

OXlHeF6Ipe9jIDugPGWJ9wRuYsQ5ufi6MRlJPZwk0-SHgVUiCjHiD2RLgZrKnNWbIGuuCUAONRM48l8j6xQtTZtvoseqGSwc4WbXr8pylEBwQn9LeZjuf8HvAcmOA~eOXaLaOBQh2LFjuDO7FSS0nmRY2Q-ay8oyC4IzQlBpS6bE6j3cRB7EoGT2JSXonqdWY2G3m8ipaeUF~EV2pAI4VTC0Zto5RgbADNG-2W7MPJSTVB31zZap-XQEhgGQ72bFIUwHihs6ODbZCIBNVbK30kd1lREg &Key-Pair-Id=APKAJLOHF5GGSLRBV4ZA#page=1174 (accessed September 25, 2020).

[109] Shane Alan Runyon, "3. FLORIDA'S FUGUTUVE SLAVE POLICY AND FORT MOSE," in *Fort Mose: The Free African Community and Militia of Spanish St. Augustine* (Bozeman, MT: Montana State University-Bozeman, 1999, Masters Thesis), 36-68, https://scholarworks.montana.edu/xmlui/bitstream/handle/1/8563/31762104216096.pdf?sequence=1&isAllowed=y (accessed October 29, 2021).

[110] Christopher Beats, "CHAPTER THREE: BACKGROUND: ST. AUGUSTINE'S HISTORY AND TREATMENT OF SLAVES," in *African Religious Integration in the First Spanish Period* (Orlando: University of Central Florida, 2007), 32-51, M.A. Thesis, https://stars.library.ucf.edu/cgi/viewcontent.cgi?article=4076&context=etd (accessed July 30, 2021).

and accepted enslaved Africans who escaped to Florida and integrated with the community… *if* they converted to Catholicism. Beats also notes that, even though the Spanish viewed Africans as good fighters fit for military recruitment, the colonizers still perceived them with distrust.[111]

Academic sources about Fort Mose and its connection to the Gullah/Geechee do exist. Much of that information concerns their relations with Native Americans in the coastal regions in the colonial period. The Maroon community in Florida represented a transculturated group of African (Gullah/Geechee) people who escaped the plantations of coastal South Carolina and Georgia and mixed with the Seminole Indians in the eighteenth and nineteenth centuries. Based on the available information, many Maroon members later went on to become tribal chiefs and fight in major conflicts in the nineteenth century: most notably, participating in the Seminole Wars (1817-1858).[112]

Some have suggested that the Gullah/Geechee link extends far beyond the Corridor into places like Texas and Mexico. However, not everyone agrees with those diasporic aspects of Gullah/Geechee history. Pablo Correa and Brian Graves indicate in their ethnographic research that, even though Floridian Gullah/Geechee people view the Anglophone Caribbean connections to their culture (via the Bahamas) with certainty, some exhibit more skepticism about stateside connections far removed from the Corridor.[113] Additionally, like with Fort Mose, the Native American and Gullah/Geechee connection remains mostly shrouded in

---

[111] Christopher Beats, 32-51.

[112] Anthony E. Dixon, *Black Seminole Involvement and Leadership During the Second Seminole War, 1835-1842* (Bloomington: Indiana University, 2010), PhD Dissertation, https://scholarworks.iu.edu/dspace/bitstream/handle/2022/7603/umi-indiana-1694.pdf?sequence=1 (accessed September 25, 2020).

[113] Pablo Correa and Brian Graves, " Articulating Cultural Belonging at the Border of the Heritage Corridor: Communication and Preservation of North Florida's Gullah/Geechee Culture," *Florida Communication Journal* 43, No. 1 (2015), https://d1wqtxts1xzle7.cloudfront.net/40858091/Florida_Gullah_Geechee_FSU.pdf?1450934142=&response-content-disposition=inline%3B+filename%3DArticulating_Cultural_Belonging_at_the_B.pdf&Expires=1600981707&Signature=RLPzvz12xrSpjWjRnZ9zravBbuVPYmwK4n~naubmygOp6ZhQmVDOeriu0jEKrjRJC~~WTyr7mwWV0BlVarLzuyJN6ieCu6GDyc~4naBN~Y7IRJQjsHFDy261zQuXs2vm8VyW41F4CNDJFzbIwgyzQoy~havDZWxxpnuYx3BfdtfXt0bEn2Ihrx2q-lXeSIzfms7dIrzAc8pUolA1rqSfON9MahUHS6nhMPOwkpZu27TzM5S7BBa88SalV0Qtfrp0IrZeaG0eVSV6SKl0OsvwP3HWgnl0L7T8o6EbyrTVzkb~C-jLpJC14CMJESypoWf5lDXv0uZ3lToz5wopmz7DTw__&Key-Pair-Id=APKAJLOHF5GGSLRBV4ZA (accessed September 24. 2020).

obscurity and needs more public, non-exploitative exposure for audiences to gain interest in this facet of American history and culture.

Figure 10: "Walkway to Freedom" at Ft. Mose (1752 Estimated Location)—St. Augustine, Florida

Figure 11: Re-enactors at Ft. Mose (During COVID-19)—St. Augustine, FL

I do not suggest that Florida has not tried to demonstrate the Gullah/Geechee presence in the state. They *have* attempted to exhibit cultural visibility to present more balanced depictions of the Gullah/Geechee so that people in the United States and the world will listen to their part of the community. This is not some new problem, either. As I will show later in my research, some archival materials from the Library of Congress subtly illustrate that extant Gullah/Geechee community through field recordings dating from the 1930s. In the twenty-first century, people from the Gullah/Geechee community in Jacksonville, Florida have attempted to re-establish themselves within the Corridor and educate the public about their culture through festivities and discussing cultural connections with the Spanish and Native Americans… *without* resorting to exploration and assimilation.

Regardless of the contemporary documentation about the Gullah/Geechee people and culture, I have noticed the tendency for some sources to discuss the Gullah/Geechee in passing or in pessimistic terms as a community threatened by industrialization in and around the areas of the Corridor. Some research from the 2010s refers to land preservation and constant disputes with the Gullah/Geechee and areas of coastal Georgia and South Carolina: most notably, Sapelo Island. Another aspect of such scholarship concerns the perception of the Gullah/Geechee people as a "disappearing" community. Such sentiments also appear in select sources from the 2010s.[114] Despite this mistake, most research from the twenty-first century has attempted to address Gullah/Geechee culture without applying stigmatization or factually dubious narratives.

I have no doubts that the Gullah/Geechee constantly face threats due to overdevelopment through modernization, cultural exploitation, and assimilation. These invasive changes in lifestyle have impacted the Gullah/Geechee since the 1950s. What concerns me more is how contemporary readers and scholars alike must approach information about the Gullah/Geechee from a more critical lens. That means determining *who* is interpreting the history and culture of the Gullah/Geechee people by analyzing the tone of the writing. Consider the reliability of the information by determining whether the resource stems from the emic perspective of the insider (someone who personally knows the culture in

---

[114] Vice News, "A Vanishing History: Gullah Geechee Nation," *YouTube* (January 6, 2016), https://www.youtube.com/watch?v=SqDTJogdWmA (accessed October 13, 2020). While this video *does* employ ethnographic fieldwork and input from members of the Gullah/Geechee communities, I find the results and overall tone questionable.

question) or from the etic perspective of an outsider. Let us briefly concentrate our attention now on Latin America and the Caribbean. Despite the geographical differences, the societal and governmental actions imposed upon Afro-Latin people in Brazil, Cuba, and Puerto Rico demonstrate striking (though not exact) similarities to what occurred with the Gullah/Geechee in the United States. Also, like what has occurred with the Gullah/Geechee, I must address some assumptions about Afro-Latin history and culture that demand reexamination.

1) Slavery did not exist in Latin America and the Hispanophone Caribbean.

Wrong. Scholars who specialize in Latin America and the Caribbean or African Studies have written extensively about slavery and its connections to Spanish and Portuguese colonialism and imperialism. This information is often presented to readers as physical proof that slavery formed a part of stabilizing the economy and trade in Latin America and the Caribbean, albeit at the expense of human lives. These sources often address the effects of the Transatlantic Slave Trade by country or region and tend to concentrate on the types of systems imposed, products cultivated via enslavement (diamonds, gold, sugar, chocolate, coffee, etc.), punishments for disobedience, and efforts for promoting abolition in the nineteenth century. Some areas noticeably receive more attention than others based on the amount of documentation available, like Brazil and Cuba. Concerning Puerto Rico, readers must recall what I referred to earlier in thinking about slavery on the island (and Afro-Latin identity) beyond the nineteenth century.

To enforce the policies behind slavery in the Spanish-speaking areas of the New World, the Spanish Crown established the *Codigo Negro* (Black Codes) in 1704 and revised them in 1723. Spain drew inspiration for these rules and restrictions—about sixty in total—after the *Code Noir*, enacted by the French Crown under Louis XIV in 1685.[115] Besides adapting the parameters of the text to apply to Spanish colonies (because the Code Noir only applied to the colonies controlled by France), the Codigo Negro enumerates a plethora of social restrictions against enslaved Africans. According to the Code, Spanish colonizers perceived enslaved Africans as their property with *no* human rights. The enslaved could not

---

[115] M. Swift, "El Código Negro and the Royal Decree of Graces of 1789." *Black Then* (July 7, 2018), https://blackthen.com/el-codigo-negro-royal-decree-graces-1789/ (accessed April 5, 2019).

own, buy, or sell items. These restrictions also included weapons. They could not drink alcohol. They also could not marry, but the male enslaver could marry an enslaved female under the condition that the enslaver raped her. Enslavers also discouraged enslaved Africans from reading or writing, for fear that they might cause insurrections with their newfound knowledge.[116]

Puerto Rico did not prove an exception to applying slavery on the island. Like other areas of Latin America and the Hispanophone Caribbean, older texts from the early twentieth century would produce revisionist, heavily romanticized versions of Puerto Rican history by claiming that slavery did not happen. More contemporary resources from the 2000s and 2010s contradict these false notions and selective memories. Using concrete evidence (often in the form of slaveholding and baptismal records on the island, as well as other relevant accounts), they demonstrate that enslaved Africans (and Free Blacks) played a role in helping to boost the economy on the island by cultivating products like sugar and coffee.[117]

Like many sources that explain the consequences of slavery in Latin America and the Caribbean, Puerto Rican scholars address that the abolition of slavery on the island occurred in 1873. This does *not* suggest, however, that that year presents the first time that Afro-Puerto Ricans attempted to obtain freedom. Decrees enacted by the Spanish Crown, like the 1789 *Real Cedula de Gracias* (Royal Decree of Graces)[118] provided strict rules where Afro-Puerto Rican slaves or fugitives could buy their freedom. The rules established in these decrees did not come without exceptions,

---

[116] M. Swift, 2018.

[117] Guillermo A. Baralt and Christine Ayorinde (English Transl.). *Slave Revolts in Puerto Rico: Conspiracies and Uprisings, 1795-1873*. Princeton: Markus Wiener Publishers. 2007.

[118] M. Swift, "El Código Negro and the Royal Decree of Graces of 1789." *Black Then* (July 7, 2018), https://blackthen.com/el-codigo-negro-royal-decree-graces-1789/ (accessed April 5, 2019); The 1789 decree should not be confused with the 1815 Real Cedula de Gracias, which the Spanish Monarchy enacted to improve the economy in Puerto Rico. This decree also encouraged foreign immigrants from Europe and other areas of Latin America to settle on the island, create businesses, and (if applicable) acquire slaves. Guillermo A. Baralt and Christine Ayorinde (English Transl.), "Chapter VI. Boom and Crisis in the Sugar Industry: 1790-1850," in *Slave Revolts in Puerto Rico: Conspiracies and Uprisings, 1795-1873* (Princeton: Markus Wiener Publishers. 2007), 53-62.

however. The Codigo Negro, for instance, came equipped with several conditions:

- The Council of the Indies or the enslaver had the power to accept or deny the decision for freedom.
- The enslaver determined the price for manumission that the slaves had to pay.
- Africans who bought their freedom had to convert to Christianity (Catholicism) through Baptism.
- Enslaved or fugitive Africans and Blacks who bought their freedom had to swear their allegiance to the Spanish Monarchy.[119]

2) Because slavery did not exist in Latin America and the Caribbean, Afro-Latin Americans also did not revolt against or resist slavery.

This is also incorrect. Contemporary research on this topic shows that forms of enslavement and resistance to slavery and colonial oppression took place *all over* Latin America and the Caribbean. Many of the revolts had been motivated by the effects of the Haitian Revolution (1791-1804). Documented evidence illustrates that the enslaved Afro-Puerto Ricans had planned insurrections on the island since 1795 with similar goals to those of the Stono Rebellion in the American colonies controlled by the British in the 1730s: obtaining freedom by any means necessary, even if that meant killing people and destroying property.[120] Many rebellions also transpired in Brazil and Cuba in the nineteenth century. Brazil had instances like the Malê Revolt of 1835 in Salvador da Bahia. That specific failed insurrection involved the *Malê* (*imalê*) population of Muslim Afro-Brazilians: many of whom, as Narlan Matos and Dale T. Garden indicate, consisted of scholars and workers who planned to attack the city of Salvador towards the end of the Ramadan holiday in late January 1835 and enslave the citizens… which included Africans who did not conform to their Muslim beliefs.[121]

---

[119] M. Swift, "El Código Negro and the Royal Decree of Graces of 1789." *Black Then* (July 7, 2018), https://blackthen.com/el-codigo-negro-royal-decree-graces-1789/ (accessed April 5, 2019.

[120] Guillermo A. Baralt and Christine Ayorinde (English Transl.), "Chapter I. The Seditious Seeds of Haiti and the 1795 Slave Conspiracy in Aguadilla," in *Slave Revolts in Puerto Rico* (Princeton: Markus Wiener Publishers, 2007), 3-11;

[121] Narlan Matos, "The Malê Rebellion in Bahia: Brazils African Muslim Uprising," Smithsonian Folklife Festival (May 19, 2020), https://festival.si.edu/blog/male-rebellion-african-muslim-brazilian-uprising (accessed August 4, 2021); Dale T. Graden, "An Act 'Even of Public Security': Slave Resistance, Social Tensions, and

Cuba had the Ten Years' War (1868-1878) and War for Independence (1895-1898). Those specific conflicts involved ending slavery AND colonial ties to Spain and featured active participation from both enslaved Africans and White Cubans tired of Spanish colonial rule.[122]

Research from the 1980s and 2000s has also encouraged readers to stop perceiving Afro-Puerto Rican slavery as a period when the people did not fight back against their oppressors. Guillermo A. Baralt notes in his research on the subject that, contrary to popular belief, many planned slave insurrections took place all over Puerto Rico from the 1810s to 1870s.[123] This is important for several reasons. It demonstrates that enslaved Afro-Puerto Ricans could resist the Spanish Monarchy and Puerto Rican Government to make their voices heard and actions known. Several of the insurrections in that period functioned as responses to imposed imperial regulations or coincided with periods of crisis for the sugar cash crop on the island. Additionally, they served as reactions to other revolts in different areas of the Caribbean: mainly, the Haitian Revolution.[124]

This does not suggest that the information from Guillermo A. Baralt is perfect and completely clear. While he does use historical records from archives in Puerto Rico across multiple areas, he also addresses how most of the accounts of the slave insurrections are shrouded in mystery or inconsistent.[125] I said the word "planned" when describing the slave revolts on the island because the available documentation reveals that these revolts failed. The enslavers eventually uncovered each plot and alerted the mayor of their respective city or municipality to stop everything. To make matters worse, some revolts failed because other enslaved Afro-Puerto Ricans, some of whom did not mind living in captivity, betrayed the cause by revealing the conspiracies to their enslavers. Those who conspired in multiple slave revolts were either imprisoned or publicly executed, while

---

the End of the International Slave Trade to Brazil: 1835-1856," *Hispanic American Historical Review* 6, 2 (1996), 249-282 (accessed May 6, 2021).

[122] Henry Louis Gates, Jr. "Cuba: The Next Cuban Revolution," in *Black in Latin America* (New York: New York University Press, 2011), 17-222.

[123] Guillermo A. Baralt and Christine Ayorinde (English Transl.), *Slave Revolts in Puerto Rico: Conspiracies and Uprisings, 1795-1873* (Princeton: Markus Wiener Publishers. 2007).

[124] Guillermo A. Baralt and Christine Ayorinde (English Transl.), "Chapter I, The Seditious Seeds of Haiti and the 1795 Conspiracy in Aguadilla," in *Slave Revolts in Puerto Rico: Conspiracies and Uprisings, 1795-1873* (Princeton: Markus Wiener Publishers. 2007), 3- 10.

[125] Guillermo A. Baralt and Christine Ayorinde (English Transl.), "Chapter V, From the Bomba Dance in Ponce to the New Reglamento de Esclavos de Puerto Rico of 1826," in *Slave Revolts in Puerto Rico: Conspiracies and Uprisings, 1795-1873* (Princeton: Markus Wiener Publishers. 2007), 41-52.

the enslaved people who revealed the plots would obtain their freedom and compensation.[126]

Abolishing slavery in Puerto Rico in 1873 also did not guarantee true freedom for Afro-Puerto Ricans. Their situation of racial discrimination on the island, such as the established "vagrancy" laws in the late nineteenth century, mirrored the problems that African Americans encountered in the mainland United States in the Reconstruction period. The effects of governmental restrictions through racial discrimination also impacted music for Afro-Puerto Ricans on the island by affecting how and where they could perform the *bomba* music and dance. [127] Understanding this point requires investigating the reasons why the bomba underwent censorship in Puerto Rico in the nineteenth century.

Scholars, historians, and specialists in Puerto Rican music have written extensively about the bomba in relation to its historical connections with slavery in Puerto Rico and musical components. Besides serving as a recreational form for Afro-Puerto Rican communities on the island[128], the bomba contains a deeper context than merely variants of music and dance. It originally functioned as more than a "call and response" format with vocal repetition and percussive patterns, similar to the Ring Shout applied by the Gullah/Geechee people from the mainland United States. Afro-Puerto Rican slaves in the 1820s applied secret codes to the bomba in either the drumming, or in singing: performing hidden messages in the town square and communicating with other Afro-Puerto Ricans about revolting against their masters. The discovery of these plots by the enslavers eventually led to the banning and relocation of the bomba as a communal activity. These restrictions lasted well into the 1910s, when Afro Puerto Ricans could finally perform the bomba in public.[129]

---

[126] Guillermo A. Baralt and Christine Ayorinde (English Transl.), 41-52.

[127] Luis A. Figueroa, "7. Conflicts and Solidarities on the Path to Proletarianization," in *Sugar, Slavery, and Freedom in Nineteenth-Century Puerto Rico* (Chapel Hill, NC: University of North Carolina Press, 2005), 175-199.

[128] Luis A. Figueroa, 175-199; Guillermo A. Baralt and Christine Ayorinde (English Transl.), "Chapter V, From the Bomba Dance in Ponce to the New Reglamento de Esclavos de Puerto Rico of 1826," in *Slave Revolts in Puerto Rico: Conspiracies and Uprisings, 1795-1873* (Princeton: Markus Wiener Publishers. 2007), 41-52.

[129] Luis A. Figueroa, 175-199; Guillermo A. Baralt and Christine Ayorinde (English Transl.), 41-52.

3) Latin America and the Caribbean did not exhibit forms of racial discrimination against Africans and Blacks in the late nineteenth and early twentieth century, like the United States did.

That assumption is also false. I argue that the anti-Black and anti-African racism in Latin America and the Caribbean in the late nineteenth and early twentieth centuries bears striking similarities to what happened in the United States in the Reconstruction era. I say that because the Latin American and Caribbean histories reveal governmental tactics used to suppress the African and Black populations. It is ironic that, after abolishing slavery in these respective areas, these governments enacted forms of racial segregation and discrimination.

These forms of suppression appeared in both overt and covert kinds of systemic racism. The process usually involved transforming identity politics by focusing on White or Creolized Latin American and Caribbean cultures while simultaneously excluding or demonizing Africans and Blacks. It also included concocting romanticized ideas about Latin American and Caribbean history and society to distract from the reality of racial inequity and inequality. Abolishing slavery in these areas did not mean abolishing racial discrimination. Instead, the respective Latin American and Caribbean governments sought to ignore or wipe African history, identity, and culture from existence. Puerto Rico, Brazil, and Cuba have *all* partaken in anti-Black racism, which persists today: from the *Brujeria* hysteria in Cuba in the nineteenth and early twentieth centuries, to the notion that Brazil functions as a "Racial Democracy" (despite constant discrimination), to denying racism and promoting nationalist concepts in Puerto Rico.[130] As I mention later in this investigation, the Africanized syncretic religions and musical practices did not escape this backlash in these regions. If anything, the respective governments cited the religious and musical practices as "evidence" for cultural exclusion via "de-Africanization" and arrests.

---

[130] Mariela A. Gutierrez, "Y yo, ¿Dónde me pongo? El negro en la sociedad cubana desde la trata (1451-1870) hasta el Nuevo Orden (1898-1912)," Warsaw: Revista del CESLA. Num 9 (2006), 101-113, https://www.revistadelcesla.com/index.php/revistadelcesla/article/view/219/217 (accessed February 13, 2021); Henry Louis Gates, Jr., "1. Brazil: May Exu Give Me the Power of Speech,'" in *Black in Latin America* (New York: New York University Press, 2011), 12-58; Marta I. Cruz-Jansen, "Out of the Closet: Racial Amnesia, Avoidance, and Denial- Racism Among Puerto Ricans," *Race, Gender & Class* 10, No. 3 (2003), 64-81, https://www.jstor.org/stable/41675088 (accessed May 6, 2021).

4) Enslaved Afro-Latin people did not form their own autonomous colonies.

Again, this is also wrong. Similar situations occurred with the Afro-Latin American side of historiography in Cuba, Brazil, and Puerto Rico regarding Maroon communities of escaped enslaved Africans. I have encountered documentation concerning Brazilian *quilombos* and Cuban *palanques*, which consisted of goals like those of the Gullah/Geechee colonies in the United States: establishing autonomous communities while simultaneously avoiding capture, re-enslavement, and repatriation to the plantations. Regarding this form of resistance in the Afro-Puerto Rican population in the colonial era, I noticed instances of autonomy and economic stability.

David M. Starke notes in his research from the late 2000s that the Afro-Puerto Rican population from the 1660s to 1790s largely consisted of Africans and Blacks who immigrated from *other* areas of the Caribbean: mainly, the regions controlled by the French and Danish. They did so primarily to escape drought and famine, or to avoid slavery and obtain their freedom. Those who escaped got their freedom often in the same way as the Africans and Blacks in Fort Mose in Florida: through conversion to Catholicism and allegiance to Span via military service.[131] What concerns Starke more in his research stems from two key points. First, Afro-Puerto Ricans established their own community on the island via San Mateo de Cangrejos (what is now Caguas) near the capital city of San Juan. San Mateo de Cangrejos was officially recognized as a municipality in 1773.[132] In a sense, San Mateo de Cangrejos parallels the Gullah/Geechee colonies of Mitchelville, South Carolina and Cosmo in Jacksonville, Florida. All these places consisted of free Blacks and escaped slaves living together in their own society. San Mateo de Cangrejos also functioned as an economically stable community that openly conducted business with the rest of Puerto Rico through fishing and trading goods.[133]

San Mateo de Cangrejos proved quite successful as a community for several decades. If that was the case, then why did it fade into obscurity? What factors led to its disappearance? Why does San Mateo de Cangrejos no longer exist as a thriving Afro-Puerto Rican municipality? Part of the problem stemmed from the changes in immigration policy from

---

[131] David M. Starke, "Rescued from Their Invisibility: The Afro-Puerto Ricans of Seventeenth-and Eighteenth-Century San Mateo de Cangrejos, Puerto Rico," *Americas* 63, No. 4 (2007), https://www.jstor.org/stable/4491299 (accessed October 2, 2020).

[132] David M. Starke, 2007.

[133] David M. Starke, 2007.

Spain in the late 1700s, specifically because of secret negotiations that they established with the Danish.[134] Over time, Puerto Rico stopped accepting and converting escaped slaves from other parts of the Caribbean and would return them to the respective Caribbean region of their slave master. The nineteenth century also foresaw economic struggle with San Mateo de Cangrejos, leading to its partition by the Puerto Rican Government in the 1860s to form parts of San Juan.[135]

5) Afro-Latin people had to learn Spanish and Portuguese, abandoning the languages from their native countries in the process.

While it *is* true that many West Africans forcibly brought to the New World learned the Spanish and Portuguese languages, their approach to interpreting these languages dialectically bears some similarities to the Gullah/Geechee. Why do I say that? Like the Gullah/Geechee community in the southeastern United States, language serves as an important factor in cultural preservation among Afro-Latin American and Caribbean people. I have encountered credible information for this investigation that points to the *Bozal* language as evidence. Bozal, or Bozal Spanish, functions like the Afro-Latin equivalent of Gullah/Geechee, in that these names refer to both a language *and* a community of people. In relation to Bozal, the name refers to people born in Africa who arrived with the Spanish to the New World as enslaved people or workers in the colonial period.[136] John M. Lipski has written extensively about Bozal as a language since the 1980s. The Bozal language ("bozal" meaning the Spanish word for "muzzle") refers to an archaic derivation of Spanish and Portuguese spoken by African people forcibly brought to areas of Latin America and the Caribbean, including Puerto Rico. The language has since become endangered or extinct by the late twentieth century, with few Latin American countries speaking remnants of the language by the 2000s.[137]

---

[134] David M. Starke, 2007.

[135] David M. Starke, 2007.

[136] Guillermo A. Baralt and Christine Ayorinde (English Transl.). "Glossary," in *Slave Revolts in Puerto Rico: Conspiracies and Uprisings, 1795-1873* (Princeton: Markus Wiener Publishers. 2007), 169.

[137] John M. Lipski, "On the Construction ta + Infinitive in Caribbean 'Bozal' Spanish," *Romance Philology* 40, No. 4 (1987), https://www.jstor.org/stable/44942858 (accessed October 16, 2020); "Chapter 20: Where and how does *bozal* Spanish survive?" in *Spanish in Contact: Policy, Social, and Linguistic Inquiries*, edited by Kim Potowski and Richard Cameron (Amsterdam: John Benjamins Publishing Company, 2007), 359-375,

In a manner that bears similarities to Gullah/Geechee, Bozal could also be perceived as a creolized language. The exception with Bozal, however, stems from combining African languages with Spanish and Portuguese instead of English or English linguistic cognates. Lipski indicates in his research that Bozal serves as an adaptation of colonialist language as the result of enslavement.[138] In another way related to Gullah/Geechee, Bozal could be misinterpreted by some non-native speakers as a "regressive" or "broken" dialect. It is true that Bozal combines the Spanish and Portuguese languages, but it does so by mixing up the grammatical structure and can present convoluted results. That dialectical Spanish has the tendency to invert tenses, truncate nouns, or verbs, and obscure the overall meaning of words and phrases through letter substitutions or removals (eg., pronouncing *r*s as *d*s).[139]

---

http://php.scripts.psu.edu/faculty/j/m/jml34/newbozal.pdf (accessed October 16, 2020).

[138] John M. Lipski, 1987; John M. Lipski, 359-375.

[139] John M. Lipski, 1987; John M. Lipski, 359-375.

(Re)Interpreting Gullah/Geechee Culture, Religion, and Music

Ethnographic Attempts in the Early Twentieth Century

The information presented in the previous chapter clearly demonstrates what I said at the beginning of this book. History should be understood as a constantly evolving process rather than something static. Factoring in ethnographic research adds another significant step to this process: one that also involves applying or questioning the methodologies and historical accuracies of firsthand accounts from interviews in the past. As I demonstrated with the problems surrounding the WPA Slave Narratives, some ethnographers from the early twentieth century would get too carried away with how they presented information. Such problems also manifested themselves in fieldwork from that era concerning the Gullah/Geechee. Approaches to understanding that specific community at that time would rely heavily on assumptions and public opinions about their religious beliefs and music to the point that these external influences marred the credibility of the information.

Preliminary investigations into Gullah/Geechee religion and music reveal several oddities and errors in terms of documentation. On one end, research on the Gullah/Geechee people focuses on Christianity (African Baptist) as part of the social structure in the community. On the other end, I have noticed some academics addressing how the Gullah/Geechee also apply conjure, hoodoo, and voodoo through certain external interpretations of beliefs and practices: primarily, through root doctors, home remedies, and dream interpretations.[140] In the more extreme cases, some sources have tried equating the Gullah/Geechee use of conjure to a form of spirit possession. Such discussions illustrate the social problem of dismissing and stereotyping these practices as "superstitious." [141]

Part of the problem with this kind of stereotyping stems from the public and academic perceptions from the early twentieth century concerning music, religion, and the Gullah/Geechee community from

---

[140] Peggy MacLeod Vogel, *Biculturalism and Identity in Contemporary Gullah Families* (Blacksburg, VA: Virginia Tech, 2000), https://vtechworks.lib.vt.edu/bitstream/handle/10919/37496/dissert2.pdf?sequence=1 (accessed October 13, 2020), PhD. Dissertation.

[141] Keith Cartwright. "Voodoo Hermeneutics/The Crossroads Sublime: Soul Musics, Mindful Body and Creole Consciousness," *Mississippi Quarterly* 57, No. 1 (2003-04). https://www.jstor.org/stable/26466953 (accessed January 11. 2021).

people *outside* the region. The observational biases and racialized assumptions about the Gullah/Geechee and their customs in early field research demonstrate a lack of understanding and racist tendencies. Despite efforts from ethnographers like Melville Herskovitz to try and correct these mistakes, much of the field research from the early twentieth century would view the Gullah/Geechee in exoticist terms.[142]

Melissa Cooper addresses early twentieth century ethnography concerning the Gullah/Geechee in her research from 2012. Cooper focuses specifically on the Gullah/Geechee from Sapelo Island in Georgia and the popular misconceptions about voodoo in the United States and other parts of the world. Referring to U.S. newspaper articles and crime reports from the 1920s and 30s (both from national newspaper presses and presses owned and operated by African Americans), Cooper illustrates the racialized depictions in the United States towards voodoo and its practitioners through media by stressing the exaggerated "connections" between African identities and the occult.[143] Cooper looks at this historical period through multiple angles via the effects of U.S. imperialism in Haiti, U.S. ethnocentric views of Afro-Cubans, and the impact of the transnational migration of African Americans from the southern U.S. to the northern regions. In many instances, newspapers (specifically, those run by White Supremacists) would often try to link voodoo to increased crime rates and murders in the United States[144]

Thinking within the context of research from Miles and Brown which I referred to several chapters earlier, the transnational aspect of voodoo could additionally help to provide readers with an understanding of ethnicization via internal class struggles. Cooper refutes the essentialist assumption that African Americans from different areas of the United States got along with each other in the early twentieth century. Instead, she demonstrates that African American communities in the north frequently resented southern African Americans who arrived in their region in "The Great Migration," which began in the 1910s. Such disdain stemmed from the fear of rising hate crimes and cultural stereotyping in the northern United States. Newspaper presses run by Black Americans in areas like New York City and Chicago would often warn the public against voodoo

---

[142] Melissa Cooper, "Chapter 3: The Voodoo Craze: Popular Media Interprets African Survivals During the 1920s and 30s," in *"They Made Gullah": Modernist Primitivist and the Discovery and Creation of Sapelo Island, Georgia's Gullah Community, 1915-1991* (New Brunswick, NJ: Rutgers University, 2012), 107-145. PhD Dissertation.

[143] Melissa Cooper, 2012.

[144] Melissa Cooper, 2012.

practitioners living in the U.S., despite also frequently refusing to publicly reprint false stories from newspapers operated by White people.[145]

Cooper also quickly points out the hypocritical nature of (White) Americans who demonized voodoo, hoodoo, and conjure and their practitioners. She notes that, even though White people in the United States attacked and arrested African Americans for these "occult" practices and beliefs, many White people had adhered to the Spiritualist movement since the 1840s. This is significant because Spiritualism used some of the same approaches as voodoo, hoodoo, and conjure: primarily, summoning and communicating with the dead.[146] In other words, the simultaneous American fixation on and denunciation of voodoo, hoodoo, and conjure were primarily grounded in racialized ideas.

The skewed portrayals of the Gullah/Geechee people helped to further perpetuate stereotypes about the community in the "Modernist Primitivism" artistic movement and ethnographic research on Sapelo Island from the 1920s and 30s. This approach aimed to reexamine and elevate aspects of African culture in the United States, albeit from predominantly Western and culturally ignorant perspectives via exploitation.[147] That specific problem persists in the twenty-first century and should not be dismissed as something from a bygone era.

In discussing the respective ethnographic works from W. Robert Moore, Lydia Parrish and Lorenzo Dow Turner, Melissa Cooper compares their markedly different approaches to understanding and interacting with the Gullah/Geechee people. Cooper notes that Moore and Parrish, as outsiders to the community (They came from the midwestern and northern United States via Michigan and New Jersey), both exhibit instances of observational biases in their works: primarily as ways to entice (White) readers unfamiliar with the culture.[148] Their tactics also serve as

---

[145] Melissa Cooper, 2012.

[146] Melissa Cooper, 2012, 111.

[147] Melissa Cooper, "Chapter 1: From Wild Savages to Beloved Primitives: Modernists Recast African Blacks' Africanness," in *"They Made Gullah": Modernist Primitivist and the Discovery and Creation of Sapelo Island, Georgia's Gullah Community, 1915-1991* (New Brunswick, NJ: Rutgers University, 2012), 33-65. PhD Dissertation.

[148] Melissa Cooper, "Chapter 4- Hunting Survivals: W. Robert Moore, Lydia Parrish, and Lorenzo D. Turner Discover Gullah Folk on Sapelo Island," in *"They Made Gullah": Modernist Primitivist and the Discovery and Creation of Sapelo Island, Georgia's Gullah Community, 1915-1991* (New Brunswick, NJ: Rutgers University, 2012), 150-184. PhD Dissertation.

reminders for what aspiring ethnographers in the twenty-first century should avoid doing when conducting field research with informants.

What exactly do Moore and Parrish do wrong in their respective investigations? Looking more closely at how they address the Gullah/Geechee, these researchers commit several blunders. Their methodologies often apply essentialist ideas about Gullah/Geechee connections to Africa, mannerisms, and historiographies about slavery. In certain instances, their approaches involve committing Libel by misquoting what informants said and tampering with field research data. Melissa Cooper illustrates these problems in her description of the 1934 field research on coastal Georgia from W. Robert Moore and his interview with the Johnson family: members of the Gullah/Geechee community. By referring to their feedback about the interview, Cooper notes how Moore attempted to manipulate his informants by defaming their character and altering photographs to give the appearance of authenticity.[149]

Gullah/Geechee music also did not escape scrutiny in ethnography from the early twentieth century. This music functions primarily as an oral tradition that does not rely on Western musical notation or transcriptions of lyrics. While documents like those from the early twentieth century do exist, those kinds of sources derive mainly from scholars and folklorists not affiliated with the Gullah/Geechee. Such is the case with the research from W. Robert Moore and Lydia Parrish. Moore talks about Gullah/Geechee music in disparaging terms via assumptions about Africa, slavery, and Christianity: "disparaging" in the sense that his work appealed mainly to the racialized imaginations of White people in that era and in how he incorrectly implies that Gullah/Geechee Christianity serves as a form of cultural assimilation to European Christianity.[150]

Lydia Parrish, who produced a catalog of African American slave songs in coastal Georgia, expresses similar sentiments in her ethnomusicological work. Even though the research from Parrish presents a decent effort, her work does not come without its fair share of problems. She demonstrates archaic social attitudes and errors that most likely would not work in the twenty-first century. Lydia Parrish conducted her research

---

[149] Melissa Cooper, 2012, 150-166.
[150] Melissa Cooper, 2012, 150-166.

in the 1930s and 40s and had to gain trust from the Gullah/Geechee and African American communities so that she could conduct her work. [151]

What tarnishes the credibility of her research stems from her misguided approach towards the African American community in the southern United States and her misinterpretation of their dance and musical practices. She often talks about African American music culture in essentialist terms or dismissing customary song and dance, like the Ring Shout, as completely meaningless: partially because she does not understand the significance of the Gullah/Geechee language and customs. In other instances, Parrish would comment on the reluctance of her Gullah/Geechee informants to sing and dance for her for the purpose of her research.[152] That approach to ethnographic scholarship would be considered careless and unethical in the 2020s. Still, readers need to think within the contexts of the period in which Parrish wrote her research and the limited scope of knowledge that she had as an outsider to the southeastern region of the United States.

Where does that leave Lorenzo Dow Turner? He is included in many investigations about the Gullah/Geechee because of how he approaches their language and culture out of respect for the community: *not* to manipulate the people, as others had done.[153] Turner approached his ethnographic interviews with members of the Gullah from a professional standpoint with concrete data instead of erroneous preconceived notions. Even though Turner worked with Lydia Parrish in the 1930s, he did not allow observational biases to influence his ethnography. Turner was also an outsider, although an African American and one who gained the trust of the Gullah/Geechee people so that he could pursue his work.[154]

Why does language matter in this discussion when this chapter focuses on religion and music? The answer to that question lies in how Turner describes the Gullah/Geechee people. He does more than provide a deep study of the linguistics. His work breaks the stereotypes about the

---

[151] Melissa Cooper, 2012, 166-184; Art Rosenbaum and Lydia Parish "Foreword," in *Slave Songs of the Georgia Sea Islands* (Athens, GA: Brown Thrasher Books, University of Georgia Press, 1992), xiii-xx.

[152] Art Rosenbaum and Lydia Parish "Foreword," in *Slave Songs of the Georgia Sea Islands* (Athens, GA: Brown Thrasher Books, University of Georgia Press, 1992), xiii-xx.

[153] Melissa Cooper, "Chapter 4- Hunting Survivals: W. Robert Moore, Lydia Parrish, and Lorenzo D. Turner Discover Gullah Folk on Sapelo Island," in *"They Made Gullah": Modernist Primitivist and the Discovery and Creation of Sapelo Island, Georgia's Gullah Community, 1915-1991* (New Brunswick, NJ: Rutgers University, 2012), 185-198. PhD Dissertation.

[154] Melissa Cooper, 185-198.

Gullah/Geechee and their cultural customs, *including* religion. Concerning this last part, Turner did not begin his research by crafting false ideas about voodoo, hoodoo, and conjure. His work from the 1930s and 40s additionally does not explicitly indicate assumptions about these religious practices within the Gullah/Geechee community.[155]

While I also mentioned that the Gullah/Geechee language functions as a Creolized combination of African dialects and English, this simple surface definition does not suffice. One must also understand *why* such connections to African dialects exist within the Gullah/Geechee community, besides the West African links via enslavement and forced migration. Contemporary research on and comprehension of the Gullah/Geechee language mainly derives from *Africanisms in the Gullah Dialect* (1949) by Lorenzo Dow Turner. While Katherine Wyly Mille and Michael B. Montgomery indicate that others had previously documented details about the Gullah/Geechee people and their language in the nineteenth and early twentieth centuries, many of the sources from those periods are suspect when compared to the work by Turner. Both fictional narratives and scholarly works of the time—that is, before *Africanisms*— did not resist racist or revisionist tendencies about Africa, African Americans, and the Gullah/Geechee. These usually arose in the forms of incorrect statements (that all Black Americans had no African ancestry) and anglicized, insulting ethnocentrism (referring to the Gullah/Geechee language as regressive and infantile derivations of British and American English).[156]

Lorenzo Dow Turner changed perceptions of the Gullah/Geechee language and people by ignoring the stereotypes and conducting real ethnographic research. He additionally gained the trust of the Gullah/Geechee community as an African American linguist: someone from the etic perspective (Turner was born in North Carolina), but who was motivated by curiosity rather than by exploitation and greed. His decades of research and interest about the Gullah/Geechee language originated in the late 1920s while pursuing a university teaching position in Orangeburg, South Carolina. Years later, in the early 1930s, Turner was tasked with compiling southern dialects for the *Linguistic Atlas of the United States and Canada*. Many of the audio recordings that formed part of his

---

[155] Melissa Cooper, 185-198.

[156] Katherine Wyly Mille and Michael B. Montgomery (Eds.), "Introduction." in *Africanisms in the Gullah Dialect* (Columbia, SC: University of South Carolina Press, 1949, 2002), xi-xlix. Lorenzo Dow Turner, "Chapter 1. BACKGROUNDS," in *Africanisms in the Gullah Dialect* (Columbia, SC: University of South Carolina Press, 1949, 2002), 1-14.

research survive in the Library of Congress under the *American Dialectical Society* collection, such as the two-part "Interview with Dave White, St. Simons Saint Simons Island, Georgia (Gullah), July 26, 1933."[157] I discuss these specific wire field recordings in relation to their benefits (and drawbacks) as sound artifacts for preserving Gullah/Geechee cultural memory and speech at a later point.

The focus of *Africanisms* stems from Turner researching and corroborating the cultural connections with the Gullah/Geechee and West African languages: of which, there exist multiple types in the latter region. His research proves that Gullah/Geechee functions as a Creole African language with English-sounding elements. Additionally, Gullah/Geechee uses a grammatical structure and principles.[158] Regarding the methodology that Turner applies for his research, the process largely would involve recording and documenting speech patterns and conversations with informants from within the Gullah/Geechee community in South Carolina and Georgia. These interviews often consisted of questionnaires with selected people (primarily, the elderly) about Gullah/Geechee society and culture or recollections of slavery. In every case, Turner initially had to ask for permission from the informants before recording and dictating what they said.[159]

Lorenzo Dow Turner does not limit his informants in *Africanisms* to only members of the Gullah/Geechee in Georgia and South Carolina. He realized during his research that he also needed to include African informants and languages from the continent and other Creole and transculturated dialects from Europe (France and Portugal) and Latin America (Brazil). To learn these languages and prove his findings to his audience, especially White people who still accepted erroneous notions

---

[157] Katherine Wyly Mille and Michael B. Montgomery (Eds.), "Introduction," in *Africanisms in the Gullah Dialect* (Columbia, SC: University of South Carolina Press, 1949, 2002), xi-xlix; Lorenzo Dow Turner, "Interview with Dave White, St. Simons Island, Georgia, July 26, 1933 (part 1 of 2)." Library of Congress, https://www.loc.gov/item/afc1984011_afs25666a/ (accessed October 5, 2020); "Interview with Dave White, St. Simons Island, Georgia, July 26, 1933 (part 2 of 2)," Library of Congress. https://www.loc.gov/item/afc1984011_afs25666b (accessed October 5, 20200.

[158] Lorenzo Dow Turner, "Chapter 2. PHONETIC ALPHABET AND DIACRITICS," in *Africanisms in the Gullah Dialect* (Columbia, SC: University of South Carolina Press, 1949, 2002), 15-29.

[159] Katherine Wyly Mille and Michael B. Montgomery (Eds.), in *Africanisms in the Gullah Dialect* (Columbia, SC: University of South Carolina Press, 1949, 2002), xi-xlix.

about African culture, Turner physically travelled abroad to areas like Europe, the United Kingdom, parts of West Africa, and Brazil.[160] I will discuss an example of the ethnographic contribution that Turner made to recording and preserving Afro-Brazilian Candomblé at a later in this investigation.

It is evident that the research that Lorenzo Dow Turner presents in *Afircanisms* features vastly significant ethnography that remains useful in more contemporary times. However, this does not suggest that his work is completely perfect. *Africanisms* is limited by the scope of the period in which Turner conducted his research: the 1930s and 40s. That research occurred decades before the construction of bridges in the 1950s, which linked the Gullah/Geechee land and people to the rest of the United States and the world. *Africanisms* should also not be considered the *only* scholarly source on Gullah/Geechee language and culture. Wyly Mille and Michael B. Montgomery demonstrate that the scholarship on that topic continued and expanded upon what Turner encountered in his research long after his death in the 1970s.[161] One must also consider the more contemporary linguistic and archival work on the Gullah/Geechee today by incorporating digital technology, social media, and streaming platforms through efforts from scholars like Sunn m'Cheaux.[162]

Lorenzo Dow Turner never intended to exploit the Gullah/Geechee through his linguistic fieldwork. Melissa Cooper nonetheless addresses some minor problems with his book. Turner sought to study the Gullah/Geechee as an isolated community on the basis that their language and culture required preserving so that *outsiders* could understand them. In this way he could physically disprove previous

---

[160] Katherine Wyly Mille and Michael B. Montgomery (Eds.), xi-xlix.

[161] Katherine Wyly Mille and Michael B. Montgomery (Eds.), xi-xlix; Kendra Hamilton, "Mother Tongues and Captive Identities: Celebrating and 'Disapearing' the Gullah/Geechee Coast," *Mississippi Quarterly* 65, No. 1 (2012), https://www.jstor.org/stable/26467170?Search=yes&resultItemClick=true&searchText=gullah&searchText=geechee&searchText=music&searchUri=%2Faction%2FdoBasicSearch%3FsearchType%3DfacetSearch%26amp%3Bcty_journal_facet%3Dam91cm5hbA%253D%253D%26amp%3Bsd%3D%26amp%3Bed%3D%26amp%3BQuery%3Dgullah%2Bgeechee%2Bmusic&ab_segments=0%2Fdefault-2%2Fcontrol&refreqid=search%3A42dff46f866b6678b1dd5f90ccec0f74&seq=1#page_scan_tab_contents. (accessed July 8, 2019).

[162] Sunn m'Cheaux. "The Pros and Cons of Code-Switching for Creole Speakers," *YouTube* (October 7, 2020), https://www.youtube.com/watch?v=movQMdB7hY0 (accessed October 13, 2020).

ideas about the Gullah/Geechee.[163] That is why part of the ethnographic research from Turner features written samples and audio recordings from informants talking about religion and daily life customs. Some of these samples have been preserved and digitized by the Library of Congress and are currently available online in electronic formats.

The Ring Shout

What about the musical aspects in the Gullah/Geechee community? That documentation for this research suggests a reliance on sacred music: primarily, of spirituals and Ring Shouts. However, sources often do not take into consideration the possibility of secular music to present a more even view of Gullah/Geechee music culture. Additionally, the scholarly attention on Gullah/Geechee music presents a contradiction. Music forms a vital component of Gullah/Geechee society through cultural festivals and recordings, but its inclusion in some Gullah/Geechee scholarship is approached more like an afterthought. Music usually gets included within the larger, broader spectrum of "the Arts" in Gullah/Geechee culture and society or within the context of African influences in the United States. Topics concerning history, land preservation, and language usually take precedence and receive more attention because of more extant documentation.

Most resources on Gullah/Geechee sacred music, regardless of the scant amount and inconsistencies, concentrates on the Ring Shout and audio recording preservation. Katrina Hazzard-Donald discusses the Ring Shout within the context of African American religious dance. Hazzard-Donald primarily aims to aid readers in reframing their comprehension of dance in the United States. Throughout her article, she attempts to establish a connection with the combination of hoodoo and Christianity: a connection that, as we have seen, proved problematic in the early twentieth century due to misinterpretations and racism.[164] According to Hazzard-Donald, this combination of religious influences eventually led to an Americanization of ancient African dance practices. While Hazzard-

---

[163] Melissa Cooper, "Chapter 4- Hunting Survivals: W. Robert Moore, Lydia Parrish, and Lorenzo D. Turner Discover Gullah Folk on Sapelo Island," in *"They Made Gullah": Modernist Primitivist and the Discovery and Creation of Sapelo Island, Georgia's Gullah Community, 1915-1991* (New Brunswick, NJ: Rutgers University, 2012), 150-184. PhD Dissertation.

[164] Katrina Hazzard-Donald, "Hoodoo religion and American dance traditions: rethinking the ring shout," *Journal of Pan African Studies* 4, No. 6 (2011), p. 194+, http://www.jpanafrican.org/docs/vol4no6/4.6-11HoodooReligion.pdf (accessed October 13, 2020).

Donald does reveal pieces of information about the historiography and performance aspect of the Ring Shout, I encountered one glaring omission from her research. She neglects to specify the impact of the Gullah/Geechee people.[165]

Mason Stewart also discusses the Ring Shout, but from the perspective of history and performance practice. Stewart mentions the processes behind the Ring Shout, which combines the sacred "call and response" format of the Shout with the secular dance format of the Ring Play. Besides discussing the connections of the Ring Shout to slavery and emancipation in the U.S., he also mentions how the dancing needed some modifications to conform to the restrictions of Protestant Christianity. These changes were deemed necessary, because excessive dancing was perceived as evil and distracting.[166] To support his work, Mason Stewart cites examples of spoken or sung texts and provides ethnographic insight from members of the Gullah/Geechee community like Griffon Lotson (whom I describe in more detail later in this investigation). Stewart notes that, since the 1980s, people from the Gullah/Geechee community have formed Ring Shout ensembles to try and preserve the music for future generations.[167]

Based on research from Margalit Fox, the Ring Shout (See rhythmic example in Figure 12) functions as a sacred dance performed by a group of people in a circle, often danced in counterclockwise motion. Fox indicates that the term "Shout" in the Gullah/Geechee language derives from the Arabic word *Saut*, which refers to a type of dance rather than a vocalization. In this case, "Shout" refers the process of crossing the feet.[168] The National Parks Service corroborates this information in their description of the Ring Shout, noting its distinct connection to West Africa:

The shout consists of call- and- response singing and rhythmic dance movements in a counterclockwise circle. Shouters progress around

---

¹⁶⁵ Katrina Hazzard-Donald, 2011.

¹⁶⁶ Mason Stewart, "The Story of the Shout," *Elegant Island Living Media Group* (January 27, 2017), http://www.elegantislandliving.net/ssi-archives/the-story-of-the-shout/ (accessed October 13, 2020).

¹⁶⁷ Mason Stewart, 2017.

¹⁶⁸ Margalit Fox, "RING SHOUT" (oldest surviving African-American performance tradition of any kind), Original People (April 1, 2013), https://originalpeople.org/ring-shout-oldest-surviving-african-american-performance-tradition-kind/?fbclid=IwAR3IPkWCt-gv58RsSyvweZlIcKehhDu4Zj4bu4ODlhBFUTuJb8rVKU_iN68 (accessed October 13, 2020).

the circle with a shuffling movement wherein feet are never crossed and never leave the ground. There are interlocking, percussive body rhythms and a type of group devotion embedded in the shout that has made it a lifeline to the West African cultural legacy through times of slavery and into the 21st century. Shouters of today move in a counter clockwise (sic.) circle, pounding canes on the wooden floor or a sheet of plywood in a manner not unlike early foot drums.[169]

Ring Shouts form an important component of Gullah/Geechee religious practices, which partially draws inspiration from Baptist and Methodist religions from colonial America in the time of the "Great Awakening" in the 1750s. The Gullah/Geechee initially performed Ring Shouts strictly in private spaces of worship: what would eventually be renamed "praise houses."[170] Praise houses served as public areas for religious and secular services that combined West African and European Christian practices and ceremonies. For instance, members of the Gullah/Geechee community were often required to take long journeys into the woods in hopes of experiencing a dream or spiritual awakening. Members, then, had to return to the praise house to retell their experience from memory.[171] The secular purpose of the praise house served as a public space for settling disputes with family members or neighbors within the community. One can get a sense of the praise house structure by visiting the historic Mitchelville Freedom Park near Hilton Head, South Carolina.[172]

Some may wonder why the Ring Shout features simple instrumentation. Why does this music incorporate clapping, sticks and wash basins instead of drums and other instruments? It turns out that there is a valid historical reason for using these "found" instruments: one that relates to the colonialism and forms of resistance that I described in the previous chapter. Amy Lotson Roberts and Patrick J. Holladay, in addition to the National Parks Service, note that the White plantation enslavers in the southern United States forbade Gullah/Geechee people from using drums.

---

[169] National Park Service, "2. Affected People and Environment," in *Low Country Gullah Culture Special Resource Study and Final Environmental Impact Statement* (Atlanta, GA: NPS Southeast Regional Office, 2005), 69-70.

[170] Margalit Fox, 2013.

[171] Peggy MacLeod Vogel, *Biculturalism and Identity in Contemporary Gullah Families* (Blacksburg, VA: Virginia Tech, 2000), https://vtechworks.lib.vt.edu/bitstream/handle/10919/37496/dissert2.pdf?sequence=1 (accessed October 13, 2020), PhD. Dissertation.

[172] "About Us," *Historic Mitchelville Freedom Park* (No Date), https://exploremitchelville.org/about-us (accessed September 24, 2020).

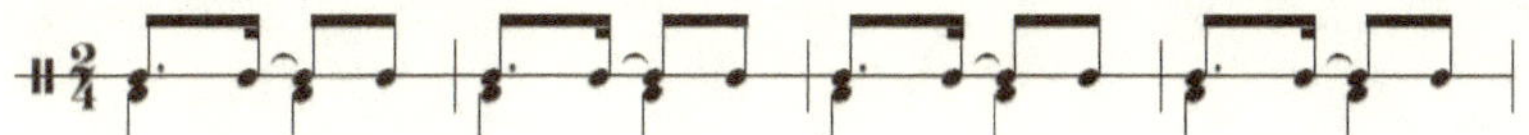

Figure 12: Ring Shout Rhythm[173]

Figure 13: Praise House in Mitchelville, South Carolina

---

[173] This is a notated approximation of the rhythm involved in the Ring Shout through the hands (top) and feet (bottom). I have seen other notated interpretations that use this pattern, but as one measure with forward and backward repeats.

Figure 14: Church Sermon (Display) at Boone Hall Plantation Slave Quarters—Mt. Pleasant, South Carolina

Roberts and Holladay indicate that this decision arose because of the tendency for the enslaved West Africans to use drumming as coded messages for insurrection.[174] This reasoning proves logical given what I previously discussed about insurrections like the Stono Rebellion earlier in this study.

Erica Lanice Washington confirms this information in her research on the Ring Shout. She specifies that, because of the effects of the Stono Rebellion in 1739, the British colonizers enacted laws the following year that disallowed drums for *any* kind of communal gathering or service. As a result, the enslaved West Africans in the southern United States used their bodies and whatever items that they had at their disposal as practicable alternatives for musical instruments.[175] Readers should not misinterpret the restrictions on drumming as something exclusive to the

[174] Amy Lotson Roberts and Patrick J. Holladay, PhD., "Part I. An Introduction to the History of the Golden Isles," in *Gullah Geechee Heritage in the Golden Isles* (Stroud, UK (?): HISTORY Press, 2019), 26-28; National Park Service, "2. Affected People and Environment," in *Low Country Gullah Culture Special Resource Study and Final Environmental Impact Statement* (Atlanta, GA: NPS Southeast Regional Office, 2005), 69-70.

[175] Erica Lanice Washington, "CHAPTER II. RING SHOUT IN U.S. SLAVE COMMUNITIES," in *"Shabach Hallelujah!": The Continuity of the Ring Shout Tradition as a Site of Music and Dance in Black American Worship* (Bowling Green, OH: Bowling Green State University, 2005), 26-55, https://etd.ohiolink.edu/apexprod/rws_etd/send_file/send?accession=bgsu11310 54976&disposition=inline (accessed May 20, 2021).

United States, though. Similar instances occurred in Latin America and the Caribbean for similar reasons. For example, Afro-Puerto Ricans in the nineteenth century had used bomba music and dance as vehicles for protesting enslavement. The Spanish imperial government at the time also placed restrictions on performing these musical genres in public.[176]

[176] Guillermo A. Baralt and Christine Ayorinde (English Transl.), "Chapter V. From the Bomba Dance in Ponce to the New Reglamento de Esclavos de Puerto Rico of 1826," in *Slave Revolts in Puerto Rico* (Princeton: Markus Wiener Publishers, 2007), 41-52.

Research on Afro-Latin Syncretic Religions and Music

Figure 15: African Drum—Possibly Batá, or Djembe

"You must judge a man by the work of his hands."

~African Proverb

"He who is his own judge never finds a reason to condemn."

~Hebrew Proverb

Much has been written about African syncretic religions in Latin America and the Caribbean. Most of the scholarship tends to present myriad (and confusing) information that tries to explain what syncretic religions are. They also focus on the historiography and politicization of such beliefs: primarily, how societies tried to silence these practices through public bans or framing them within the contexts of a reconfigured identity and exploitative cultural tourism.[177] Despite the differences in geography and names (Cuban Lucumí, Brazilian Candomblé, and Puerto Rican Espiritismo), I have located recurrent patterns in the perceptions of these syncretic religions: many of which

---

[177] J. Rausenberger, "Santurismo: The Commodification of Santeria and the Touristic Value of Afro-Cuban Derived Religions in Cuba," *Almatourism Special Issue* N. 8 (2018), 150-171, https://almatourism.unibo.it/article/view/7775 (accessed June 22, 2021).

parallel discussions about the Gullah/Geechee with Christianity, voodoo, hoodoo, conjure, and root medicine. It is equally interesting that scholars like Erica Lanice Washington have tried connecting syncretic religion and Catholic influences with the Gullah/Geechee and the Ring Shout, versus what she views as the more prominent English Protestant impact on that community.[178]

Sources from the past and present have associated Afro-Latin syncretic religions with spirit possession and magic. From a historical standpoint, such associations with the occult have been negatively attributed to Afro-Latin Americans by outsiders to attempt to disparage and erase their cultural identities. Of course, Afro-Latin communities are aware of these harmful cultural portrayals. That is why they have been attempting to restore their image and teach the public about these practices from their own perspectives.

I must mention several important points about Afro-Latin syncretism to prevent confusion. Concerning the syncretic religion called Spiritism, credit for creating the religion has often gone to Allan Kardec. However, more contemporary research indicates that the *real* credit should go to the indigenous and African groups who brought their syncretic religious practices to Latin America and the Caribbean. Kardec did not establish Spiritism. He merely devised the *philosophical principles* to apply to forms of Spiritism.[179]

Christianity and much of the scholarship from researchers outside the Afro-Latin communities frequently refer to African syncretic religions as "cults." This word, along with the use of the name "Santeria" as a derivation of these syncretic religions functions as a derogatory term. Concerning the availability of information about syncretic religions, Cuba and Brazil often receive more scholarly attention than Puerto Rico. Even though extant information about this topic in relation to that island exists, such research often involves looking beyond the surface descriptions and expanding the linguistic

---

[178] Erica Lanice Washington, "CHAPTER II. RING SHOUT IN U.S. SLAVE COMMUNITIES," in *"Shabach Hallelujah!": The Continuity of the Ring Shout Tradition as a Site of Music and Dance in Black American Worship* (Bowling Green, OH: Bowling Green State University, 2005), 26-55, https://etd.ohiolink.edu/apexprod/rws_etd/send_file/send?accession=bgsu11310 54976&disposition=inline (accessed May 20, 2021).

[179] Alexander Moreira-Almeida, "Spiritism: The Work of Allan Kardec and Its Implications for Spiritual Transformation," *metanexus* (September 2, 2008), https://metanexus.net/spiritism-work-allan-kardec-and-its-implications-spiritual-transformation/ (accessed October 19, 2021).

parameters to include relevant academic sources in Spanish. Some academic research on syncretic religions in Puerto Rico date from the late 1990s to 2010s, like the respective academic works from Marta Moreno Vega, Bettina E. Schmidt, and José Santana.[180] These scholars all illustrate, in one form or another, the constant struggle to acknowledge African identity in Puerto Rico and to fight against racialization and oppression.

Many discussions about African syncretic religions in Latin America and the Caribbean also take areas of the Francophone (French-speaking) and Anglophone (English-speaking) Caribbean into consideration: places like Haiti and Jamaica, often in relation to hoodoo and voodoo. The historiography concerning syncretic religions in Cuba, Puerto Rico, and Brazil focuses largely on their social misinterpretations and governmental suppression. This is both problematic and necessary, because these moments in history illustrate how societies thought about syncretic religious practices. Recent activism from Latin American and Caribbean syncretic religions serves to (re)educate the public, prevent stereotyping, and peacefully protest hate crimes. These procedures are necessary, because syncretic religions are still being persecuted or misused in the era of social media and rampant misinformation.

Understanding the Different Types of Spritism and Social Perceptions of Afro-Latin Syncretic Religions

All three geographical regions discussed in this chapter apply similar approaches to honoring African deities, albeit with linguistic differences. Cuba and Puerto Rico refer to the deities as "orishas" or "orichas," while Brazil uses the Portuguese spelling of "orixas." In these regions and elsewhere across Latin America and the Caribbean, the syncretic religions honor the Seven African Powers: Eshu

---

[180] Marta Moreno Vega, " Espiritismo in the Puerto Rican Community: A New World Recreation with the Elements of Kongo Ancestor Worship," *Journal of Black Studies* 29, No, 3 (1999), 325-353, https://www.jstor.org/stable/2668062 (accessed June 25, 2021); Bettina E. Schmidt, "The Power of the Spirits: The Formation of Identity based on Puerto Rican Spiritism, *Revista de Estudos da Religao* No. 2 (2006), 127-154, https://www.pucsp.br/rever/rv2_2006/p_schmidt.pdf (accessed June 25, 2021); José Santana, "An Absent History: The Marks of Africa on Puerto Rican Popular Catholicism (Dayton, OH: University of Dayton, 2017), 1-104, Master's Thesis, https://etd.ohiolink.edu/apexprod/rws_etd/send_file/send?accession=dayton150048226 1688046&disposition=inline (accessed June 25, 2021).

Elegbara, Ogun, Obatala; Yemaya, Oshun, Shango, and Oya.[181] I should note, however, that people must not perceive syncretic religions in absolutist and homogenous terms. Syncretism consists of multiple types of religious belief systems and practices based on African (and indigenous) rituals. Spiritism presents a good example of this. Despite how some scholars in the past would try to erase the African connections to Spiritism, the African links nonetheless remain an integral part of this syncretic religion. Spiritism also should not be interpreted as only one type. It consists of many different subsets practiced all over Latin America and the Caribbean.

 Scientific Espiritismo, also referred to as *Table Spiritism* or *White Table ("Mesa Blanca") Spiritism* originated in Cuba. However, it is also applied in other Latin American and Caribbean regions like Puerto Rico. Scientific Espiritismo follows the philosophical principles espoused by Allan Kardec and involves group communication with the deceased (via a séance) while seated around a white table. It also involves spirit possession through a medium, (who answers questions from participants and tries to resolve certain problems) and incorporates moments of prayer, hymns, and music.[182]

 Espiritiso de Cordon refers to a type of Spiritism used for healing that involves multiple processes: things like bodily movements (joining hands via walking in a circle, stomping, vocal chanting, noises, etc.) and purification by using water administered by a Head Medium to cleanse participants in the ritual space from evil spirits. At first glance, parts of this description sound like the procedures incorporated in the Ring Shout via the Gullah/Geechee from the United States. The Ring Shout also applies stomping and chanting, but it does *not* involve spirit possession due to its connections to Christianity. Some scholars also suggest that Espiritismo de Cordon contains closer links to the Taino Indian *areito* ritual ceremony rather than to African connections.[183]

---

[181] Federal Bureau of Prisons, "Orisha Manual," https://www.bop.gov/foia/docs/orishamanual.pdf (accessed February 23.2021). I have found it perplexing that there is no key explanation as to why Federal Bureau of Prisons has access to a digitized guidebook about African Orishas.

[182] Marta Moreno Vega, " Espiritismo in the Puerto Rican Community: A New World Recreation with the Elements of Kongo Ancestor Worship," *Journal of Black Studies* 29, No, 3 (1999), 325-353, https://www.jstor.org/stable/2668062 (accessed June 25, 2021)

[183] Jorge Luis Morejón, "From the *Areito* to the *Cordon*: indigenous healing dances," *Revista Brasileira de Estudos da Presença* 8, No. 3 (2018), 563-591,

Espiritismo Cruzado, by contrast, *does* have links to Africa by combining Catholicism with Afro-Cuban *Palo* religious practices. It combines religious elements from both Scientific Spiritism and Espirismo de Cordon and is used for initiating Lucumí priests in Regla de Ocha. Of particular importance is the Mass for the Dead, which encourages deceased ancestors to cross over to the afterlife and communicate with living family members about dream interpretations.[184] This last part demonstrates another possible connection with the Gullah/Geechee. I mentioned earlier that they, too, stress the importance of honoring their ancestors and interpreting dreams, albeit as an individual spiritual epiphany. It deserves mention that other versions of Spiritism also present more combinations of religious practices. This is also seen in *Santerismo*, which fuses procedures from Santeria with Spiritism. Santerismo also involves forms of spirit possession through a medium and communication with members of the afterlife. Scholarship on Santerismo indicates that this syncretic religion has manifested in places like Puerto Rico and transnationally in Cuban and Puerto Rican communities in the United States.[185]

Concerning Puerto Rico and its place in the syncretic religion spectrum, I hinted that the island features Scientific Spiritist practices

---

https://www.scielo.br/j/rbep/a/WS5vKQPZPp9D454fj8NkFKx/?format=pdf&lang=en (accessed October 18, 2021).

[184] Yalexy Castañeda Mache, Escenificación: Vida y Muerte *Misa spiritual en el Espiritismo Cruzado*" Centro de Investigaciones Psicologicas y Sociologicas (CIPS) (1999), https://core.ac.uk/reader/35230410 (accessed October 19, 2021).

[185] Bettina E. Schmidt, "The Power of the Spirits: The Formation of Identity based on Puerto Rican Spiritism, *Revista de Estudos da Religao* No. 2 (2006), 127-154, https://www.pucsp.br/rever/rv2_2006/p_schmidt.pdf (accessed June 25, 2021); Erwan Dianteill, "Deterritorialization and Reterritorialization of the Orisha Religion in African and the New World (Nigeria, Cuba and the United States)," *International Journal of Urban and Regional Research* 26, 1 (2002), https://d1wqtxts1xzle7.cloudfront.net/47930509/1468-2427.0036720160809-30095-xv08gj-with-cover-page-v2.pdf?Expires=1634663416&Signature=P0bOqjJIqPOxJVoJjmZV4l~W6Z2eKVmYlpFbiatk7iGoTcg5T~8tPh~veXHNoDgBf6E9Hlb08V7wYByRay5RD-kV5ac3SYWR6cqWdteadnTGC34~oWZLNbMtjBcwK4lBMg-gVDwupuLbc~y5l6ol8RgLT2dwEE1avEek~q4YZvImQqcOfebcsC65Sh-U78K33KiXXMQ5nLptO7jGX86wKuS4PC7KNVZMeBO1IYJt2SFXpEQLsOtYmypOceiOCghHdI5CUoprxw0ovGZzrSWxbSXXZ8UhnBgUQ1nlVDifOr2Zyxt9BZOBDbat53HsdeGqFmBhksM2DYrbKvNaHuoq~A__&Key-Pair-Id=APKAJLOHF5GGSLRBV4ZA (accessed October 19, 2021).

and other types of Spiritism derived from Cuba. Puerto Rico clearly has more than that. Consider *Indigenous Espiritismo*, which applies practices derived from Taino, African, and European Spanish cultures. Consider that Indigenous Espiritismo uses a *Bohique*, or medicine man, to administer procedures via magic, massages, or tobacco. Myriad contemporary research on Spiritism in Puerto Rico concentrates on root medicines as valuable forms for healing: an approach that could also allude to the similarities behind root medicines and the Gullah/Geechee in the U.S.[186] It also helps to consider that Puerto Rico has adopted other forms of Spiritism from other parts of Latin America and the Caribbean, like the ones that I previously mentioned.

Readers should also consider that the African influences on Christianity (Catholicism and Protestantism) in Puerto Rico consist of multiple forms of reverence. Although Puerto Rico has applied different forms of Espiritismo (Spiritism) on the island since the nineteenth century, there are other African-based religious customs in Puerto Rico besides Espiritismo. Contemporary research from José Santana reveals the significance of "Popular Catholicism" and the African influence of paying respects to deceased ancestors. Referring to contemporary research on Latin American and Caribbean Theology, Santana mentions several important points. Popular Catholicism reflects an *adapted* version of Catholicism by the colonized and culturally oppressed (Afro-)Puerto Rican communities. In this way, Popular Catholicism combines sacred and folkloric features that people on the island understand and can interpret in their own way.[187]

José Santana presents several examples of Popular Catholicism and African connections to Puerto Rico in his research from 2017. He mentions the *Fiesta de Santiago Apóstol* (Feast of Saint James the Apostle) in Loiza and *Carnaval* (Carnival) in the southern city of Ponce. These celebrations, which last for several days in winter and summer respectively, combine aspects of Catholic practices (like devotion to

---

[186] Mario A. Núñez Molina, "Community healing among Puerto Ricans: Espiritismo as a therapy for the soul," *Healing Cultures* (2001), https://academic.uprm.edu/~marion/SOULHEAL.htm (accessed October 18, 2021).

[187] José Santana, "An Absent History: The Marks of Africa on Puerto Rican Popular Catholicism (Dayton, OH: University of Dayton, 2017), 1-104, https://etd.ohiolink.edu/apexprod/rws_etd/send_file/send?accession=dayton150 0482261688046&disposition=inline (accessed June 25, 2021).

Saints) with Africanized cultural customs (like performing *bomba* music and ancestral reverence). The Fiesta de Santiago Apóstol commemorates the (historically mythologized) vanquishing of the Moors in the Crusades by St. James in the Middle Ages. Carnaval (like in Brazil, Cuba, the U.S., and other parts of the world) serves as the final celebration before Ash Wednesday and the start of fasting in Lent.[188] José Santana refers to these events as forms of Popular Catholicism because of how they fuse and adapt European Catholicism for the (Afro-)Puerto Rican public. Music contributes immensely to disseminating Popular Catholicism in Puerto Rico. In addition to the celebrations previously mentioned, José Santana also talks about the *baquine* and bomba as ways to musically interpret Catholicism through death and other religious customs. I find this interesting, considering that it encourages readers to expand their understanding of bomba music beyond the secular context.

Regarding the bomba and its place as a musical genre in Puerto Rico, I explained at the beginning of this book that bomba music incorporates a duple meter rhythm (with beats felt "in two") and can consist of different rhythmic types, like the "Bomba Sica" (See Figures 1 and 2). The instrumentation for bomba music consists of barrel drums and other occasional procession, like a log drum known as a *cua*, to complement the vocal "call and response" and dancing components: aspects that also manifest themselves in the Gullah/Geechee Ring Shout, but with different rhythms. I also referred to how the bomba initially functioned in the nineteenth century as a tool for transmitting coded messages among enslaved Afro-Puerto Ricans to indicate forms of rebellion and emancipation. I must add to this that bomba music and dance have existed for centuries since the 1500s.[189] Bomba in the twenty-first century is now considered a genre that encourages communal participation through *bombazos* meant for everyone in Puerto Rico. It should not be interpreted as music and dance exclusively for the Afro-Puerto Rican population. Bomba is also frequently used in modern, stylized settings and (in certain cases) gets combined with other genres through the

---

[188] José Santana, 1-104.

[189] Juan Cartagena, "When Bomba Music Becomes the Music of the Nation…" *Centro Journal* *XVI, num. 1* (2004), 14-35.

transnational lens of the mainland United States through genres like hip hop.[190]

During my travels across Puerto Rico in the 2010s, I encountered different towns and municipalities that strive to preserve the African identity on the island. The small town of Loiza, like the Gullah Geechee Cultural Heritage Corridor, is an enclave with rich African cultural traditions. The Centro Cultural Loiza (est. 1963) is a good example of this. This center preserves their traditions of the bomba music and dance. In addition to collecting instruments like bomba barrel drums, it has also documented festivities associated with the *Fiesta de Santiago Apóstol.*

Another example of non-invasive cultural preservation in Loiza stems from what locals call the "Batey de Los Hermanos Ayala." ("Batey" is a Puerto Rican Taino Indian word meaning "patio" or "communal space"). Understanding the significance of this place requires exploring the historical impact of the Ayala Family through their dance troupe Ballet Folklórico Hermanos Ayala[191]. Founded in 1959 by Castor Ayala Fuentes, the organization serves to revive the public African musical presence on the island. The batey consists of a small house that consists of an accompanying museum gift shop that highlights the African handmade items related to syncretic religion, like painted *vejigante* masks constructed from coconuts. These types of masks represent an important feature in both the Fiesta de Santiago Apóstol and Carnaval. The vejigante depicts a demon, meant to poke fun at the Moors as a reference to the Crusades, who carries a stick with an inflated cow bladder with which to hit random audience members. This process contains Christian symbolism because it is often used as a warning for people to do good deeds in life and go to Church.[192]

---

[190] Barton Halbert, "A Challenge to Puerto Rican Music: How to Build a Soberao for Bomba," *Centro Journal XVI, num. 1* (2004), 68-89; Juan Cartagena, "When Bomba Music Becomes the Music of the Nation…," *Centro Journal XVI, num. 1* (2004), 14-35.

[191] Ayala Brothers Folkloric Ballet

[192] José Santana, "An Absent History: The Marks of Africa on Puerto Rican Popular Catholicism (Dayton, OH: University of Dayton, 2017), 1-104, https://etd.ohiolink.edu/apexprod/rws_etd/send_file/send?accession=dayton150 04822261688046&disposition=inline (accessed June 25, 2021).

The Ballet Folklorico Hermanos Ayala and the batey are currently headed by descendants Raul and Raquel Ayala. Ballet Folklorico has helped archive Afro-Puerto Rican music and culture via bomba to the public through televised performances.[193] In this respect, their efforts to educate the community about their heritage, both on the island and overseas, parallel the educational work from the Gullah/Geechee communities through groups like the Geechee Kunda Center and the Geechee Gullah Ring Shouters singers and dancers based in coastal Georgia.

Information about syncretic religions and the orishas are currently available in print and electronic formats. Audio recordings of music used in Regla de Ocha and Candomblé from Cuba and Brazil are also currently accessible online via streaming services.[194] However, people need to exercise caution concerning the validity of some of these sources. These range from manuals and guides detailing the basic information, like which orishas are honored on which specific day and what procedures to follow, to more questionable commercial resources associating syncretic religions with magic and superstition.[195] In many respects that last part reflects the early writings about syncretic religions. Even though they do adhere to rituals involving ancestral worship, there has been the tendency for outsiders to completely misunderstand the original contexts. Such sources from the past contain flaws in terms of credible scholarship, but they also cannot be ignored as historical artifacts. Readers must understand the problems

---

[193] Feria del Barrio, "Ballet Folklorico Hermanos Ayala," *Feria del Barrio* (August 8, 2019) https://feriadelbarrio.org/2019/08/08/ballet-folklorico-hermanos-ayala/ (accessed November 5, 2021).

[194] Abbilona y Tambor Yoruba, *Eleggua, Ogun y Ochosi I* (Miami: Caribe Productions Inc., 1999; Stolkholm: Spotify, 1999), https://open.spotify.com/album/6PaZKP3MJOJBWzy12qQiGX (accessed June 22, 2021); Mestres Navagantes, *Candomble Ketu (Edicao Bahia/ vol.2)* (Vila Mariana, Sao Paolo, BR: Zapipa Producoes, 2019) (Stockholm: Spotify, 2019), https://open.spotify.com/album/3ylcymg08wg6iOBr0AsWHJ (accessed June 22, 2021). Finding musical resources related to Puerto Rican Espiritismo (Spiritism) becomes more complicated.

[195] Federal Bureau of Prisons, "Orisha Manual," https://www.bop.gov/foia/docs/orishamanual.pdf (accessed February 23.2021); "Seven African Powers," *Occult World*, 2020, http://occult-world.com/seven-african-powers (accessed February 23. 2021).

in the older academic materials and the mindset of the specific eras. To

Figure 16: Sra. Raquel Ayala (Right) at the Batey de Los Hermanos Ayala—
Loiza, Puerto Rico

Figure 17: Vejigante Masks—Loiza, Puerto Rico

Figure 18: Banner Commemorating the 2019 *Fiesta de Santiago Apóstol* and
Tricentennial of the city of Loiza, Puerto Rico

do that, I partially return to my discussion about Fernando Ortiz and his writings about Afro-Cuban society and religion at a later point. I focus more specifically on his perceptions of Afro-Cuban religious syncretic practices in the nineteenth and twentieth centuries.

To comprehend the significance of Lucumí in Cuba, because of the complex variants found in Afro-Latin syncretic religions, one must first look at the purpose(s) behind it. Javier Diaz mentions that Lucumí (what he refers to as "Regla de Ocha" and "Santeria") primarily involves attempting to accomplish good deeds to appease God, Nature, and the African ancestors to maintain a happy afterlife. Some of that process involves harnessing and accruing spiritual energy (*ashé*) from the natural environment.[196] Diaz describes Lucumí as a process involving three steps: honoring ancestors (*Egun*), praising the ancestors, and praising the deity Orunmila through the Yoruba syncretic religion known as *Ifá*. Diaz describes Orunmila as an important oricha in Lucumí because he is the deity that determines the lives and goals of humans. Despite this valuable description, the author nonetheless commits the mistake of referring to the Africanized syncretic religion as a "cult": a word that, as I mentioned earlier in this investigation, should not be used when referring to Africanized religious practices due to its culturally offensive contexts.[197]

Music functions in the Afro-Cuban Lucumí religion both to communicate with the orichas (deities) and to connect with the community. Afro-Cuban syncretic religious practices consist of both private and public events and often employ strict procedures. According to Diaz, this process features singing and dancing to honor specific orichas, although not necessarily at the same time.[198] It is equally important to understand that Lucumi/Regla de Ocha often involves preparing the way for communicating with certain deities at specific moments. Through the information provided by Diaz, he indicates that the process behind the rituals is imperative. Lucumi priests and community members cannot simply pick or summon a

---

[196] Javier Diaz, "Chapter 1: Preliminary Information," in *Meaning Beyond Words A Musical Analysis of Afro-Cuban Bata Drumming* (New York: CUNY Academic Works, 2019), 7-35, https://academicworks.cuny.edu/cgi/viewcontent.cgi?article=4024&context=gc_etds (accessed June 22, 2021).

[197] Javier Diaz, 7-35.

[198] Javier Diaz, 7-35.

deity at random in certain instances. When talking about honoring Oshain, for instance, Diaz mentions that the Lucumí priest must initially create a purification liquid called *omíero* and chant to the deity Elegba to open the musical communication with Oshain.[199]

In terms of the musical elements behind Lucumi, there is the emphasis on "call and response" chanting and percussion via specific consecrated and non-consecrated drums like the *batá* and *bembe*. Ritual ceremonies can be performed in private locations, like in the homes of Lucumí priests, or in public outdoor areas on specific occasions, like to celebrate or give thanks to specific orichas.[200] Readers should not jump to conclusions about Afro-Cuban Lucumí customs, however. Although song and dance are often performed together in ceremonies, that is not always the case. In a similar manner, readers should not perceive the music and instrumentation in Lucumí as homogeneous across other areas of Latin America. Javier Diaz clarifies this point by briefly demonstrating the differences between Regla de Ocha in Cuba versus Candomblé in Brazil. While both countries feature stringent procedures to musically honor deities, Diaz notes that Afro-Brazilian Candomblé musicians do not use batá drums as part of their ensemble.[201] Even though Diaz concentrates on batá drumming as the basis for his academic investigation and even though consecrated versions of these drums are often used in Cuba to initiate priests, he also illustrates the batá are not used for all ceremonies.[202]

These clarifications may lead some readers to wonder what Cubans outside of the Lucumí community in the past thought about the Africanized syncretic religion. Upon reading the historical contexts of how Cuba interpreted Lucumí in the late 1800s into the 1900s, it becomes clear that the governing powers and some intellectuals not affiliated with the Afro-Cuban community knew little to nothing about syncretic religion. Earlier in this study, I mentioned that Cuba attempted to distance itself from anything related to African culture and replace it with Cuban nationalist ideas. This process included persecuting African tribes and established religions, like the Lucumí. Some of that religious persecution involved scholarly writing from academics who openly condemned the Afro-Cuban population and

---

[199] Javier Diaz, 7-35.

[200] Javier Diaz, 7-35.

[201] Javier Diaz, 7-35.

[202] Javier Diaz, 7-35.

attacked their religious beliefs: intellectuals like Fernando Ortiz, the same person who developed transculturation theory.

It is true that the anthropological works by Fernando Ortiz on Cuba and Afro-Cuban culture in the 1940s and 50s serve as important resources on understanding the history, culture, and customs of the island. Javier Diaz notes that Ortiz was also one of the first anthropologists to extensively provide a musical ethnography about instruments derived from Africa and their impact on Cuba: this, despite having no musical training, nor fully understanding what he was talking about most of the time.[203] While Ortiz mostly presents a Positivist view of Afro-Cubans in that period, he did not always exhibit that same attitude in previous decades, specifically, the 1900s. To understand why Ortiz changed his views about Afro-Cubans in his later works like *Cuban Counterpoint*, readers must study his early writings on Criminology and Spiritism. From these sources, a more culturally oblivious and intolerant Fernando Ortiz emerges. This intolerance falls in line with the anti-African sentiments in Cuba in the late nineteenth and early twentieth centuries.

Why do the early writings by Fernando Ortiz matter in this discussion? They illustrate that Ortiz was influenced by the Spiritistic philosophy from Allan Kardec. Additionally, Ortiz was one of many people at the time who openly voiced his opposition to the African cultures and religions in Cuba. He served at the forefront of the *Brujería* (witchcraft or sorcery) panic on the island in the 1900s by elevating the fear and distrust through his rhetoric.[204] It deserves mention that, even though he lived in Cuba and wrote about the sociological situations there, Ortiz spent most of his academic studies *off* the island. What is more, the attacks on Brujería and those who supposedly practiced it in Cuba were not something new. A similar situation previously occurred in Cuba in the nineteenth century under Spanish colonization.[205] What aggravated the attacks in the early twentieth century stemmed from how the rhetoric denouncing syncretic religions functioned as a "justification" for a new, racialized Cuban identity.

---

[203] Javier Diaz, 7-35

[204] Mariela A. Gutierrez, "Y yo, ¿Dónde me pongo? El negro en la sociedad cubana desde la trata (1451-1870) hasta el Nuevo Orden (1898-1912)," Warsaw: *Revista del CESLA* Num 9 (2006), 101-113; https://www.revistadelcesla.com/index.php/revistadelcesla/article/view/219/217 (accessed February 13, 2021).

[205] Mariela A. Gutierrez, 101-113.

As an example of this last point, take *Hampa afro-cubana: los negros brujos*[206] from 1906 by Fernando Ortiz. Reading through this work, the scholarly critiques of it, and the overviews of racial discrimination in early modern Cuba, one gets the sense that Ortiz does not fully understand the scope of Afro-Cuban culture and religion. This is not just about him discussing the topic as an outsider, an aspect that many scholars have criticized him for decades after his death.[207] The problem lies in his methodology.

Fernando Ortiz writes *Hampa afro-cubana* from the perspectives of Criminology, Anthropology, and Spiritism: all the while espousing racist ideas. Bearing this in mind, Ortiz views the Afro-Cuban population in an unfavorable light, to the point where his descriptions portray the people as animalistic and inhuman. To Ortiz in the 1900s, he candidly perceives Afro-Cubans as superstitious, savage, and incompetent people. He also advocates for their cultural assimilation in the country. In that period, he believed that the Afro-Cubans descended from slaves would intentionally *forget* their ancestry and religious practices because of the imposition of Catholicism and European influences on the island.[208] This perception clearly denotes both racialization and racism against Afro-Cuban people. Ortiz does not stop there, though. He also does not value the Afro-Cuban syncretic religions as official sacred practices. Instead, he perceives Africanized syncretic religion more as a secularized version of Christianity, which he perceives as something to completely avoid.[209]

Contrast that criticism with how Ortiz cites the practice of Spiritism from Allan Kardec. Ortiz interprets (Kardecian) Spiritism as a compromise between Africanized syncretic religion and Catholicism. That type of Spiritism, as I said before, functions as a more philosophical version of spirituality, as opposed to what Ortiz (mis)understands as the innate occult nature of Afro-Cuban religions. This presents some irony, considering that Spiritism involves

---

[206] This title roughly translates in English to *Empty Afro-Cuban: The Black Sorcerers.*

[207] Fernando Ortiz, *Hampa Afro-Cubana: Los Negros Brujos (Apuntes para un estudio de etnología criminal.)* (Madrid: Librería de Fernando Fé, 1906); Javier Diaz, "Chapter 1: Preliminary Information," in *Meaning Beyond Words A Musical Analysis of Afro-Cuban Bata Drumming* (New York: CUNY Academic Works, 2019), 7-35, https://academicworks.cuny.edu/cgi/viewcontent.cgi?article=4024&context=gc_etds (accessed June 22, 2021).

[208] Fernando Ortiz, *Hampa Afro-Cubana: Los Negros Brujos (Apuntes para un estudio de etnología criminal.)* (Madrid: Librería de Fernando Fé, 1906).

[209] Fernando Ortiz, 1906.

connecting with dead ancestors and the temporary reincarnation of the human soul into other bodies through possession: traits found in many Afro-Latin syncretic religions. It was not until the 1930s, through the encouragement of a group of Cuban artists that Ortiz befriended, that he began to reassess his perceptions of African cultures.[210]

The rampant attacks against Brujería in Cuba did not exclude Spiritism. On the contrary, the colonial Spanish and Cuban governments, in addition to the Catholic Church, also went after the Spiritists by issuing arrests and denying practitioners Christian Sacraments. However, as Reinaldo Román illustrates in his study of anti-Spiritist persecution in the nineteenth and twentieth century Cuban newspapers, reporters often inflicted their vitriol at Afro-Cuban practitioners while showing more leniency towards others.[211] Román reinforces this point by addressing a case involving two Spiritist "man-gods" from the 1900s from different backgrounds: one Afro-Cuban (Hilario Mustilier Garzon) and the other Spanish (Juan Manzo). Román reveals that, even though the Cuban press distrusted both spiritual leaders and even though they both faced arrests for their work, Manzo received more respect as a Spiritist, while Garzon became demonized and frequently received public scorn in the press. This problem further plays into the racialized ideas in Cuba of "de-Africanizing" the island at the turn of the century.[212]

Looking into the impact of Africanized syncretic religions in Brazil, I encountered similarities in terms of social misunderstanding and religious persecution. The Candomblé religious practice combines aspects of Afro-Latin syncretism with Catholicism. Like Lucumí from Cuba, Brazilian Candomblé should also be perceived more as a form of *resistance* rather than complete subjugation to Catholicism. To the Portuguese in colonial Brazil, *they* interpreted the orixas as *Saints*. The

---

[210] Robin Moore, "Representations of Afrocuban Expressive Culture in the Writings of Fernando Ortiz," *Latin American Music Review* 15, No. 1 (1994), http://www.jstor.com/stable/3085947 (accessed December 28, 2019); Arcadio Díaz Quiñones, "Fernando Ortiz and Allan Kardec: Transmigration and Transculturation," in *Cultures of the Hispanic Caribbean*, ed. James Conrad and John Perivolaris (Gainesville, FL: University Press of Florida, 2000) 9-27; Henry Louis Gates, Jr. "6. Cuba: The Next Cuban Revolution," in *Black in Latin America* (New York: New York University Press. 2011), 179-222.

[211] Reinaldo Román, "Governing Man-Gods: Spiritism and the Struggle for Progress in Republican Cuba," *Journal of Religion in Africa* 37 (2007), 212-241, https://www.jstor.org/stable/27594414 (accessed June 23, 2021).

[212] Reinaldo Román, 212-241.

processes behind Candomblé, especially the musical processes, involve a lot more than that simple description.

Many scholars have studied the musical aspects of Candomblé, among them Lorenzo Dow Turner: the same person who conducted his ethnographic study on the Gullah/Geechee people and language in the 1930s and 40s. He also concentrated part of his linguistic project on the African diaspora by travelling to different parts of the world, like Brazil. From that experience, he recorded and collected ethnographic field recordings of Afro-Brazilian Candomblé for his research. While his approach demonstrates an etic perspective because Turner was not native to Brazil, his aural documentation nonetheless demonstrates cultural respect because he does not try to commercialize and exploit Afro-Brazilian culture. He links the cultural experience in Brazil to that of the Gullah/Geechee in the United States.[213]

Many of the hundreds of Candomblé recordings that Turner amassed for his research are housed at the Archives of Traditional Music at the University of Indiana Bloomington. In the 2010s, they also underwent digitalization, restoration, and cultural repatriation to Brazil. This ethnographic effort currently exists via a compilation project entitled, *Memórias Afro-Atlânticas: as gravações de Lorenzo Dow Turner na Bahia (1940-1941)*. This project was compiled on a grant from the Brazilian Ministry by ethnomusicologists Xavier Vatin, who initially visited ATM at IU in 2012, and Cassio Nobre. *Memórias Afro-Atlânticas* consists of a two-volume set of Candomblé field recordings from Lorenzo Dow Turner and his trip to Bahia, Brazil. It also consists of an accompanying documentary film, completed by Vatin in 2019. Vatin publicly presented the documentary in early 2021 through his YouTube channel for educational use via the Zumbi Series from the Cultural Center African Diaspora Institute (CCADI) in New York.[214]

---

[213] Katherine Wyly Mille and Michael B. Montgomery (Eds.), "Introduction," in *Africanisms in the Gullah Dialect* (Columbia, SC: University of South Carolina Press, 1949, 2002), xi-xlix.

[214] Michelle Crowe, "'Precious' 1940s recordings travel back to Brazil," *Indiana University Bloomington Archives of Traditional Music* (November 5, 2019), https://libraries.indiana.edu/precious-1940s-recordings-travel-back-brazil (accessed June 23, 2021; Couraca Criaçoes, "Memorias Afro Atlanticas: as gravacoes do Lorenzo Dow Turner na Bahia 1940 1941 Vol.1 (Full Album)," *YouTube* (Nov 21, 2017), https://www.youtube.com/watch?v=diZHAx5rhRs

Xavier Vatin provides plenty of critical information in his documentary about Candomblé and the Lorenzo Dow Turner field recordings from ethnomusicologists (himself included) and informants. Concerning the informants, he focuses mainly on talking with people who actively participated in the Turner recordings in Chacoeira, Bahia, Brazil: many of whom were children when the recordings took place in the 1940s. Vatin also devotes time in the documentary to talking to the descendants of the Candomblé priests who participated in the recordings.[215]

Several other significant aspects of the documentary deserve mention in relation to this study. The first, and perhaps most obvious, derives from its aural and visual components. From the very beginning audiences get the opportunity to hear and see Afro-Brazilians in the *tereiros* (temples) in Bahia performing the religious ceremonies through "call and response" chants and percussive performances via drums and the *agogo* (metallic belled percussion).[216] The second most important part of the documentary, as it concerns my work, concentrates on linguistic and historical preservation through (selective) cultural memory. Scholars like Yeda Pessoa de Castro stress that the African languages and dialects form an important part of Candomblé because they inform the type of appropriate vocabulary and geography. Castro also tries to clarify misconceptions about Candomblé by noting that the syncretic religion largely originated from the Yoruba people in West Africa and not from the Bantu people in South Africa. She indicates that *that* misunderstanding resulted from the effects of colonization in the 1700s through linguistic categorization. Castro and others interviewed for the documentary also mention that the linguistic nature of Candomblé has gradually become lost in translation and meaning through generations as the decades pass. People chant the

---

(accessed June 23, 2021); Couraca Criacões, "Memórias Afro-Atlânticas: as gravações do Lorenzo Dow Turner na Bahia 1940 1941 Vol.1 (Full Album)," *YouTube* (Nov 21, 2017), https://www.youtube.com/watch?v=hG3yBT9oq84 (accessed June 23, 2021); Xavier Vatin, "Memórias Afro-Atlânticas / Afro-Atlantic Legacies (Zumbi Series, CCADI, NY, 14/12/2020)," *YouTube* (Feb 1, 2021), https://www.youtube.com/watch?v=EaJi63AYscA (accessed June 23. 2021).

[215] Xavier Vatin, "Memórias Afro-Atlânticas / Afro-Atlantic Legacies (Zumbi Series, CCADI, NY, 14/12/2020)," *YouTube* (Feb 1, 2021), https://www.youtube.com/watch?v=EaJi63AYscA (accessed June 23. 2021).

[216] Xavier Vatin, 2020.

words, but few fully understand what they signify.[217] This problem presents similarities to the misinterpretations of certain Gullah/Geechee sacred music, like "Kumbaya": a song that I go into more detail later in this study.

Speaking of the Gullah/Gechee, Xavier Vatin openly acknowledges the visibility of this community in the United States via his documentary on Lorenzo Dow Turner. This proves logical given the monumental impact that Turner had on uncovering information about the Gullah/Geechee language and people in a way that also demonstrated respect. The documentary features a moment where Vatin speaks with Queen Quet, who reinforces some of the points which I have previously discussed in this investigation:

1) Scholars need to reframe how they talk about the Gullah/Geechee people, because the community is not "disappearing."

2) The Gullah/Geechee language is not "broken English."

3) To adapt to modernization, many in the community had no choice but to conceal their Gullah/Geechee identity from a society that (for the most part) did not understand their culture.[218]

Although Vatin and Nobre originally compiled the Lorenzo Dow Turner audio recordings on compact discs, they have also issued intangible, digital versions of their restoration efforts to promote accessibility for audiences from around the world. The field recordings that Lorenzo Dow Turner produced in Bahia do not illustrate stylized, popularized, or nationalized versions of Candomblé. His work drastically contrasts with the nationalist governmental approach to Afro-Brazilian musical identity (specifically, the *samba*) occurring the same time under the Getulio Vargas dictatorship in the 1930s and 40s.[219] The Turner Candomblé recordings represent examples of the

---

217 Xavier Vatin, 2020.
218 Xavier Vatin, 2020.
219 Lisa Shaw, "*São Coisas Nossas*: Samba and Identity in the Vargas Era (1930-45), *Portuguese Studies* 14 (198), 152-169, https://www.jstor.org/stable/41105089 (accessed June 24, 2021); (Xavier Vatin), "Memorias Afro Atlânticas: as gravações do Lorenzo Dow Turner Bahia, Brazil," *Soundcloud* (2017-2018), https://soundcloud.com/memoriasafroatlanticas (accessed June 23, 2021).

ceremonial music in its raw form from the informants who lived in Brazil. These recordings also demonstrate an expansive Afro-Brazilian demographic from all age groups and genders: men, women, and children. From these Candomblé field recordings, listeners also get the sense of the instrumentation involved in the syncretic religious practice: vocals for "call and response," drumming, and other percussion, like the *shekere* (beaded gourd) and agogo.

Figure 19: Type of Shekere

Candomblé also incorporates visuals through dancing to honor the orixas. This is best exemplified in both the documentary by Vatin and more recent ethnographic research from Everton Barreiro. In February 2021, Bereiro released his five-volume documentary film series entitled *Brazil, The Untold Story*. At its core, this documentary series aims to educate audiences about the African presence in Brazil while simultaneously dispelling false and racist ideas about the country. Barreiro accomplishes these tasks by following a similar approach to what Henry Louis Gates employed in his ethnographic research in Brazil: interviewing informants from within the Afro-Brazilian communities and getting *their* perspectives about daily life and customs in their own words. Barreiro does not taint his research with personal biases and assumptions. Instead, he shows audiences the people from the communities speaking in the Brazilian Portuguese language (subtitled in English for certain viewers) and presenting unfiltered commentary about their lived experiences.

The first documentary in *Brazil: The Untold Story* ("Candomblé") primarily concentrates on Candomblé practitioners from the terreiro of Ilê Axé Odé Aladê Ijexá in Ilheus, Bahia, Brazil. From this documentary, viewers receive commentary about the tense relationship between syncretic religion and Christianity: both Catholicism and Protestantism. In "Part I" of the documentary, Ya Darabi (Cristina Soares) talks about growing up impoverished and initially raised in the Catholic faith (She does not specify a decade). She explains how she originally felt betrayed by Catholicism in her childhood: specifically, an incident where she was denied the Eucharist at Mass because she had not been baptized, even though she was suffering from hunger practically every day.[220] That sense of disillusionment eventually led Darabi to find solace in syncretic religion through Candomblé after connecting with a friend, as well as to reconsider the impact of Christianity on her life. Darabi encountered a similar experience while on a mission trip decades later in Argentina administering the Eucharist to the people. What she found after recanting her childhood experience to others was that the problem did not lie with the Catholic Church, but with *individual people* who tried to represent it and prevent her from participating.[221]

Everton Barreiro presents the musical aspects of Candomblé in "Part I" and "Part II" of *Brazil: The Untold Story*. In these segments, he shows responses and performances from the *ogãs*, or musicians and dancers who offer respect to different orixas representative of the natural elements. The musical form and instruments involved feature the same kinds that I referred to earlier when talking about the Lorenzo Dow Turner Candomblé field recordings: "call and response" chanting, barrel drumming, the shekere, and the agogo. "Part II" ("Yoruba") consists of several accompanied chants to different deities who control the natural environment.[222] While the informants speak in

---

[220] Everton Barreiro, "Alba Darabi in Candomble/Brazil, the untold story, " *YouTube* February 26, 2021), https://www.youtube.com/watch?v=4kaSZ5KVEII (accessed August 2, 2021).

[221] Everton Barreiro, 2021.

[222] Everton Barreiro, 2021.

Brazilian Portuguese for most of the documentary, this specific section presents a linguistic barrier where the English subtitles offer no assistance. The practitioners sing in an Africanized language, but the subtitles only specify which deity that they honor.[223] Nevertheless, Barreiro provides valuable insight about Candomblé. He also avoids using his documentary to exploit the practitioners in the terreiro.

One would think that this new ethnographic information would suggest an increase in cultural respect for Candomblé and African culture in contemporary Brazil. Unfortunately, that has not been the case. Religious intolerance towards Candomblé and its practitioners has grown in the twenty-first century. Based on what I have encountered throughout this study, the religious tension between Candomblé and Christianity still permeates Brazil. Only, this time, Candomblé has faced persecution by Evangelical Christianity: more specifically, the Pentecostal religion. In more extreme cases, this persecution has led to countless attacks on terreiros in the country to the point where such events have caught international attention. That leads to yet another problem. While there have been some scholars who have addressed the topic of Evangelical Christianity and Candomblé[224], I have noticed that most sources that talk about this derive from commercial news sources, which are not always reliable in the academic realm. I argue that the current religious persecution of Candomblé in Brazil demands further academic investigation so that more people know what has been occurring in the country via concrete evidence. Newer scholarly research needs to present the full scope of the situation.

What I have described in this chapter should serve as an introduction to understanding the impact of syncretic religions and the complex relationship between African and European customs in forming and (mis)understanding religious practices. Based on the information uncovered, it becomes clear that syncretic religions feature many different categories and subcategories Some of these religious belief systems take from and combine ritualistic components with each

---

[223] Everton Barreiro, 2021.

[224] Kristina Hinz et al, "The rise of Brazil's neo-Pentecostal narco militia," *Open Democracy* (May 6, 2021), https://www.opendemocracy.net/en/democraciaabierta/rise-narco-militia-pentecostal-brazil-en/ (accessed August 2, 2021).

other. One also notices the mentality and tactics that Christian and governmental powers in Latin America and the Caribbean have used to subdue Afro-Latin syncretic religions and communities: perceiving these customs as evil due to fear and misunderstanding by implementing bans and restructuring national identities that ignore the African cultures. This does not suggest, however, that Catholicism has been the only defining religious influence in Latin America and the Caribbean. I had hinted at the Protestant presence in these regions through religious persecution. Places like Puerto Rico also encountered such influences on the island in the nineteenth century through external mission trips and mainland United States involvement.[225] These topics extend beyond the scope of this investigation and could be addressed for future research.

[225] Bettina E. Schmidt, "The Power of the Spirits: The Formation of Identity based on Puerto Rican Spiritism, *Revista de Estudos da Religao* No. 2 (2006), 127-154, https://www.pucsp.br/rever/rv2_2006/p_schmidt.pdf (accessed June 25, 2021)

Ìí á ó Ìṣ ùń àà àń ò [226]

~Yoruba Proverb

Some may recall that I provided a series of questions in the beginning of this book concerning the ethics associated with preserving Gullah/Geechee and Afro-Latin cultures through audio. They mainly focused on which organizations and people had access to and controlled the materials, as well as the purposes for use. Preliminary investigations about this topic reveal that people have used these audio recordings both to teach audiences and as inspiration for musicians. *How* people and organizations have applied these materials in those contexts presents more complicated situations.

Washington, D.C. features many Gullah/Geechee aural fragments via the American Folklife Center at the Library of Congress. The research guide entitled, "Gullah/Geechee History and Culture" from the Library of Congress, proves most valuable for locating and obtaining historical artifacts concerning aspects of the Gullah/Geechee people. This series of archival collections, digitized in an online format in late 2018 and updated the following year, features myriad books, articles, maps, and audio recordings from the early twentieth century.[227] While the Library of Congress often encourages people to visit and peruse these collections in person, "Gullah/Geechee History and Culture" also contains clickable links to these materials that people can access remotely from a computer. The "Digital Collections" portion of the archive serves as an especially useful tool for the current study. It features multiple field recordings and written testimonials from the 1930s from African Americans who

---

[226] One does not engage in a dyeing trade in Ìṣokùń people there wear only white. (Wherever one might be, one should respect the manners and habits of the place.) University of Nebraska Lincoln, *The Good Person: Excerpt from the Yorùbá Proverb Treasury*, http://yoruba.unl.edu/yoruba.php-text=1b&view=0&uni=1&l=1.htm (accessed July 28, 2021).

[227] Todd Harvey, "Gullah/Geechee collections at the American Folklife Center," *Library of Congress*, (February 25, 2019), https://guides.loc.gov/gullah-geechee-folklife, (Accessed January 7, 2020), Archival Collection Guide.

Figure 20: Record Player (Photo by Lee Campbell on Unsplash)

lived through enslavement in the nineteenth century. These historical artifacts provide contemporary listeners and readers with the opportunity to experience the power of ethnography and cultural memories.[228]

This does not suggest that the Library of Congress is the only archival site preserving Gullah/Geechee sound artifacts. Coastal Carolina University in Conway, South Carolina has spent the past few years planning another Gullah/Geechee archive situated more at the local level along the Gullah Geechee Cultural Heritage Corridor. The *Gullah Geechee Digital Project* (2018-2022) is currently working together with the Library of Congress, American Folklife Center, and the Association for Cultural Equity (ACE) to create a digital archive with thousands of plantation records and testimonies from members of the Gullah/Geechee community. The project, led by Eric Crawford and Ali Crandell, aims to provide a diverse look at the South Carolina area

---

[228] Todd Harvey, 2019.

of the Gullah/Geechee communities and educate people about their historical and cultural significance.[229]

The online version of the "Finder's Guide" for the *Gullah-Geechee Collections at the American Folklife Center* (in draft form from 2018) provides a list of different collections of documents, audio recordings and other media with materials related to the Gullah/Geechee. The collections span from Florida to South Carolina. They recently underwent an update in early 2019 with limited online access.[230] These collections do contain a few noticeable problems, however. They demonstrate a partial representation of the Gullah/Geechee Cultural Heritage Corridor. Collections available at the AFC present more information about South Carolina and Georgia, but they do not include many details about the Gullah/Geechee in Florida. As of 2019, the AFC does not provide information about the Gullah/Geechee presence in North Carolina.

Another glaring problem with the *Gullah/Geechee Collections at the American Folklife Center* is its overall sporadic organizational approach. The archival materials related to the Gullah/Geechee often get mixed with other aspects of southern U.S. culture and music. The "Finders Guide" attempts to alleviate this confusion by highlighting the Gullah/Geechee resources available from within each collection. Access to the collections listed in the guide often proves complicated: mainly, with matters concerning music and speech. The AFC presents lists of audio recordings in specific collections, but they also imply that researchers must travel in person to listen to the recordings. I encountered this problem when trying to access field recordings by John and Ruby Lomax collected from their trips across the southern United States in the 1930s.[231] Recordings and field notes related to the

---

[229] Charles Joyner Institute (Coastal Carolina University), "Projects and Research," (Conway, SC: Coastal Carolina University, 2021), https://www.coastal.edu/joynerinstitute/projects/ (accessed August 24, 2021).

[230] Todd Harvey, "Gullah/Geechee collections at the American Folklife Center," *Library of Congress*, (February 25, 2019), https://guides.loc.gov/gullah-geechee-folklife, (Accessed January 7, 2020), Archival Collection Guide; Todd Harvey and Riley Calcagno, "Gullah/Geechee collections at the American Folklife Center, Library of Congress," *Gullah-Geechee Corridor* (February 2018), https://www.gullahgeecheecorridor.org/wp-content/uploads/2018/02/Gullah-Geechee-Finders-Guide.pdf, (accessed October 1, 2019), Draft Document.

[231] Todd Harvey, 2019; Todd Harvey and Riley Calcagno, 2018.

Gullah/Geechee could only be accessed by physically visiting the American Folklife Center.

Researchers should not assume, though, that all Gullah/Geechee recordings from the American Folklife Center or Library of Congress are completely restricted to the public or scholars. Some collections of audio recordings and texts are readily available electronically from the Library of Congress website for people to access from the comfort of their own home. Typing in the word "Gullah" and searching under the "Audio Recordings" category reveals a plethora of field recordings and interviews from the 1920s to 1970s from different folklorists and ethnomusicologists. Clicking on these results can often lead to a page containing a digital version of the recording and, in the case of recorded audio interviews, supplemental transcripts in "PDF" or "XML" formats. Some recordings can also be downloaded as "MP3" or "WAV" files.

Selected Gullah/Geechee Audio Recordings from the Library of Congress:

Robert Winslow Gordon and Henry Wiley, "Come by Here" (1926)

Contemporary sources from the twenty-first century frequently credit the 1926 field recording of "Come by Here" from folklorist Robert Winslow Gordon as one of the first known audio recordings of Gullah/Geechee music. Listeners might remember this song by its more familiar title, "Kumbaya," which surged in popularity as part of the folk music revival in the 1950s and 60s. Since the 2010s, the Library of Congress has officially recognized "Come by Here" as a song of Gullah/Geechee origin.[232] "Come by Here," as performed by Henry Wiley on the wax cylinder recording located at the Library of Congress, partially represents the preservation of the Gullah/Geechee oral musical tradition. The Georgia State Senate recognized "Come by Here" as the official State Historical Song of Georgia (as "Kumbaya"), thanks to efforts from the mayor of Darien, Georgia and Griffin

---

[232] Stephen Winnick, "Kumbaya: History of an Old Song," *Library of Congress* (February 6, 2018), https://blogs.loc.gov/folklife/2018/02/kumbaya-history-of-an-old-song/ (accessed December 16, 2019); House of Representatives, "Recognizing the Song 'Kumbaya' Congressional Record Vol. 163, No. 200 (December 7, 2017), *Congress.* https://www.congress.gov/congressional-record/2017/12/07/house-section/article/H9714-1 (accessed January 7, 2020). Public Domain.

Lotson: Federal Commissioner of the Gullah Geechee Cultural Heritage Corridor Commission.[233]

Stephen Winick from the American Folklife Center, where Robert Winslow Gordon served as its first archivist in 1928, indicates that Gordon collected four different wax cylinder recordings of "Come by Here." Winick also concentrates on the significance of the lyrics to the song. He mentions that Gordon received a version of the words via correspondence letters from fellow part-time folklorist Julian Parks Boyd the year before in 1927. Boyd obtained a transcription of the lyrics from his student Minnie Lee the year before while Boyd served as a high school principal in North Carolina. The lyrics in question, however, present a different version entitled, "Oh Lord, Won't You Come By Here." Winick argues that, despite differences in the texts, "Oh Lord, Won't You Come By Here" shares the same structure as "Come by Here/Kumbaya."[234]

The Library of Congress features the audio recording of "Come by Here" on their website as a digital restoration of one of the wax cylinder recordings. Accompanying liner notes for the song, however, neither provide a specific date nor location: only the year in which Gordon recorded it (1926).[235] This information proves misleading for several reasons. First, sources indicate that Gordon spent time in Darien, Georgia and interacted with members of the Gullah/Geechee community at the time of the recording. Second, Griffin Lotson provides crucial details that clarify the ambiguity of the liner notes to "Come by Here." In an interview conducted with the British Broadcasting Corporation (BBC) in 2018, Lotson mentions that the song title for "Come by Here" at the Library of Congress is a mistranslation: specifically, the substitution of the English word "Here" for the Gullah/Geechee word "Ya." Third, Lotson also

---

[233] Kristina Torres, "Good Lord: Georgia lawmakers are recognizing 'Kumbaya,'" *Atlanta Journal Constitution* (February 23, 2017), https://www.ajc.com/news/state--regional-govt--politics/good-lord-georgia-lawmakers-are-recognizing-kumbaya/dTCImxIonvY2I7bod9TtFP/ (accessed January 7, 2020).

[234] Stephen Winnick, "Kumbaya: History of an Old Song," *Library of Congress* (February 6, 2018), https://blogs.loc.gov/folklife/2018/02/kumbaya-history-of-an-old-song/ (accessed December 16, 2019).

[235] Robert Winslow Gordon and H. Wylie. *Come by Here.* 1926 (Date of Recording), Library of Congress, https://www.loc.gov/ihas200197143./ (accessed September 1, 2019), Audio.

explicitly states that, in the original recording, Henry Wiley mentions the exact date of his performance: "…April 17, 1926."[236] This conflicting data illustrates that researchers should not completely accept the liner notes that Robert Winslow Gordon provides to "Come by Here" as definitive historical material.

The digital version of "Come by Here" derives from one of the original wax cylinder audio recordings that Robert Winslow Gordon collected in the 1920s. It also consists of sound quality problems due to the degradation of the wax cylinder over time. At around the "0:21" mark of the field recording, listeners will immediately detect skipping and scratching noises that interfere with the music.[237] Upon closer examination of the digitized version, I noticed another glaring omission. Playing the track online leads directly to Henry Wiley singing. It does not include the verbal introduction from Wiley providing the date of the recording.[238]

"Come by Here" demonstrates one of the earliest attempts at archiving Gullah/Geechee music via audio recording technology. As I have shown, the recording available at the Library of Congress website does contain a few problems. Listeners and scholars must speculate the purpose and sociocultural visibility of the preserved song. The field recording of "Come by Here" functions primarily as an academic tool for ethnomusicologists and curious researchers who want to know more about Gullah/Geechee music. Additionally, the Library of Congress includes a disclaimer under the "Rights and Access" section of each archived recording in respective collections.[239] Like every other culture documented there, the Library of Congress states that researchers must respect the culture and their privacy when using the materials in question.

---

[236] Newsday, "Descendants of African slaves trace the origins of Kumbaya," *BBC* (February 13, 2018). https://www.bbc.co.uk/programmes/p05xzmx5 (accessed November 15, 2019).

[237] Robert Winslow Gordon and H. Wylie. *Come by Here.* 1926 (Date of Recording), Library of Congress, https://www.loc.gov/ihas200197143./ (accessed September 1, 2019), Audio.

[238] Robert Winslow Gordon and H. Wylie, 1926.

[239] Robert Winslow Gordon and H. Wylie, 1926.

Despite this precaution, one must consider additional questions. Thinking within the contexts of transculturation and cultural appropriation, does mistranslating the title for "Come by Here" from Gullah/Geechee to English constitute a form of cultural disrespect? Is it merely human error? What about not including details about the performer and the actual performance date in the liner notes, other than through ambiguous references to the name of the performer and the year? If the musician mentions the performance date on the wax cylinder of "Come by Here," then why is this detail removed in the digital version on the Library of Congress website?

I do not doubt the work that Robert Winslow Gordon conducted to collect and preserve the recording of "Come by Here." At the same time, though, where are all the details about Henry Wiley: the informant who performs on the field recording? Not much is known about him as a person. Although the "Finders Guide" for the *Gullah/Geechee Collections at the American Folklife Center* mentions Wiley at the beginning of the document, it does so in relation to Robert Winslow Gordon and to the history of the American Folklife Center.[240] Wiley indirectly becomes an accessory who helps to interpret Gullah/Geechee music for audiences outside of the culture. Listeners get the extent of Henry Wiley as a *voice* associated with Gullah/Geechee culture: a voice preserved (or, suppressed?) in time, because listeners are not given enough details about the performer. That presents a problem because it gives the wrong impression that the *archivist* takes credit for what the *performer* does on the recording. Over time, other ethnographers have tried to shift focus away from themselves and more on acknowledging their informants.

The Lorenzo Dow Turner Field Recordings from the Library of Congress Website

I explained the significance and purposes of Lorenzo Dow Turner and his research in the 1930s for what would eventually become his *Africanisms in the Gullah Dialect*. I must refer to Turner again to highlight his application of audio recording technology as historical, linguistic, and cultural preservation. The field recordings that Turner produced

---

[240] Todd Harvey and Riley Calcagno. "Gullah/Geechee collections at the American Folklife Center, Library of Congress." *Gullah-Geechee Corridor* (February 2018). https://www.gullahgeecheecorridor.org/wp-content/uploads/2018/02/Gullah-Geechee-Finders-Guide.pdf., (accessed October 1, 2019), Draft Document.

in the 1930s served as valuable tools for understanding the Gullah/Geechee people and their language in their own words. They also function as good resources for researchers in the twenty-first century, because the recorded anecdotes represent the preservation of cultural memory and bygone eras: primarily, the nineteenth and early twentieth centuries. Most important, the archived recordings predate research conducted in the late 1930s with the Works Progress Administration (WPA) Federal Writers' Project: specifically, the collection of historical narratives by formerly enslaved African Americans.[241]

Digitized audio ethnographic interviews with members of the Gullah/Geechee community play a significant part in the audio collections at the Library of Congress. Many available recordings have been preserved and converted from their original acetate phonograph disc and wire recording formats. The Library of Congress website currently features a plethora of audio field recordings in multiple parts from the early 1930s that form a section of the ethnographic research that Turner conducted for the *Linguistic Atlas of the United States and Canada* and *Africanisms*.[242]

Like the Robert Winslow Gordon field recording and most other early attempts at recording the Gullah/Geechee in the twentieth century, Lorenzo Dow Turner also wrote about the Gullah/Geechee and recorded their voices when the community was still in isolation. Remember that bridges did not connect the Gullah/Geechee community in the Low Country to the rest of the United States until the late 1950s.[243] Turner concentrates his attention on the

---

[241] Todd Harvey. "Gullah/Geechee collections at the American Folklife Center." *Library of Congress*, February 25, 2019. https://guides.loc.gov/gullah-geechee-folklife, (Accessed January 7, 2020); Library of Congress. "Born in Slavery: Slave Narratives from the Federal Writers' Project, 1936 to 1938," *Library of Congress* (2000-2001), https://www.loc.gov/collections/slave-narratives-from-the-federal-writers-project-1936-to-1938/about-this-collection/ (accessed January 24, 2020).

[242] Katherine Wyly Mille and Michael B. Montgomery (Eds.), "Introduction." in *Africanisms in the Gullah Dialect* (Columbia, SC: University of South Carolina Press, 1949, 2002), xi-xlix.

[243] Ken Otterbourg, "Being Gullah or Geechee, Once Looked Down On, Now a Treasured Heritage." *National Geographic* (October 16, 2014). https://www.nationalgeographic.com/news/2014/10/141017-gullah-geechee-heritage-corridor-lowcountry-coast-sea-islands-sweetgrass/ (accessed January 4, 2020).

Gullah/Geechee in South Carolina and Georgia. Despite how Florida and North Carolina also represent part of the Gullah/Geechee Cultural Heritage Corridor, these states do not form part of that study. The list of Gullah/Geechee field recordings from Lorenzo Dow Turner online present a slight problem in that the Library of Congress has duplicates in other archives. This is because the recordings serve multiple purposes as linguistic artifacts and narratives from the formerly enslaved. I will briefly discuss the readily available Turner field recordings from the Library of Congress website to demonstrate the perspectives of these narratives and current issues with sound quality via digitalization. To avoid redundancies in my analyses, readers must know that each field recording contains a "Side A" and "Side B."

"Interview with Susan A. Quall, Johns Island, South Carolina, May 16, 1932"

To fully understand the context of the Lorenzo Dow Turner interviews as ex-slave narratives, one must consider the contexts of the times: that is, the eras of the informants who spoke and divulged information about their lives. They frame their recollections and experiences within the contexts of before and after "the War." When the informants mention "the War," they are referring to the Civil War from the 1860s and not to later conflicts like World War I. Many of the people that Turner spoke with about slavery and the Civil War were either children or young adults when they experienced such events. Informants like Susan Quall reveal critical details about what life was like under enslavement. On "Side A" of her interview, Quall goes into detail about the work that she was expected to do on the farm, her lack of privacy and constant travel restrictions.[244] At times, though, determining what she is talking about becomes a challenge due to sound quality problems via the digital restoration of the recording. The PDF transcription additionally presents multiple gaps and oddities through unfinished sentences and phrases. I posit that, when Quall reflects on the looming threat of getting caught during her past experience under enslavement, she could be referring to her enslaver and what he planned to do if he ever captured her.[245]

---

[244] Lorenzo Dow Turner, "Interview with Susan A. Quall, St. Johns Island, South Carolina, May 16, 1932 (part 1 of 2)," *Library of Congress*, (1932) https://www.loc.gov/item/afc1984011_afs25665a/ (accessed October 5, 2020).

[245] Lorenzo Dow Turner, 1932.

"Side B" of the same recording is less confusing in interpretation, partly because that section does not have as many problems as the previous side. Here, Quall talks about what happened when the Union troops arrived in her area of South Carolina in the Civil War, although she does not specify an exact date. This absence of information is understandable, though, because she indicates that she was just a child when the events took place. In the recordings, Quall recalls being carried on her back by her father while trying to escape the plantation with her family.[246] She also briefly talks about what happened to her after the Civil War. She later married and had a son: both of whom, at the time of the interview, had long since died.[247]

"Interview with Ann Scott, St. Helena Island, South Carolina, June 27, 1932"

Recorded in the Gullah/Geechee enclave of St. Helena Island, South Carolina, the "Interview with Ann Scott" presents an anecdote from an elderly Gullah/Geechee woman recalling her memories of life in the nineteenth century. More specifically, Scott refers to her life in the Civil War in the 1860s. One reason for this deduction stems from the accompanying field recording transcription, which uses the term "Yankee" several times.[248] In the same narrative, Scott also discusses her duties as a slave at that point in time, in addition to the church where she sang and worshiped. At certain points, she also offers moments of prayer and meditation.[249]

Regarding the sound quality of the interview, it is poor and degraded in its digitized state. This is common among the Lorenzo Dow Turner field recordings at the Library of Congress website and produces multiple problems in terms of preservation and interpretation. The "Interview with Ann Scott" features many recording gaps of empty space, or distorted passages that make it

---

[246] Lorenzo Dow Turner, "Interview with Susan A. Quall, St. Johns Island, South Carolina, May 16, 1932 (part 2 of 2)." Library of Congress (1932), https://www.loc.gov/item/afc1984011_afs25659b/ (accessed October 5, 2020).

[247] Lorenzo Dow Turner, 1932.

[248] Lorenzo Dow Turner, "Interview with Ann Scott, St. Helena Island, South Carolina, June 27, 1932 (part 1 of 2)." Library of Congress (1932), https://www.loc.gov/item/afc1984011_afs25657a (accessed October 5, 2020; "Interview with Ann Scott, St. Helena Island, South Carolina, June 27, 1932 (part 2 of 2)." Library of Congress (1932), https://hdl.loc.gov/loc.afc/afc9999001.25657b. Accessed October 5, 2020.

[249] Lorenzo Dow Turner, 1932; Lorenzo Dow Turner; 1932.

difficult to comprehend what Ann Scott or the interviewees are saying. "Side B" is especially problematic, because the "0:00" to "1:15" mark of the field recording features empty or damaged sections due to aging.[250]

At times, the textual transcription of the interview does not accurately match the words spoken in the field recording (I found myself reading "Side B" of the interview and frequently losing my place.). The transcriptions for the "A" and "B" sides of the recording are littered with question marks and unfinished segments denoted by ellipses. Perhaps, the most frustrating aspect of these field recordings stems from the skipping. "Side B" features sections where Ann Scott is talking, but the digitized recording captures the error of the skipping 78 RPM record in places like "1:44-1:54." The PDF transcription from the Library of Congress lists these moments as the disc skipping.[251] That description needed to be included in the transcript because what the informant says at that point cannot be properly determined and is lost to history.

"Interview with Samuel Polite, St. Helena Island, South Carolina, June 27, 1932"

Samuel Polite reveals myriad telling, if at times convoluted, details about slavery. Like the testimony from Susan Quall, Polite mentions his experience working on farms before, during, and after the Civil War. Much of his work at that point in his life involved tending to the crops and animals, often while working under harsh conditions. Polite devotes parts of his interview to talking about plowing the fields with manure, growing vegetables, and planting trees. Of course, Polite does not forget to mention the punishments that he would receive for disobedience. At one point in "Side A," he mentions that his enslaver would whip him if he refused to follow his orders.[252] One must study the audio recording and textual transcriptions to discern these anecdotes. This procedure is necessary because the inconsistencies and

---

[250] Lorenzo Dow Turner, "Interview with Ann Scott, St. Helena Island, South Carolina, June 27, 1932 (part 2 of 2)." Library of Congress (1932), https://hdl.loc.gov/loc.afc/afc9999001.25657b. Accessed October 5, 2020.

[251] Lorenzo Dow Turner, 1932.

[252] Lorenzo Dow Turner, "Interview with Samuel Polite, St. Helena Island, South Carolina (Gullah), June 27, 1932 (part 1 of 2)." Library of Congress. https://www.loc.gov/item/afc1984011_afs25656a/ (accessed October 5, 2020).

empty spaces in the field recording do not clarify these points in the recording.

When I talked about the Robert Winslow Gordon recording of "Come By Here," I indicated that the information listed in the liner notes for the recording ought to be analyzed with suspicion because it removes crucial details. I propose a similar warning regarding the digitized Lorenzo Dow Turner Gullah/Geechee field recordings and textual transcriptions. The Library of Congress provides scholars and students with the PDF transcriptions to decipher what the informants say on the respective recordings. However, the more I investigated these transcriptions, the more I noticed their many inaccuracies.

Readers must know the following when assessing the digitized versions of the recorded material from Lorenzo Dow Turner. Turner includes a selection of his ethnographic field interviews from South Carolina and Georgia in *Africanisms in the Gullah Dialect*: both in a phonetic version of the Gullah/Geechee language and in English. This includes his interview with Samuel Polite.[253] The transcriptions that Lorenzo Dow Turner provides in his book stem from an era when the phonograph recordings that he produced in the 1930s were still in good condition. The digital versions of the field recordings at the Library of Congress website attempt to salvage the tangible materials, which have undergone decades of wear and tear through sound degradation. Despite efforts from the Library of Congress, the preservation and archiving do not fix the problems with sound quality (skipping, scratching, recording gaps, etc.). The accompanying PDF texts of the Turner interviews from the Library of Congress website refer to the transcriptions of the *digital* versions of the field recordings.[254] *These* transcriptions indicate the gaps and problems within each recording through question marks, segments in parentheses that try to explain who is talking on the recording, indications in parentheses that a given recording is of bad quality, and indications of when the recording starts skipping or features a gap.

---

[253] Lorenzo Dow Turner, "9: GULLAH TEXTS ('Making Manure on St. Helena Island')," in *Africanisms in the Gullah Dialect* (Columbia, SC: University of South Carolina Press, 1949, 2002), 285-286.

[254] Library of Congress, "Interview with Samuel Polite, St. Helena Island, South Carolina (Gullah), June 27, 1932," AFS t25, 656A, https://tile.loc.gov/storage-services/service/afc/afc1984011/afc1984011_afs25656/afc1984011_afs25656a.pdf (accessed October 16, 2020).

Concerning the "Interview with Samuel Polite," the PDF transcription of the field recording does match the text to the same interview presented in *Africanisms in the Gullah Dialect*. Readers and scholars looking for a more thorough version of the interview should consult and compare the text from Chapter 9 of *Africanisms* with the text presented by the Library of Congress.[255] According to the text presented in *Africanisms*, readers get a better sense of the kind of agricultural tasks that Samuel Polite had to accomplish on the farm where he worked. He clearly explains creating layers of garbage, mud, and straw for composting. The Library of Congress transcription, which relies on the degraded recording, leaves the bulk of the textual material incomplete.[256] This means that people reading the text must exercise their judgements and hypothesize what is being said. Of course, that approach is unnecessary because Lorenzo Dow Turner includes the full transcription in *Africanisms*. I must also mention that the Library of Congress does not cite *Africanisms* when cataloging the "Interview with Samuel Polite." What they do, instead, is refer to other archives within the Library of Congress and American Folklife Center where people can locate the same material: archives like the American Dialect Society Collection.[257]

"Interview with Dave White, St. Simons Island, Georgia (Gullah), July 26, 1933"

This ethnographic interview consists of a conversation with a Gullah/Geechee preacher. Like the "Interview with Ann Scott," this interview in question also functions as the preservation of oral history

---

[255] Lorenzo Dow Turner, "9: GULLAH TEXTS ('Making Manure on St. Helena Island')," in *Africanisms in the Gullah Dialect* (Columbia, SC: University of South Carolina Press, 1949, 2002), 285-286; Library of Congress, "Interview with Samuel Polite, St. Helena Island, South Carolina (Gullah), June 27, 1932," AFS t25, 656A, https://tile.loc.gov/storage-services/service/afc/afc1984011/afc1984011_afs25656/afc1984011_afs25656a.pdf (accessed October 16, 2020).

[256] Lorenzo Dow Turner, 285-286; Library of Congress, 1932.

[257] Lorenzo Dow Turner and Dave White. "Interview with Dave White, St. Simons Island, Georgia, part 1 of 2. Saint Simons Island, Georgia, None , 7, 1933." *Library of Congress.* https://www.loc.gov/item/afc1984011_afs25666a/. (accessed September 1, 2019), Audio, PDF; "Interview with Dave White, St. Simons Island, Georgia, part 2 of 2. Saint Simons Island, Georgia, None , 7, 1933." *Library of Congress.* https://www.loc.gov/item/afc1984011_afs25666b/ (accessed September 1, 2019), Audio, PDF.

and slave narratives.[258] This does not mean, though, that the "Interview with Dave White" does not contain problems. Even though the field recording is digitized for the twenty-first century, this does not alleviate matters concerning its overall poor sound quality. At times, it becomes difficult to tell which person in the recording is speaking (either Lorenzo Dow Turner, or his informant Dave White). One also must take into consideration that this preserved recording originates from a degraded record from over eighty-five years in the past. Some words or phrases in the recorded interview sound muffled or inaudible. Listeners must hypothesize what is being said in the recording.

Supplemental transcriptions of the interview attempt to capture the original text as best as possible. However, the copies of the text on the Library of Congress website do not specify which archivist provided the electronic version of the transcriptions. Because of the plethora of gaps in the recordings, due to the sound degradation over time, the transcribed texts also quickly transform into an enigmatic puzzle because the written texts are based on what people hear in the recordings. Sentences and phrases get truncated or left incomplete. "Side B" of the interview represents such poor sound quality that the PDF transcription indicates that problem at the outset of the recording. Passages that sound awkward or indeciphcrable are followed by question marks. The transcription also features bracketed sections that describe to readers the contexts and mannerisms of Dave White during the interview.[259]

"Interview with Wallace Quarterman, St. Simons Island, Georgia (Gullah), August 5, 1933"

This interview represents one of the oldest Gullah/Geechee informants whom Lorenzo Dow Turner recorded as part of his field research. Like the other digitized recordings that I have previously mentioned, Wallace Quarterman talks about slavery and his life at that time working on the farm and planting crops. The recording also features numerous problems by capturing the scratchy sound quality and disc skipping. What differentiates the "Interview with Wallace Quarterman" stems from how Quarterman mentions the hunting and foraging techniques that people used in the area where he worked in

---

[258] Lorenzo Dow Turner and Dave White, 1933; Lorenzo Dow Turner and Dave White, 1933.

[259] Lorenzo Dow Turner, 1933; Lorenzo Dow Turner, 1933.

the nineteenth century. On "Side A" of the field recording, Quarterman discusses the dangerous possibility of encountering bears and fighting them off with sticks.[260]

"Side B." by contrast, presents a short and confusing section of the interview. Quarterman briefly mentions reading the Bible and his scholastic education, although he does not necessarily provide a definitive description about the latter part. The last half from this section makes no logical sense, based on what the Library of Congress PDF transcription gives to readers and scholars. Lorenzo Dow Turner starts talking to Quarterman, but the effects of aging on the recording prevent listeners from hearing and knowing what he says (The transcription simply indicates that the sound of his voice on the recording suddenly fades). To add to this awkward moment, Quarterman begins listing months and numbers.[261] It is unclear why he does this because there is no direct context for what he is talking about. Perhaps, Quarterman is referring to his work schedule during his time as a slave. Perhaps, it could be that he is talking about how long he has worked planting crops on St. Simons Island. The recording in its current digital condition does not present listeners with clear answers and forces people to form educated guesses.

Stetson Kennedy and Herbert Halpert, "Church Door-Opening Song" (1939)

Other Gullah/Geechee field recordings from the 1930s fare better in terms of the sound quality and representation. Recall earlier that I mentioned how the 2018 revision of the "Finder's Guide" for the *Gullah-Geechee Collections at the American Folklife Center* does not concentrate much on the Gullah/Geechee presence in the North Florida region of the "Corridor." Readers should not misinterpret this point as a complete absence of Gullah/Geechee recordings from Florida. "Church Door-Opening Song" clearly illustrates this exception. The 1939 shellac or acetate field recording by Herbert Halpert, assisted by Stetson Kennedy (folklorist) and Reverend Harden W. Stuckey (performer), derives from Jacksonville, Florida.

---

[260] Lorenzo Dow Turner "Interview with Wallace Quarterman, St. Simons Island, Georgia, August 5, 1933 (part 1 of 2)," Library of Congress, https://www.loc.gov/item/afc1984011_afs25665a. (accessed October 5, 2020).

[261] Lorenzo Dow Turner "Interview with Wallace Quarterman, St. Simons Island, Georgia, August 5, 1933 (part 2 of 2)," Library of Congress, https://www.loc.gov/item/afc1984011_afs25665b/ (accessed October 5, 2020).

"Church Door-Opening Song" does not contain an accompanying textual transcription. However, it does provide detailed liner notes that specify the exact date and location of the recorded performance (June 18, 1939 at the Federal Music Office in Jacksonville, Florida). In the field recording Reverend Harden W. Stuckey explains and sings a song sung in Gullah/Geechee used after a church sermon. Unlike the Lorenzo Dow Turner "Interview with Dave White" from 1933, which proves difficult to hear, "Church Door-Opening Song" remains mostly intact because of slightly better sound quality.[262]

Gullah/Geechee Audio Field Recordings from John and Ruby Lomax

The field recordings from Alan Lomax are often regarded by many scholars and ethnomusicologists as valuable documents for comprehending different cultures and musical genres from around the United States and the world. His ethnographic work also played a vital role in disseminating the music of the Gullah/Geechee to external audiences on his trips across the southeastern U.S. in the 1930s, 50s, 60s, and 80s. To assume that Alan Lomax was the *only* family member involved in this process proves grossly incorrect, however. While I do mention about his accomplishments in this area, I initially demonstrate how his father and mother, John and Ruby Lomax, also recorded music from the Gullah/Geechee Heritage Corridor in the 1930s. I do this by discussing the collections from the Library of Congress that contain these recordings and their accessibility for scholars and the general public. In discussing the contributions of the Lomax family to preserving Gullah/Geechee music and speech, I must also consider other organizations and resources. I also mention the Association for Cultural Equity (co-chaired by Anna Lomax Wood, the daughter of Alan Lomax[263]), the *Voices in Time* YouTube channel, and other available audio recordings in alternate formats. It also deserves mention in passing that Bess Lomax Hawes, the sister of Alan Lomax, also conducted ethnomusicological research. While Alan often receives credit for collaborating with Bessie Jones, who I will discuss later, Bess

---

[262] Stetson Kennedy, Herbert Halpert and Harden W Stuckey, "Church Door-Opening Song. Jacksonville, Florida, 1939." *Library of Congress.* https://www.loc.gov/item/flwpa000040/ (accessed September 1, 2019), Audio.
[263] I had the opportunity to correspond with Anna Lomax Wood via e-mail while gathering resources for my lecture at the 2020 International Gullah Geechee and African Diaspora (IGGAD) Symposium at the Coastal Carolina University in Conway, South Carolina.

Lomax Hawse also worked with Jones for the book *Step It Down: Games, Plays, Songs, and Stories from the Afro-American Heritage.*[264]

The Library of Congress houses valuable archives of collected field recordings from John and Ruby Lomax respectively, some of which include materials related to the Gullah/Geechee. The *John A. Lomax Southern States Collection, 1933-1937* and *Southern Mosaic: The John and Ruby Lomax 1939 Southern States Recording Trip* each contain hundreds of audio recordings and documented materials collected from ethnomusicological trips across the southern United States. Like the previous archives that I have mentioned in this study, both collections feature digitized versions of select audio recordings from their field trips. The first collection contains a different version of "Come by Here" from 1936, recorded in Raiford, Florida and performed by Ethel Best with a chorus (not credited). This recording is available online to the public and is slightly longer than the Robert Winslow Gordon 1926 recording. Concerning the liner notes to this version, John A. Lomax does not mention a connection to the Gullah/Geechee. Instead, he refers to the music as "African American."[265]

The Library of Congress is not the only place that has access to materials from John and Ruby Lomax. The *Voices in Time* YouTube channel features Gullah/Geechee field recordings from John and Ruby Lomax from their ethnographic field trip to Murrels Inlet, South Carolina: an area pertaining to the Gullah/Geechee people. According to the "About" page of the channel, the people who have uploaded the videos for *Voices in Time* have complied with the copyright laws from the Library of Congress and use the material for educational purposes.[266] For example, the description for the recording to "You

---

[264] John Szwed. "Chapter 15: The Science of Folk Song," in *Alan Lomax: The Man Who Recorded the World: A Biography* (New York: Penguin Books, 2010), 339.

[265] John A. Lomax and Ethel Best, "Come by Here," (May 1936), *John A. Lomax Southern States Collection, 1933-1937*, https://www.loc.gov/item/ihas.200197362/ (accessed January 7, 2020); Library of Congress, "About This Collection," *Southern Mosaic: The John and Ruby Lomax 1939 Southern States Recording Trip*, https://www.loc.gov/collections/john-and-ruby-lomax/about-this-collection/ (accessed January 7, 2020).

[266] Voices in Time, "About," *YouTube* (March 31, 2016), https://www.youtube.com/channel/UClpH81HFHrKxtY0V7Tds53g/about (accessed October 1, 2019).

Gots to Move" performed by Annie Holmes is the same as it is on the Library of Congress website. Those details appeared when I typed the name of the song in the search.

At the same time, however, the recordings pertaining to Murrels Inlet on *Voices in Time* are organized in playlists on the channel. These playlists often mix Gullah/Geechee music with other aspects of southern music that are not related. The channel groups "You Gots to Move" as part of southern United States folk music and not as distinctly Gullah/Geechee.[267] Listeners and researchers must investigate these playlists and hypothesize which songs (most of which are unaccompanied) belong to the Gullah/Geechee community.

A more accessible approach to locating Gullah/Geechee music recorded by John and Ruby Lomax stems from digital compilation albums. Many of these digitized, intangible versions are currently available to listeners via music streaming services. The Alan Lomax Collection features a series of unaccompanied Gullah/Geechee spirituals from Murrels Inlet on the album *Deep River of Song, South Carolina, "Got the Keys to the Kingdom."* From this collection, listeners can grasp the feel of the "call and response" technique or congregational participation on songs like "Gonna' Take a Ride on the Chariot Wheel," or "Heaven is a Beautiful Place, I Know." The album also reveals the significance of faith and Christianity within the Gullah/Geechee communities, because these spirituals are performed for the purpose of uplifting people.[268]

The digitally restored field recordings on *Deep River of Song, South Carolina, "Got the Keys to the Kingdom"* derive from acetate discs. Like the ethnographic recordings that I previously discussed from Robert Winslow Gordon to Herbert Halpert, the sound quality of some of the tracks produces scratching or hissing noises because of degradation. The restored versions (as presented via the music

---

[267] Voices in Time, "American Folk Music (Southern): You Gots to Move." *YouTube* (May 16, 2016), https://www.youtube.com/watch?v=IzHDuQrdvMk (accessed January 7, 2020).

[268] D.W. White, "Gonna' Take a Ride on the Chariot Wheel," *Deep River of Song, South Carolina, "Got the Keys to the Kingdom—The Alan Lomax Collection*, Rounder Records, 2002. https://open.spotify.com/album/6biFA55hl5SLuernZOI9oA (accessed January 7, 2020); Hannah Besselieu and Mittie Doctor, "Heaven is a Beautiful Place, I Know," *Deep River of Song, South Carolina, "Got the Keys to the Kingdom—The Alan Lomax Collection*, Rounder Records, 2002.

streaming services) also do not include the performers initially explaining who they are and providing the recording dates.[269]

Alan Lomax, the Gullah/Geechee, and the Association for Cultural Equity

Another organization connected to the Lomax family and their work is the Association for Cultural Equity, or ACE. This organization, based in New York City as part of Hunter College, features websites dedicated to preserving folk music cultures from all over the world. Originally founded by Alan Lomax in the 1980s, ACE is currently co-chaired by his daughter, Anna Lomax Wood (b. 1944).[270] The ACE website contains multiple accessible visual and interactive resources (videos posted to social media, podcasts, "The Global Jukebox" interactive musical map, and others). Concerning the Gullah/Geechee, the *Alan Lomax Archives* YouTube channel contains a playlist of eight videos dedicated to his visual field research from 1983 in St. John's Island, South Carolina.[271] The videos currently on display in the YouTube channel feature fragments of a Gullah/Geechee church service.

The Association for Cultural Equity also features thousands of audio recordings from ethnographic field trips that Alan Lomax conducted from the 1940s to 1990s. This expansive sound archive has been made free and open to the public since 2012. Researchers can find digitized field recordings by the following categories: Collection/Session. Group, Artist, Genre, Location, Culture, and Tape Number.[272] Clicking on the "Location" link leads to a webpage with a list of alphabetized countries and territories where Alan Lomax recorded music for his ethnographic research. Each country contains nested links, with "United States" listed towards the end. Clicking the

---

[269] Hannah Besselieu and Mittie Doctor, "Heaven is a Beautiful Place, I Know," *Deep River of Song, South Carolina, "Got the Keys to the Kingdom—The Alan Lomax Collection*, Rounder Records, 2002. https://open.spotify.com/album/6biFA55hl5SLuernZOI9oA (accessed January 7, 2020).

[270] Association for Cultural Equity (ACE), http://www.culturalequity.org/ (accessed September 16, 2019).

[271] Alan Lomax Archive, "1983: St. Johns Island," *YouTube* (April 24, 2012), https://www.youtube.com/watch?v=NXY3PqVbNLU&list=PLA3B7461E3337D45E (accessed November 1, 2020).

[272] Association for Cultural Equity, "Research Center: Sound Recordings," *Association for Cultural Equity*, 2018. http://research.culturalequity.org/home-audio.jsp (accessed October 1, 2019).

"+" icon reveals recordings from thirteen states, the commonwealth of Puerto Rico and a subsection listed as "… United States (unspecified)."[273] What does this information have to do with the Gullah/Geechee? ACE does contain audio recordings of Gullah/Geechee music as part of the archive, albeit under strange categories. Gullah/Geechee music is available on the website under "Georgia" via "United States." Looking under "Culture," however, I noticed that the website lists Gullah/Geechee music as "Georgia Sea Islands" and not by the correct designation of the people.[274]

The Georgia Gullah/Geechee field recordings by Alan Lomax in the ACE sound archives originate from the 1950s and 60s from his second trip to St. Simons Island, Georgia. Sources frequently refer to his collaborations with Bessie Jones (1902-1984), an African American blues, spiritual and folk singer whom Alan Lomax met and befriended in 1959 on his second ethnomusicological trip to the Golden Isles of coastal Georgia. Lomax previously travelled there in the 1930s, working with Zora Neal Hurston and Mary Elizabeth Barnicle. According to Joh Szwed, that specific trip to Georgia that Lomax took represented part of his ethnographic field research across the southern United States and as part of his work with the Archive of American Folk Song at the Library of Congress.[275]

The Library of Congress website features one readily accessible digitized field recording from the first Georgia field trip that Alan Lomax took: an ethnographic interview with Wallace Quarterman at Fort Federica in St. Simons Island, Georgia in June 1935. This is the same Wallace Quarterman whom Lorenzo Dow Turner interviewed two years earlier for his research on Gullah/Geechee language.[276] The

---

[273] Association for Cultural Equity, 2018.

[274] Association for Cultural Equity, 2018.

[275] John Szwed. "Chapter 4: Travels with Zora Neal Hurston and Mary Elizabeth Barnicle" in *Alan Lomax: The Man Who Recorded the World: A Biography* (New York: Penguin Books, 2010), 77-92.

[276] Alan Lomax, Zora Neale Hurston, and Mary Elizabeth Barnicle. "Interview with Wallace Quarterman, Fort Frederica, St. Simons Island, Georgia, June 1935 (part 1 of 2)." *Library of Congress*, 1935, https://www.loc.gov/item/afc1935001_afs00342b/. Accessed January 16, 2020; "Interview with Wallace Quarterman, Fort Frederica, St. Simons Island, Georgia, June 1935 (part 2 of 2)." *Library of Congress*, 1935, https://www.loc.gov/item/afc1935001_afs00342b/. Accessed January 16, 2020;

interview, primarily conducted by Zora Neal Hurston, consists of two parts: of which, only the second part is available to the public online (For some unexplained reason, the Library of Congress also lists this recording as a section in three parts). Like the Turner interview, the field recording that Lomax, Hurston, and Barnicle produced functions as a preservation of ex-slave narratives. The difference here stems from the fact that Quarterman devotes time on the recording to singing a spiritual. The sound quality, however, suffers from unavoidable background noise (A dog starts barking in the beginning of "Side A") and sound degradation due to aging.[277]

If one ignores the scratchiness of the sound quality, the recording functions as another preserved history of life in the nineteenth century from someone who experienced it. Wallace Quarterman talks about freedom from his enslavement and life in the Reconstruction Era. The interview transcription, however, does not provide many context clues regarding the period that Quarterman is talking about. He mentions voting for a Democratic president at one point, but it is unclear if he is referring to the nineteenth century or the 1930s, nor which person.[278] Given what I just said earlier, it is plausible that Quarterman is referring to life in the nineteenth century under Reconstruction. Within this historical context, he could be referring to the racism and "Jim Crow" laws imposed by the Democratic Party at that point in time.

Other aspects of the 1935 Quarterman interview reveal instances of the Gullah/Geechee linguistic dialect and other Georgia connections. He mentions that his former enslaver lived in Skidaway Island and Savannah, Georgia.[279] Concerning the transcription, it serves as both a help and a hinderance. Reading the text reveals what the informant says, albeit as written and interpreted by the interviewees and the Library of Congress. The grammar and speech by Quarterman

---

Lorenzo Dow Turner, *Africanisms in the Gullah Dialect*. Columbia, SC: University of South Carolina Press, 1949, 2002.

[277] Alan Lomax, Zora, Neal Hurston, and Mary Elizabeth Barnicle, "Interview with Wallace Quarterman, Fort Frederica, St. Simons Island, Georgia, June 1935 (part 2 of 2)," *Library of Congress*, 1935, https://www.loc.gov/item/afc1935001_afs00342b/ (accessed January 16, 2020).

[278] Alan Lomax, Zora Neal Hurston, and Mary Elizabeth Barnicle, 1935.

[279] Alan Lomax, Zora Neal Huston, and Mary Elizabeth Barnicle, 1935.

additionally demonstrate the Gullah/Geechee language as a Creolized language that applies English. At the same time, the transcription inadvertently reinforces the mistaken notion of Gullah/Geechee as a "regressive" or "broken" language.[280] Some readers could quickly misinterpret the text from Quarterman as "improper" English through his use of verbs and pronouns.

Regarding Zora Neal Hurston and her involvement with Alan Lomax in the 1930s, there is a valid reason why Hurston speaks on the field recording and not Alan Lomax. John Szwed indicates that Hurston had more qualifications to navigate her way across the African American communities in the southern United States. That is not to say that she got along with all African Americans. Szwed also mentions how her candid criticism of Black intellectuals (like W.E.B. DuBois), coupled with her unorthodox ethnographic methodology by simply talking to people, often led to her communal alienation.[281]

Many of the Alan Lomax Gullah/Geechee recordings from the 1950s and 60s have been preserved on the ACE website. Lomax recorded audio interviews and performances with Bessie Jones and contributed to the formation of the Georgia Sea Island Singers in the 1960s. "Folk music," in the context of Bessie Jones and this ensemble, often applies to Gullah/Geechee music or African American spirituals. The performances by this musical group helped initiate the folk music revival in that era.[282] Bessie Jones and the Georgia Sea Island Singers were not the only group performing Gullah/Geechee music that Alan Lomax recorded. He also spent time working with the Moving Star Hall Singers from South Carolina the same decade. This group also performed their music live outside the geographical scope of the Gullah/Geechee Cultural Heritage Corridor. One specific album from 1967 demonstrates the group performing as far as California.[283]

---

[280] Alan Lomax, Zora Neal Hurston, and Mary Elizabeth Barnicle, 1935.

[281] John Szwed. "Chapter 4: Travels with Zora Neal Hurston and Mary Elizabeth Barnicle" in *Alan Lomax: The Man Who Recorded the World: A Biography* (New York: Penguin Books, 2010), 77-92.

[282] Peter Stone and Ellen Harold. "Bessie Jones" *Association for Cultural Equity*, [2018 (?)] http://www.culturalequity.org/alan-lomax/friends/jones-0 (accessed January 15, 2020).

[283] Moving Star Hall Singers, *Moving Star Hall Singers Live in San Fransisco 1967*. Westside. 2016. Accessed August 27, 2019. https://open.spotify.com/album/2cAbzWsCHQJ6aodzqEvX5d.

It should be noted that Bessie Jones interprets Gullah/Geechee music from an etic perspective. Concerning her involvement with the Georgia Sea Island Singers and Alan Lomax respectively, Jones primarily aimed to educate the public about African American music and culture through audio recordings, live concerts, and stories.[284] In addition to audio recordings, the ACE website also contains digitized versions of interviews that Jones participated in with Lomax and Antoinette Marchand. The interview originates from 1961 in New York City, in which Jones presents an oral autobiography and selected performances. This interview, conducted in three months and originally recorded on reel-to-reel audio tapes, consists of thirteen large sections: each one divided into multiple subsections. Part of the audio interview exhibits Bessie Jones talking about music that she grew up listening to and creating in her childhood. These personal anecdotes can be heard in "Bessie Jones I, 10/61: 8." Commentary by Bessie Jones on homemade musical instruments." I find it intriguing how she goes into detail describing the different types of musical instruments that she heard and played (like the quill woodwind instrument, akin to the panpipe).[285] Readers must take into consideration that Jones discusses these instruments from the perspective of African American culture and not necessarily from that of the Gullah/Geechee.

Many previous sources concentrate on clapping and singing as the predominant aspects that define Gullah/Geechee music.[286] While this may be true in areas like coastal South Carolina, not all Gullah/Geechee people from the Corridor use the same instrumentation. Throughout my investigation, I have encountered the use of additional instruments in ensembles like the Geechee Gullah

---

[284] Peter Stone and Ellen Harold. "Bessie Jones" *Association for Cultural Equity*, [2018 (?)] http://www.culturalequity.org/alan-lomax/friends/jones-0 (accessed January 15, 2020).

[285] Bessie Jones, Alan Lomax, and Antoinette Marchand, "Bessie Jones I, 10/61: 8. Commentary by Bessie Jones on homemade musical instruments." *Association for Cultural Equity* (2018) http://research.culturalequity.org/get-audio-detailed-recording.do?recordingId=23065 (accessed October 1, 2019).

[286] Erica Lanice Washington, "'Shabach Hallelujah!': The Continuity of the Ring Shout Tradition as a Site of Music and Dance in Black American Worship." Bowling Green, OH. Bowling Green State University, 2005, Master's Thesis, https://etd.ohiolink.edu/!etd.send_file?accession=bgsu1131054976&disposition=inline. (Accessed August 28, 2019).

Ring Shouters from Riceboro, Georgia. They apply a stick and wash board *in addition to* clapping and singing.[287]

One can see that Alan Lomax cared deeply about preserving the music of foreign, unknown, or marginalized cultures. One can also notice that Lomax tried his best to maintain a level of respect for these cultures, something that he frequently talked about in personal interviews later in his life.[288] However, this did not mean that his ethnographic research went perfectly without interruptions or problems. While conducting his field trips across the southeastern United States, like his work in 1935, Lomax frequently got arrested and released from prison. Consider that he conducted his research in the "Jim Crow" era, where a White person working together with Black scholars or informants could be perceived as threatening.[289] This kind of mentality has not really disappeared in the United States in the twenty-first century. It has merely evolved through the incorporation of technology via misinformation, suppression of African American historical narratives (like the opposition to the 1619 Project [290]), hate speech, and violence.

Aside from constantly running out of funding and internal disputes during his time as Archivist at the Library of Congress, Alan Lomax also had to face the constant threat of harassment by the Federal Bureau of Investigation (FBI). This was due, in part, to the relentless efforts by the House Un-American Activities Committee (HUAAC). This committee greatly distrusted Lomax with his folk music research and recordings that demonstrated to audiences the different aspects of American society and culture, accusing him of

---

[287] Geechee Gullah Ring Shouters. "Home," *Geechee Gullah Ring Shouters* (N.D.) https://www.geecheegullahringshouters.com/ (accessed January 15, 2020).

[288] Terry Gross and Alan Lomax, "Folklorist Alan Lomax: Everyone Has a Story," *Fresh Air* (January 7, 2011, Rebroadcast) https://www.npr.org/2011/01/07/132733850/folklorist-alan-lomax-everyone-has-a-story (accessed January 15, 2020). Transcript.

[289] John Szwed. "Chapter 4: Travels with Zora Neal Hurston and Mary Elizabeth Barnicle" in *Alan Lomax: The Man Who Recorded the World: A Biography* (New York: Penguin Books, 2010), 77-92.

[290] PBS, "What Trump is saying about 1619 Project, teaching U.S. history," *PBS News Hour* (September 17, 2020), https://www.pbs.org/newshour/show/what-trump-is-saying-about-1619-project-teaching-u-s-history (accessed October 21, 2020), Transcript.

promoting and spreading Communist and Anti-American sentiments.[291]

It might seem laughable and preposterous to some readers in the twenty-first century that a person could be blacklisted for promoting folk music. Unfortunately, that is exactly what happened to Alan Lomax in the 1940s and 50s. John Szwed and Delaina Sepko mention that, in 1942, Lomax had been brought to the FBI for interrogation. The HUAAC accused Lomax of promoting Communism since the 1930s through his fieldwork, pointing to his connections to folk singers like Woody Guthrie and Pete Seeger as supposed evidence. They assumed that, because these performers attended workers rallies and protests, that Lomax sympathized with Communists: a charge which Lomax frequently denied. To try to corroborate their claims, the FBI also questioned his fellow co-workers, who also denied that Lomax had ties to Communism.[292]

Even though J. Edgar Hoover ordered that the case against Alan Lomax should be dropped, that did not prevent the HUAAC from constantly targeting him. Their unceasing harassment eventually caused Lomax and his family to temporarily leave the United States for England in the 1950s. While Lomax did conduct more field research overseas for compilation albums of international folk music, UK and European police departments also secretly maintained contact with the FBI and continued spying on him. Alan Lomax and his family did not return home until the late 1950s, by which point the musical landscape in the United States had changed via rock and roll and the folk music revival.[293]

---

[291] John Szwed, "Chapter 9: The People's War," in *Alan Lomax: The Man Who Recorded the World: A Biography* (New York: Penguin Books, 2010), 189-216.

[292] John Szwed, 189-216; Delaina Sepko, "The Archive of American Folk Song, The Library of Congress Recording Laboratory and Notions of American Identity." *Fontes Artis Musicae* 62, No. 2 (2015), https://www.jstor.org/stable/24579447?noAccessModalRRLoggedIn=true&Search=yes&resultItemClick=true&searchText=alan&searchText=lomax&searchText=fbi&searchUri=%2Faction%2FdoBasicSearch%3FQuery%3Dalan+lomax+fbi&&acc=off&&wc=on&&fc=off&&group=none&ab_segments=0%2Fbasic_SYC-5152%2Ftest&refreqid=search%3A81a49a7f35f6d9e3e56172319ef190b6&seq=1 (accessed May 12, 2020).

[293] John Szwed. "Chapter 14: The American Campaign Resumed," in *Alan Lomax: The Man Who Recorded the World: A Biography* (New York: Penguin Books, 2010), 306-323.

In the case of Alan Lomax and his collaborations with members of the Gullah/Geechee, his field recordings serve a dual purpose. They function as both educational and commercially marketable materials. The ACE website contains compilation albums from the 2010s of his field recordings from around the United States and the world: including his work with the Gullah/Geechee. This music has also appeared in earlier compilations from the 1990s, like the *Sounds of the South* album reissue from 1993. While some may dispute his ethnographic approach, Alan Lomax often believed that the musicians that he recorded deserved compensation for their work. This is evident in the digitized versions of correspondence letters that Alan Lomax and members of the Georgia Sea Island singers wrote from the 1950s to 1980s, available on the Library of Congress website. Since his death in 2002, some his field recordings of Gullah/Geechee music have also been made available through the ACE website and via digital formats through music streaming services.[294]

Gullah/Geechee Recordings from The Society for the Preservation of Spirituals

Investigations into Gullah/Geechee audio recordings from the early twentieth century additionally directed me to other areas beyond fieldwork by the ethnomusicologists whom I have previously mentioned. More importantly, this part of the research focuses on preserving Gullah/Geechee music at the local level via South Carolina. Many of the other ethnomusicologists I mentioned originated outside the Corridor in other states like Texas (the Lomax Family), or outsiders who adapted to the Gullah/Geechee environment by living in the area and gaining trust from the community (Robert Winslow Gordon, Lorenzo Dow Turner, Stetson Kennedy, and Herbert Halpert). Considering these points and the questions that I raised earlier in the beginning of the book in relation to control and access to Gullah/Geechee audio recordings, the Society for the Preservation of Spirituals presents an unusual case. My goal in this section of my research is not just to highlight the archived materials related to the Gullah/Geechee community via this organization. I mainly concentrate on the methodology behind the Society for the

---

[294] Alan Lomax, "Alan Lomax Collection, Manuscripts, Georgia Sea Island Singers. 1958-1987." https://www.loc.gov/resource/afc2004004.ms180333/?st=gallery. Accessed August 26, 2019, Manuscript/Mixed Material; Various Artists. *Sounds of the South*. Atlantic Records. 1993. Accessed October 18, 2019. https://open.spotify.com/album/2MQMLFDBfgm3CNM24sK0TT.

Preservation of Spirituals and whether they apply cultural respect or appropriation.

The Society for the Preservation of Spirituals, or the Spiritual Society, formed in 1922 in Charleston, South Carolina. This ethnomusicological organization records, collects, interprets, and preserves Gullah/Geechee and African American spiritual music. In these respects, the society aims to educate the public: primarily, outsiders unfamiliar with African American and Gullah/Geechee music cultures. Early collected field recordings date from 1936 to 1939. Additionally, the field work and performances from the Society for Preservation of Spirituals inspired John A. Lomax to research the music of the Gullah/Geechee in South Carolina.[295]

Looking through the website for the Society for the Preservation of Spirituals, one can grasp the sense of care taken in cataloging musical and ethnographic audio recordings that the group has created since the 1930s. The website also provides sample audio recordings of their work on the top of every page and examples of lyrics to spirituals in the Gullah/Geechee language, like "Silbuh Trumpet." To bring Gullah/Geechee music to the public, the society has performed as a group at the White House and on radio programs.[296]

The Society for the Preservation of Spirituals is currently led by Park Dougherty and other descendants of the original group members. These descendants seek to continue preserving Gullah/Geechee music for future generations through cultural repatriation by giving back to the Gullah/Geecchee. In 2004, the society released multiple CD recordings of Gullah/Geechee music, digitized from reel-to-reel tape recordings from the 1960s. These tapes had preserved aluminum disc recordings from the 1930s. Access to these recordings prove limited, because they are currently available at

---

[295] Samuel G. Freeman, "A Black Cultural Tradition and Its Unlikely Keepers," *New York Times* (June 17. 2011), https://www.nytimes.com/2011/06/18/us/18religion.html (accessed March 20. 2020).

[296] Society for the Preservation of Spirituals (Website), http://gullahspirituals.org/ (accessed March 20. 2020); Samuel G. Freeman, "A Black Cultural Tradition and Its Unlikely Keepers," *New York Times* (June 17. 2011), https://www.nytimes.com/2011/06/18/us/18religion.html (accessed March 20. 2020).

the Edisto Bookstore and the Preservation Society of Charleston. Audio recordings from the society are not available via online music streaming services. However, there is one compilation sample available through YouTube.[297]

The Society for the Preservation of Spirituals attempts to maintain cultural respect for Gullah/Geechee music. I have, however, also noticed some strange aspects of the society when conducting research. Many of the audio recordings on the website feature interpretations of Gullah/Geechee music... by White people. Listening to the spirituals with that context in mind, the songs begin to sound awkward because of the sense of cultural displacement. The fact that some of the current group members descended from enslavers also did not alleviate matters much.[298]

It would be tempting for me to simply focus on the problematic parts of the musical interpretations by the Society for the Preservation of Spirituals and accuse them of stealing from Gullah/Geechee culture. As outsiders to the Gullah/Geechee community (*comyahs*, even though they live in Charleston, South Carolina), they technically have no authority to interpret this music. The Gullah/Geechee music culture does not belong to them. Yes, all the key steps of the cultural theories that I mentioned many chapters earlier in this study are present in their recordings: primarily, through foreign dominance and what listeners could quickly perceive as exploitation. In many respects, the ethnographic approach from this organization can come off as tampering with the Gullah/Geechee music culture by assuming "Black" voices by White people.

I could have left my criticisms there and continued with my investigation. However, readers must understand that the members of Spiritual Society already know that the Gullah/Geechee culture does not belong to them. While their approach is questionable on the surface, the group does not aim to "speak for" or "represent" the

---

²⁹⁷ Samuel G. Freeman, 2011; The Society for the Preservation of Spirituals, n.d.; Brandon Coffey, "Spiritual Society Field Recordings, 1936-39." *YouTube* (December 4, 2016), https://www.youtube.com/watch?v=1-MU6lIzGSw&t=103s (accessed March 23, 2020). Brandon Coffey includes a disclaimer, where he explains that he intends this video to be used for entertainment or education, although he does not directly specify "Fair Use." Coffey also assumes that the recordings in the video are "Public Domain" and does not intend to commit Copyright Infringement.

²⁹⁸ The Society for the Preservation of Spirituals (Website), http://gullahspirituals.org/ (accessed March 20. 2020).

133

Gullah/Geechee. It educates people in efforts to give Gullah/Geechee music back to the community.[299] This point brings me back to what I said at the outset of this research. Readers should not jump to conclusions and assume that outsiders did not care about foreign or unknown cultures. Groups like the Society for the Preservation of Spirituals interpret Gullah/Geechee music in a way that outsiders can understand and not necessarily out of disrespect for the culture.

Sidney Robertson Cowell and Puerto Rican Field Recordings from the WPA California Music Project

Previous segments of this chapter have revealed the accessibility of locating Gullah/Geechee recorded audio via the Library of Congress website. Searching for Latin American audio field recordings, on the other hand, proves more complicated. Some extant digitized audio field recordings from the early twentieth century pertaining to Puerto Rico, for example, derive from the 1930s in California. This geographical aspect of my investigation is quite unusual, considering that most discussions about Puerto Rican migration and diaspora concentrate on areas like New York City, Chicago, Illinois and Orlando, Florida.

The available field recordings of Puerto Rican music form part of the *Works Progress Administration (WPA) California Music Project*. Led by Sidney Robertson Cowell (1903-1995), the *California Music Project* provides ethnographic research of recorded and cataloged folk music (through audio and other media) from different migrant and immigrant populations across northern California from 1938 to 1940.[300] Cowell conducted the research for the Puerto Rican segment of this project in 1939. The Library of Congress website features digital restorations of five acetate disc audio recording from two distinct informants: Aurora Calderon and Elinor Rodriguez (See Table).These informants present Puerto Rican folk and popular songs by singing them without accompaniment. Some of the songs recorded, like "Venid pastores =

---

[299] Samuel G. Freeman, "A Black Cultural Tradition and Its Unlikely Keepers," *New York Times* (June 17. 2011), https://www.nytimes.com/2011/06/18/us/18religion.html (accessed March 20. 2020).

[300] Library of Congress, "Collection: California Gold: Northern California Folk Music from the Thirties Collected by Sydney Robertson Cowell," *Library of Congress*, https://www.loc.gov/collections/sidney-robertson-cowell-northern-california-folk-music/articles-and-essays/wpa-california-folk-music-project/ (accessed October 21, 2020).

Come shepherds," function as music appropriate for celebratory occasions: in this case, Christmas.[301]

The selection from the *WPA California Music Project* presents a good portion of Puerto Rican folk music from the early twentieth century. However, I noticed something missing in the series of field recordings from Sidney Robertson Cowell. The music that she recorded represents what is often referred to in Puerto Rico as *musica jíbara*, or (as a rough English approximation) "mountain music." I have discussed the significance and impact of this musical genre in Puerto Rico and elsewhere in my previous research.[302] The reason why I address this is because these field recordings do not present the Afro-Puerto Rican side of Puerto Rican music via genres like the *bomba* and *plena*. Conducting searches via the library of Congress website with the terms "Afro-Puerto Rican" and "bomba" under "Audio Recordings" produces no results. However, typing in the word "plena" reveals a small selection that includes segments of a concert of Puerto folk music from the 1970s performed by the Conjunto de Cuerdas Tipicas de Puerto Rico in Chicago, Illinois.[303] The Library of Congress has different rules for these recordings under the respective "Rights and Access," They acknowledge that some of the songs are currently Public Domain. However, because the concert dates from the 1970s, most of the recorded material is under copyright protection and should be approached with caution.[304]

Archivo Virtual Instituto de Cultura Puertorriqueña

Turning to recording archives and compilations directly from Latin America and the Hispanophone Caribbean, there are two worth mentioning for the purpose of this study. The first stems from San Juan, Puerto Rico via the Instituto de Cultura Puertorriqueña (Institute of Puerto Rican Culture), or ICP. Their *Archivo Virtual Instituto de Cultura Puertorriqueña* features digital archives of audio recordings

---

[301] Sydney Robertson Cowell and Aurora Calderon, "Venid pastores = Come, shepherds." *Library of Congress* (1939), https://www.loc.gov/item/2017701611/ (accessed October 22, 2020).

[302] Anthony L. Sanchez, *The Jíbaro and the Gaucho United in Music and Song* (English Translation), Vancouver, BC: Ditrie Marie Bowie, 2019.

[303] Philip B. George et al, "Recording of performance by Conjunto de Cuerdas Tipicas de Puerto Rico at El Romance Club, Chicago, Illinois, part 1," *Library of Congress* (1977), https://www.loc.gov/item/afc1981004_afs20754/ (accessed July 28, 2021).

[304] Philip B. George et al, 1977.

related to Puerto Rico. That section of the ICP website can be located under the "Grabaciones" ("Recordings") link.[305]

The collections catalog for the ICP virtual audio archives is readily available online for scholars to peruse. According to that catalog, dated November 2016, the Unidad de Grabaciones de la Editorial del I.C.P. spearheaded the digitalization process of the audio recordings. These recordings derive as digital conversions from the original tangible recording formats at the ICP. This includes incorporating *all* aspects of the audio recording, like the cover art, names of performers, and recording dates. [306] While the recordings in the archive have been made public and accessible to anyone from home online, the Institute acknowledges that this virtual audio archives represents a small part of the ICP recording catalog. The institute hopes that more archiving can be completed in the future to expand the collections.[307]

The *Archivo Virtual Instituto de Cultura Puertorriqueña* features multiple sections of recordings dedicated to both music and speech: "speech," in this context referring to recorded stories and not necessarily ethnographic field research. It also includes sections devoted to Puerto Rican classical, folk, and popular music. ICP features an entire catalog of recordings of *danza* music from the nineteenth century, as well as selections from twentieth-century Puerto Rican composers like Hector Campos Parsi (1922-1998), Rafael Aponte Ledeé (b. 1937), and others.[308] The popular music presented in ICP, however, can prove misleading for those expecting to find genres from the late twentieth and early twenty-first centuries. Genres like reggaeton and hip hop are nowhere to be found. Instead, it features music from the early to mid-twentieth century with artists like Rafael Hernandez. Even though the Afro-Puerto Rican bomba *is* present in the audio archives, the folk music section concentrates (perhaps too much) on musica jíbara.[309]

While the *Archivo Virtual Instituto de Cultura Puertorriqueña* demonstrates a good effort for Latin American sound archiving, it still

---

[305] "Grabaciones," *Archivo Virtual Instituto de Cultura Puertorriqueña* (2020), https://www.archivoicp.com/coleccion-por-series (accessed October 26, 2020).

[306] "Grabaciones," *Archivo Virtual Instituto de Cultura Puertorriqueña* (2020).

[307] "Grabaciones," *Archivo Virtual Instituto de Cultura Puertorriqueña* (2020).

[308] "Grabaciones," *Archivo Virtual Instituto de Cultura Puertorriqueña* (2020).

[309] "Grabaciones," *Archivo Virtual Instituto de Cultura Puertorriqueña* (2020).

has some glaring issues. The first stems from its exclusivity to Puerto Rico via the island. More specifically, the recordings at ICP are issued under their own recording label in Puerto Rico. Additionally, it is understandable that the audio recordings there represent music from bygone eras and must be collected and restored. However, the contemporary popular music in Puerto Rico is equally important and deserves some attention: especially the protest songs and raps that have emerged in the wake of events like Hurricane Maria in 2017, the protests against corruption in the Puerto Rican Government in 2019, and addressing COVID-19 in the 2020s.[310] The archive also largely leaves out the equally significant demographic of the Puerto Rican diaspora in the mainland United States, many of whom helped to disseminate the Puerto Rican music cultures across the country. As I previously mentioned, ICP knows that their archival work has just begun. Perhaps, by including the missing information that I just discussed, they can help to expand the knowledge of Puerto Rican culture by working together with music archivists from the stateside Puerto Rican communities.

Colección Gladys Palmera

The Instituto de Cultura Puertorriquena is not the only place that offers acccss to archived audio related to Latin American music. The Coleccion Gladys Pamera represents part of a private collection of records amassed over thirty years. This collection, based in Spain and digitized in 2018, features an array of popular musical genres from Latin America and the Caribbean, with special focus on Cuban music.[311] It features everything from mambo to rock music and Afro-Latino artists (including Puerto Rico). Additionally, the collection does

---

[310] Lin-Manuel Miranda et al, "A Forgotten Spot (Olvidado)," (New York: Hamilton Uptown Limited Liability Company/Atlantic/WEA; Stockholm: Spotify, 2018), Single, https://open.spotify.com/album/6J74LJVGaniegVuVcX9tna (accessed August 19, 2021); Plena Combativa, "Candela," *Plena Combativa* (San Juan(?): Plena Combativa; Stolkhom: Spotify, 2020), Tr. 3, https://open.spotify.com/album/0hueG0Ly9bLV4qkJQ43iuD (accessed August 19. 2021); Residente, "Antes Que el Mundo Se Acabe," (Miami: Sony Music Entertainment Latin US LLC; Stockholm: Spotify, 2020), Single, https://open.spotify.com/album/6w0POUCEoPxwGYM7tLOLGM (accessed August 19, 2021).

[311] Colección Gladys Palmera, (2018), https://gladyspalmera.com/coleccion/ (accessed August 19, 2021); Caitlin Donohue, "Meet Gladys Palmera, the Woman Who Has Collected 50,000 Latin Music Records," *Remezcla* (April 10, 2017), https://remezcla.com/music/gladys-palmera-record-collection/ (accessed August 19, 2021).

not limit itself to solely the Spanish-speaking areas of Latin America. It also includes musical recordings from Brazil in the Portuguese language.[312]

One can see that the Colección Gladys Palmera demonstrates the musical diversity of Latin American and Caribbean cultures. However, people should keep several things in mind when navigating the online archive. It features some of the same problems as the *Archivo Virtual Instituto de Cultura Puertorriqueña*, because it mainly includes popular music from the twentieth century and not from artists active in the twenty-first century. While the collection is divided by categories in the "Search," like by region and musical genres, it assumes that people know what they are looking for in advance. People who use the digitized Colección Gladys Palmera should also be aware that the online version does not represent the full tangible collection. A fraction of the fifty-thousand total recordings in the private collection are displayed on the website.[313] It also does not allow complete access to the albums listed. Visitors and researchers cannot listen to albums in their entirety on the website. However, it does feature playlists of specific musical genres with selected tracks that people can listen to.[314]

---

[312] Colección Gladys Palmera, (2018), https://gladyspalmera.com/coleccion/ (accessed August 19, 2021).

[313] Colección Gladys Palmera, (2018), https://gladyspalmera.com/coleccion/ (accessed August 19, 2021); Julyssa Lopez, "One of the World's Largest Private Collection of Latin American Music Just Hit the Web," *Remezcla* (May 7, 2018), https://remezcla.com/music/gladys-palmera-collection-online-archive/ (accessed August 19, 2021).

[314] Colección Gladys Palmera, (2018), https://gladyspalmera.com/coleccion/ (accessed August 19, 2021).

Figure 21: Sound-Mixing Board (Photo by Filip Barna on Unsplash)

"A kì í fi ohun-olóhun tọrẹ bí kò ṣe tẹni."[315]

The following segments explore Gullah/Geechee music from the perspectives of popular music genres from the 1950s through the 2010s. I explore how popular musicians and groups apply and adapt Gullah/Geechee music to their specific genres as a way for expressing artistic creativity. In doing this, I demonstrate that such approaches can often produce conflicting results: in the extreme case, completely obscuring the meaning of Gullah/Geechee culture to signify something else. Using Gullah/Geechee music in popular music settings depends on the artistic or critical interpretation and whether the artists maintain respect for the culture.

---

[315] One does not make a gift of someone else's property when it is not one's own. (Never be too free with other people's property.) University of Nebraska Lincoln, *The Good Person: Excerpt from the Yorùbá Proverb Treasury,* http://yoruba.unl.edu/yoruba.php-text=1b&view=0&uni=1&l=1.htm (accessed July 28, 2021).

Let me clarify one crucial point before going any further in this discussion. The critiques of popular musicians and groups presented in this chapter do *not* attempt in any way to defame or attack their character as artists. I offer analyses and feedback concerning how they approach Gullah/Geechee music across different genres. I especially draw attention to musical artists who use Gullah/Geechee culture and, if done incorrectly or questionably, try to explain why.

It also should be noted that not everyone initially supported certain genres like the folk music revival in the 1950s and 60s. Alan Lomax had expressed extreme caution over its application in the United States as "pop" music upon returning home from his exile and research overseas in Europe. Excluding some folk artists like Bob Dylan, Lomax perceived the contemporary iteration of folk pop music as inauthentic and inaccurate. His reasoning behind these complaints stemmed from what he perceived as excessive stylization of the music and geographic displacement (e.g., hearing folk singers from New York City perform music about the South).[316] This partially explains why Lomax conducted another series of field trips and recordings across the southern United States, including coastal Georgia, in the 1950s and 60s. He wanted to demonstrate to audiences the geographical sources from which the popularized versions of folk music originated.[317]

"Kumbaya" and the Folk Music Revival

Earlier in this investigation, I explained the origins of the song "Come by Here," or "Kumbaya," as recorded by Robert Winslow Gordon and performed by Henry Wiley. Recall that the recording dated from the 1920s and how that song (as "Kumbaya") would increase in popularity several decades later in the 1950s and 60s. How exactly did people interpret "Kumbaya" within the context of the folk music revival of that specific period? To answer that question, I consider the origins of the song based on the perspectives of the 1950s and 60s. I additionally concentrate on the consequences of how "Kumbaya" transformed in its overall meaning as the decades passed.

---

[316] John Szwed, "Chapter 14: The American Campaign Resumed," in *Alan Lomax: The Man Who Recorded the World: A Biography* (New York: Penguin Books, 2010), 306-323.

[317] John Szwed, 306-323.

Researchers now know, or are mostly certain, that "Kumbaya" began as a Gullah/Geechee song. Thinking from the perspectives of the 1950s and 60s, however, sources from *that* era do not mention this cultural connection. Instead, musical artists and scholars provide opposing details concerning the geography and history of "Kumbaya." The Folksmiths suggest that the song originated in Africa, while others indicate that it was written in 1939 by Marvin Frey, a British-American composer and preacher. Stephen Winick from the American Folklife Center has disproven both origin stories as false in his research from 2010.[318]

Understanding the impact of the folk music revival on "Kumbaya" requires examining the topic from a global standpoint. While it is true that "Kumbaya" received wide popularity in the United States via folk recordings by artists like Pete Seeger (1919-2014), interpretations of the song are not exclusive to the U.S. "Kumbaya" has also been recorded and interpreted by folk musicians from overseas, like The Seekers from Australia.[319] One must additionally think about the setbacks associated with these interpretations of "Kumbaya" in the forms of cultural and contextual erasures. A plethora of recordings of "Kumbaya" from the 1950s and 60s stem from cultural outsiders: many of whom, as I said before, do not discuss its connection to the Gullah/Geechee people. Recall that, even though the field recording of "Come by Here" originated in 1926, it was not until 2017 that people began to officially recognize "Kumbaya" as belonging to the Gullah/Geechee community.[320]

"Kumbaya" additionally underwent a transformation in meaning throughout the remainder of the twentieth century. When

---

[318] Stephen Winnick, "Kumbaya: History of an Old Song," *Library of Congress* (February 6, 2018), https://blogs.loc.gov/folklife/2018/02/kumbaya-history-of-an-old-song/ (accessed December 16, 2019).

[319] Pete Seeger, "Kumbaya," *Pete Seeger: The Smithsonian Folkways Collection*, Smithsonian Folkways, 2019, (accessed January 15, 2020), https://open.spotify.com/album/2D3VqXZRrje1UzRBDwLNas?highlight=spotify:track:52dweof0R55C5KgR7QaYzX; Seekers, "Kumbaya—Remastered," *Kumbaya (Remastered)* Caribe Sound, 2018 (accessed January 15, 2020), https://open.spotify.com/album/3yABmKDU9PBX4VodAKHRYm.

[320] House of Representatives, "Recognizing the Song 'Kumbaya' Congressional Record Vol. 163, No. 200 (December 7, 2017), *Congress.* https://www.congress.gov/congressional-record/2017/12/07/house-section/article/H9714-1 (accessed January 7, 2020).

taken in its original context, the song signifies a plea to the Lord for assistance to overcome struggles. Over time, however, "Kumbaya" gradually lost its sacred meaning and changed into a secularized version. The song did not come to signify something associated with Gullah/Geechee and African American cultures. Instead, it functioned as music strictly for children or as a stereotype associated with promoting peaceful diplomacy. In many respects, this last derivation has damaged the original meaning of "Kumbaya." The song has frequently manifested itself in that format through media and politics, often with negative connotations.[321] In these respects, the folk revival of "Kumbaya" serves as indirect cultural appropriation based on the theorization posited by Richard A. Rogers. The folk recordings of "Kumbaya" that I have previously mentioned exhibit moments of cultural exchange, dominance, exploitation, and transculturation by outsiders in promoting the material as a commercial product.[322] Transculturation also appears as a linguistic fusion (Gullah/Geechee and English) coupled with contextual misinterpretations of "Kumbaya": neither comprehending where the song originated, nor its primary meaning.

Sampling in My Life in the Bush of Ghosts, by Brian Eno and David Byrne

Instances of Gullah/Geechee music and speech have appeared in popular music via avant-garde collage and sampling. The concept album, *My Life in the Bush of Ghosts* from 1981 (and re-released in 2006 with remastered and extended content)[323] presents a fitting example of this. The electronic music album serves as a collaboration between British composer and music producer Brian Eno (b. 1945) and Scottish-American musician and composer David Byrne, best known as the lead singer for his band, Talking Heads. When taken as a whole, *My Life in the Bush of Ghosts* provides listeners with impressions of

---

Linton Weeks, "When Did 'Kumbaya' Become Such a Bad Thing?" *National Public Radio (NPR)* (January 13, 2012), https://www.npr.org/2012/01/13/145059502/when-did-kumbaya-become-such-a-bad-thing (accessed January 16, 2020).

[322] Richard A. Rogers. "From Cultural Exchange to Transculturation: A Review and Reconceptualization of Cultural Appropriation." *Communication Theory* 16 (2006). http://jan.ucc.nau.edu/~rar/papers/RogersCT2006.pdf (accessed October 8, 2019).

[323] Brian Eno and David Byrne. *My Life in the Bush of Ghosts.* Nonesuch Records, Inc. 2006 (accessed October 18, 2019). https://open.spotify.com/album/0uWpq6h99OaylNLXe2KPTR.

African music through electronic soundscapes and vocal sampling from different source materials.[324]

It is for this same reason that *My Life in the Bush of Ghosts* often functions as a polarizing work. While music critics praise the album for its sampling and eclectic musical depiction of African cultures[325], academics have repeatedly cautioned listeners against interpreting *My Life in the Bush of Ghosts* as an authentic representation of African musical identities. Elizabeth Ann Lindau and Marcus Boon respectively address the fact that the musicians who created *My Life in the Bush of Ghosts* approach African music as cultural foreigners. They also criticize Eno and Byrne of applying African musical identities through Western, European avant-garde techniques: specifically, taking preexisting musical materials and rearranging them to create something that sounds new, thereby altering the contexts of the original musical sources used. [326]

In their representations of "Africaness" in *My Life in the Bush of Ghosts*, Eno and Byrne also provide examples of sampling from the Gullah/Geechee. In "Moonlight in Glory"[327], they sample directly from three tracks from the 1964 live album, *Sea Island Folk Festival: Moving Star Hall Singers and Alan Lomax*. More specifically, they take from Track 4 ("See God's Ark A-Moving"), Track 12 ("Moonlight in

---

[324] Elizabeth Ann Lindau, "Avant-gardism, 'Africa,' and Appropriation in *My Life in the Bush of Ghosts*," in *Brian Eno: Oblique Music*, Edited by Sean Albiez and David Pattie (London: Bloomsbury Academic, 2016), 193-210.

[325] John Parelles. "My Life in the Bush of Ghosts." *Rolling Stone* (April 2, 1981), https://www.rollingstone.com/music/music-album-reviews/my-life-in-the-bush-of-ghosts-252823/ (accessed January 22, 2020).

[326] Elizabeth Ann Lindau, "Avant-gardism, 'Africa,' and Appropriation in *My Life in the Bush of Gosts*," in *Brian Eno: Oblique Music*, Edited by Sean Albiez and David Pattie (London: Bloomsbury Academic, 2016), 193-2010; Marcus Boon, "On Appropriation." *CR: The New Centennial Review*, 7, No. 1 (2007). https://www.jstor.org/stable/41942891?Search=yes&resultItemClick=true&searchText=On&searchText=Appropriation&searchUri=%2Faction%2FdoBasicSearch%3FQuery%3DOn%2BAppropriation&ab_segments=0%2Fbasic_SYC-4929%2Ftest&refreqid=search%3A4dee5fd0e07c5c151414979b56b5c922&seq=1 (accessed December 30, 2019).

[327] Brian Eno and David Byrne. *My Life in the Bush of Ghosts*. Nonesuch Records, Inc. 2006. Accessed October 18, 2019, Tr. 7 https://open.spotify.com/album/0uWpq6h99OaylNLXe2KPTR.

Glory") and Track 7 ("Gullah Folk Tale: Barney McCabe").[328] Given these samples, it also becomes unusual that Eno and Byrne name their track with the same title from their second sample. In terms of musical sampling, Eno and Byrne mix all three tracks together to obscure their original contexts. A Biblical sermon about Noah and the Flood gets interspersed with seemingly random chanting about the moon and segments from a Gullah version of "Hansel and Gretel." Eno and Byrne juxtapose these re-arranged samples to the musical backdrop of African-sounding funk.[329]

What does all this mean in terms of the Gullah/Geechee culture? Consider how Brian Eno and David Byrne approach the original source materials from the 1964 Moving Star Hall Singers recording within the theoretical frame of how Richard A. Rogers defines cultural appropriation. One could easily locate instances of dominance and exploitation throughout "Moonlight in Glory" in *My Life in the Bush of Ghosts*. Aside from using the same song title word for word, this track *interprets* Gullah/Geechee music within a Westernized view of an imaginary Africa. It suggests ethnocentric cultural ideas of European (and American) superiority. Whether the artists intended to accomplish this task or not is irrelevant. The result leads to a loss of Gullah/Geechee identity at the cost of artistic creativity and demonstrates a disrespect for the Gullah/Geechee culture.

This analysis does not necessarily mean that the artists in question have retained this reckless attitude in the twenty-first century. David Byrne, for one, has had time to contemplate the significance of *My Life in the Bush of Ghosts* and some of his other works from the 1980s. Byrne has recently reflected on the controversy associated with *My Life*

---

[328] Moving Star Hall Singers and Alan Lomax, *Sea Island Folk Festival: Moving Star Hall Singers and Alan Lomax*. Smithsonian Folkways Recordings/Folkways Records. 1964, 2004. Tr. 4, 12, 7 (accessed August 27, 2019), https://open.spotify.com/album/63mDe1DpOANi3he5WwrKhT; Elizabeth Ann Lindau, "Avant-gardism, 'Africa,' and Appropriation in *My Life in the Bush of Gosts*," in *Brian Eno: Oblique Music*, Edited by Sean Albiez and David Pattie (London: Bloomsbury Academic, 2016), 193-2010. Elizabeth Ann Lindau lists this album as released in 1968. This date, however, is incorrect. Smithsonian Folkways, the record label pertaining to the Smithsonian Institution, indicates the original live recording as 1964.

[329] Brian Eno and David Byrne. *My Life in the Bush of Ghosts*. Nonesuch Records, Inc. 2006. Accessed October 18, 2019, Tr. 7 https://open.spotify.com/album/0uWpq6h99OaylNLXe2KPTR.

in the Bush of Ghosts in interviews, specifically its problem with cultural appropriation. He suggests that he now understands some of the negative critical reception behind the album.[330] In late 2020, Byrne also addressed another issue concerning work that he conducted with his band Talking Heads in the early 1980s. In discussing the Broadway production of his show *American Utopia*, Byrne also reflected on the problematic visual promotion of the *Stop Making Sense* album from 1984, where he appeared in Blackface and Brownface.[331] He has since realized the crassness of his past actions, taking to social media to issue a lengthy and sincere apology for his previously immature behavior. As a Scottish-American, he realizes the cultural diversity of the United States and the world: that humanity must do its best to maintain respect and ethical responsibility.[332]

Sampling in Play, by Moby

Musical sampling has become a common practice since the 1980s and 90s. In terms of academic discussions, some scholars focus on the dichotomy of using preexisting music for artistic expression versus the legal ramifications of sampling: usually, as it pertains to copyright law in the United States and elsewhere.[333] While that topic goes beyond the scope of what I discuss here in this section, I *will* illustrate how sampling can backfire depending on the type of creative inspiration. I

---

[330] Brian Hiatt, "David Byrne on Trump, Cultural Appropriation and Why He Won't Reunite Talking Heads," *Rolling Stone* (February 1, 2018). https://www.rollingstone.com/music/music-features/david-byrne-on-trump-cultural-appropriation-and-why-he-wont-reunite-talking-heads-203033/ (accessed December 30, 2019).

[331] Lake Schatz, "David Byrne Apologizes for Wearing Blackface in 1984 Stop Making Sense Promo Video," *Consequence of Sound* (September 1, 2020), https://consequenceofsound.net/2020/09/david-byrne-apology-blackface-video/amp/ (accessed October 23, 2020).

[332] Lake Schatz, 2020.

[333] David Hesmondhalgh, "Digital Sampling and Cultural Inequality." *Social and Legal Studies* (2006). https://s3.amazonaws.com/academia.edu.documents/12709783/53.full.pdf?response-content-disposition=inline%3B%20filename%3DDigital_Sampling_and_Cultural_Inequality.pdf&X-Amz-Algorithm=AWS4-HMAC-SHA256&X-Amz-Credential=AKIAIWOWYYGZ2Y53UL3A%2F20191209%2Fus-east-1%2Fs3%2Faws4_request&X-Amz-Date=20191209T185659Z&X-Amz-Expires=3600&X-Amz-SignedHeaders=host&X-Amz-Signature=2a1703e4ffc25a110950114c1b7013f3de8cfc8aca6ccc90b76f2d9a04cce464 (accessed September 16, 2019).

focus specifically on the 1999 electronic techno album *Play* by Moby (b. 1965). Like *My Life in the Bush of Ghosts* by Brian Eno and David Byrne, Moby draws his musical resources from African and African American musical genres as the basis for *Play*: including Gullah/Geechee music as part of the cultural macrocosm.

Play debuted in 1999 to mostly positive reviews, save for some critics who issued mediocre ratings at the time (Brent Dicrecenzo gave *Play* a "5.0" out of 10, alluding to the disorganized nature of the album and to how Moby transitioned from independent rock to techno.).[334] Moby re-issued this album fifteen years later in 2014 as *Play and Play: The B-Sides*, with the original tracks and alternate versions not featured on the 1999 version. The 2014 re-issue is more readily available through music streaming services. This is the version that I will refer to in my discussion.

Academic criticisms of *Play* that I have encountered in my research highlight three key topics, often in conjunction with each other: the musicality behind sampling, the ethical problems associated with the technique, and taking from African American musical styles for creative purposes. Discussions concerning musical sampling in *Play* focus on how Moby approaches the original source materials that he uses for the album and transforms the preexisting songs. Some of the samples that Moby uses for this album derive from the Alan Lomax field recordings from *Sounds of the South*.[335] That four-disc compilation album consists of field recordings that Lomax preserved from his trips across the southern United States in the early and mid-twentieth century. In relation to this current study, it is worth noting that some of the tracks from *Sounds of the South* feature Bessie Jones performing with the Georgia Sea Island Singers, like the song "Sometimes."[336] This song originally features vocals and clapping.

---

[334] Brent DiCrescenzo. "Moby *Play* Album Review," *Pitchfork* (June 1, 1999). https://pitchfork.com/reviews/albums/5344-play/ (accessed December 18, 2019).

[335] Moby, *Play and Play: The B-Sides.* Little Idiot, 2014 (accessed October 18, 2019). https://open.spotify.com/album/0t4ItMJbYMYLzvEO7tzt0B; Various Artists, *Sounds of the South.* Atlantic Records, 1993. Accessed October 18, 2019. https://open.spotify.com/album/2MQMLFDBfgm3CNM24sK0TT

[336] Moby, 2014; Bessie Jones, Various Artists, *Sounds of the South.* Atlantic Records, 1993. Disc 4, Tr. 17. Accessed October 18, 2019. https://open.spotify.com/album/2MQMLFDBfgm3CNM24sK0TT.

Recall earlier in this study when I highlighted the connection with Bessie Jones and the Georgia Sea Island Singers to Gullah/Geechee culture. Upon first listen, "Sometimes" appears as a song that conforms to the Ring Shout: the song and dance commonly associated with the Gullah/Geechee. However, hearing that track several times reveals that Bessie Jones and the Georgia Sea Island Singers do not apply a Ring Shout in the song. "Sometimes" features clapping that falls *directly* on the beat in duple meter in 2/4 time.[337] The Ring Shout applies clapping in groups of *three* in duple meter, with the first beat serving as the strong pulse and the other two as the weaker beats.

How does Moby handle the musical materials in "Sometimes?" He samples fragments of the song as the basis for the first track on *Play* called, "Honey." He mainly lifts parts from the "0:15" to "0:24" marks of "Sometimes" and repeats these snippets over and over in loops.[338] Listening carefully to this track on his album, one could guess that Moby pays attention to the rhythmic aspects of the vocal samples. At certain points in "Honey," Moby truncates the selected sample and applies more repetition ("1:08-1:19"). He also samples from the opening seconds of "Sometimes" and juxtaposes it with the first sample at the "1:21" mark of the track.[339]

It also helps to consider the instrumental layering that Moby uses in "Honey." Remember that "Sometimes" features only vocals and clapping. With "Honey," Moby adds the following: an electric piano (starting immediately), synthesized drum patterns ("0:10"), blues and funk guitar riffs ("0:49" and "1:21"), and random vocal shouts that have nothing to do with the original track that he sources (starting at "2:08").[340] One could argue that Moby adds these instruments to complement the rhythmic nature of the sampled vocal parts. In terms of content and contexts, *Play* suffers from the same setbacks as *My Life in the Bush of Ghosts* by Brian Eno and David Byrne. Moby presents a vision of African American music (including Gullah/Geechee)

---

[337] Bessie Jones, "Sometimes." Various Artists, *Sounds of the South*. Atlantic Records, 1993. Disc 4, Tr. 17. Accessed October 18, 2019. https://open.spotify.com/album/2MQMLFDBfgm3CNM24sK0TT.

[338] Moby, *Play and Play: The B-Sides*. Little Idiot, 2014. Track 1. Accessed October 18, 2019. https://open.spotify.com/album/0t4ItMJbYMYLzvEO7tzt0B

[339] Moby, 2014.

[340] Moby, 2014.

through an ethnocentric perspective that does not consider the historical and religious aspects of the people. Whether he means to or not, he nonetheless provides listeners with a culturally ignorant view of the music that he samples on his album.

In their respective critiques of *Play*, both concerning the compositional process and the finished product, Richard Osbourne and David Hesmondhalgh express concern over how Moby applies African American music on the album. They argue that he freely (mis)uses these musical styles as a privileged White musician through cultural appropriation. Osbourne compares the frequent appropriation of Blackness in *Play* to a contemporary version of nineteenth century United States "Blackface" minstrel shows.[341] Neither he nor Hesmondhalgh stop there in their criticism. Both point to the problems associated with creative ownership and copyright in musical sampling. One key mistake that they indicate stems from how Moby does not give any credit at all to the African American (and Gullah/Geechee) artists whom he samples from in *Play*, living or deceased: indicating his lack of cultural awareness. Instead, he thanks the Lomax family for helping him with the album and adds his name to all aspects of the production.[342]

---

[341] Richard Osbourne, "'Blackface' minstrelsy from Melville to Moby." *Critical Quarterly* (2006). https://s3.amazonaws.com/academia.edu.documents/32119407/Richard_Osborn e_Blackface_Minstrelsy_from_Melville_to_Moby.pdf?response-content-disposition=inline%3B%20filename%3DBlackface_Minstrelsy_from_Melville_to_M.pdf&X-Amz-Algorithm=AWS4-HMAC-SHA256&X-Amz-Credential=AKIAIWOWYYGZ2Y53UL3A%2F20191209%2Fus-east-1%2Fs3%2Faws4_request&X-Amz-Date=20191209T185008Z&X-Amz-Expires=3600&X-Amz-SignedHeaders=host&X-Amz-Signature=d4aad9b615e87e1e5ffecc29b48674f35b4797a42e110ee6004480fd4f6cca 8f (accessed September 16, 2019).

[342] Richard Osbourne, 2006; David Hesmondhalgh, "Digital Sampling and Cultural Inequality." *Social and Legal Studies* (2006). https://s3.amazonaws.com/academia.edu.documents/12709783/53.full.pdf?respo nse-content-disposition=inline%3B%20filename%3DDigital_Sampling_and_Cultural_Inequalit y.pdf&X-Amz-Algorithm=AWS4-HMAC-SHA256&X-Amz-Credential=AKIAIWOWYYGZ2Y53UL3A%2F20191209%2Fus-east-1%2Fs3%2Faws4_request&X-Amz-Date=20191209T185659Z&X-Amz-Expires=3600&X-Amz-SignedHeaders=host&X-Amz-Signature=2a1703e4ffc25a110950114c1b7013f3de8cfc8aca6ccc90b76f2d9a04cce46 4 (accessed September 16, 2019).

The live version of *Play* also serves to reinforce the minstrelsy mentioned by Osbourne in his research. The YouTube channel for Moby features a live performance of "Honey," uploaded in 2016. What I find bizarre about this is that it includes a Black female backup singer performing over the Bessie Jones sample. Upon closer examination of the video, though, it looks like she is lip-synching to the track. This same performer, and all the other instrumentalists, do not receive any credit for their involvement in the video in the description.[343] It is practically a repetition of what Moby does in the credits to the *Play* album.

Perhaps most troubling, Moby violates copyright law by using many of these samples. I mentioned earlier in this study that the Bessie Jones recordings with Alan Lomax originated in the late 1950s into the 1960s. This means that her recordings are currently *not* in the "Public Domain." Even though Osbourne and Hesmondhalgh write about the copyright infringement in *Play* from the perspective of the 2000s, the problem persists over two decades later because the copyrights still apply to each sampled song on the album.[344]

Some readers could also argue that, given the recent changes to copyright and sound recordings via the Music Modernization Act of 2018, the recordings that Moby samples in *Play* are now free to use. However, if one examines the wording of the Music Modernization Act further, one can see that copyright restrictions still apply. The Bessie Jones audio recordings originated as early as 1959. According to Amanda Jenkins, the Music Modernization Act attempts to reduce the strict 2067 expiration date set forth by previous copyright law, which indicated that *no* audio recordings were Public Domain. The new designation of Public Domain audio recordings under the Music Modernization Act nevertheless presents a problem. The changes apply specifically to recordings issued before 1956.[345] This means that the samples that Moby uses in *Play* still infringe upon copyright.

---

[343] Moby, "Moby- Honey," *YouTube* (May 19 2016), https://www.youtube.com/watch?v=J8CMLpUAwsk (accessed October 23, 2020).

[344] Richard Osbourne, 2006; David Hesmondhalgh, 2006.

[345] Amanda Jenkins, "Copyright Breakdown: The Music Modernization Act." *Library of Congress* (February 5, 2019), https://blogs.loc.gov/now-see-hear/2019/02/copyright-breakdown-the-music-modernization-act/ (accessed December 9, 2019).

Up to this point, I have examined the consequences of selected popular musicians applying Gullah/Geechee music. The previous examples demonstrated works from people outside of the Gullah/Geechee culture. As a result, the albums previously discussed concentrate on artistry while simultaneously diminishing or exploiting the cultural value of the Gullah/Geechee people. Those musical albums and trends either do not openly acknowledge the Gullah/Geechee presence, or they include it within the scope of a fictionalized Africa through an ethnocentric viewpoint. What about musical artists who draw inspiration from the Gullah/Geechee and do so within a positive light? Is it possible to take music from that culture and combine it with another genre while still maintaining respect?

The answer to this last question is "Yes." To illustrate why, I refer to the jazz quintet from Charleston, South Carolina known as Ranky Tanky. Since their debut in 2017, this ensemble has frequently received critical praise for their approach to combining traditional Gullah/Geechee music (like Ring Shouts, spirituals and play songs) with modern jazz instruments.[346] In this respect, the music that they produce functions as transculturation: one that does not intentionally aim to exploit the Gullah/Geechee music culture. Ranky Tanky arranges Gullah/Geechee folk music for contemporary audiences within a jazz setting to combine elements from the past and present. Following this approach, their musical interpretations serve to educate listeners who may be unfamiliar with Gullah/Geechee music.

The members of Ranky Tanky exhibit a profound sense of respect for Gullah/Geechee music culture. Their 2017 interview on National Public Radio (NPR), in which three of the five members were present (Clay Ross, Quiana Parker and Charlton Singleton) reveals the origin and purpose for the ensemble. Founder Clay Ross, who admits that he is a cultural outsider from North Carolina, created the ensemble with Parker, Singleton and the other members while college students at Charleston, South Carolina. Their fascination with Gullah/Geechee culture and the fact that most of the members grew up within the culture served as a valuable connection.[347] In this sense the works that

---

[346] Ranky Tanky, https://www.rankytanky.com/ (accessed November 1, 2019).

[347] Terry Gross, "Ranky Tanky Builds on the Music and Culture of Slave Descendants." *Fresh Air* (December 12, 2017).

they perform function as a preservation of cultural memories of the Gullah/Geechee history and heritage performed for twenty-first century audiences, but with key musical elements intact.

Ranky Tanky currently has two jazz albums in their catalogue: their self-titled debut (2017) and *Good Times* (2019), which recently won a Grammy award (ironically, not under the "Jazz" category).[348] In both instances, the ensemble features combinations of both religious and secular Gullah/Geechee music. From a linguistic standpoint, they use both Gullah/Geechee and English. They also retain key musical elements of the vocal "Call and Response" and percussive clapping techniques. This can best be heard together in their rendition of "Shoo Lie Loo."[349] In other instances, Ranky Tanky applies jazz textures and instruments (trumpets, bass, percussion and piano) to the traditional Gullah/Geechee songs like "That's Alright." Realizing that Gullah/Geechee music grew out of slavery, the ensemble also does not avoid addressing social issues on their albums. This is best exemplified by the tracks "Freedom" and "Pay Me My Money Down," which address racial equality and wage discrimination.[350]

Gullah/Geechee References in Rap

In terms of popular music, I have encountered uses and borrowings from the Gullah and Geechee from folk music to electronic dance and jazz. One must additionally factor hip hop and rap into this discussion to understand the changing trends in popular music. These can be located online and via music streaming services. Throughout this investigation I found a small selection of tracks related to Gullah/Geechee culture via rap music. However, several rappers stand out to me because of their distinct approaches to the given thematic materials and quotation: Lo' Kuntry, Dear Silas, and Q Smalls.

---

https://www.npr.org/2017/12/12/569965570/ranky-tanky-leans-on-the-music-and-culture-of-slave-descendants (accessed November 1, 2019).

[348] Sunn m'Cheaux, "Congrats RANKY TANKY, Grammy Award Winners," *YouTube* (January 26, 2020), https://www.youtube.com/watch?v=d0tCeoCD1GA (accessed October 23. 2020).

[349] Ranky Tanky, *Good Time*, Resilience Music, LLC., 2019 (accessed November 1, 2019) https://open.spotify.com/album/00U3tf4nUq23aULqpiBbZt. Tr. 12.

[350] Ranky Tanky, 2019. Tr. 10.

Lo' Kuntry is an elusive artist. Not much is known about him, except that he hails from South Carolina. Although he is active as a rapper, his social media pages do not reveal valuable biographical information in the respective "About" sections. In a similar manner, his website leads to a defective link. Despite these problems, Lo' Kuntry presents intriguing content about Gullah/Geechee culture with his track "Gullah Geechee." Released in 2015 off the *Saute (House of Fengshui)* album, "Gullah Geechee" provides listeners with a condensed history of his Gullah/Geechee heritage in three minutes. More importantly, Lo' Kuntry raps about the dangers associated with the cultural erasure of the Gullah/Geechee: from the European conquest of the New World, to linguistic suppression and assimilation.[351]

From a musical perspective, Lo' Kuntry applies trap beats for the percussion and "Auto Tune" effects for the vocals and rapping. However, it is the lyrics to "Gullah Geechee" that matter most. Lo' Kuntry attempts to present the history and struggles of the Gullah/Geechee people, his heritage, as graphically as possible. He refers to the slave market in Charleston, South Carolina and to cultural assimilation of the Gullah/Geechee as "brainwashing."[352] Some listeners might quickly dismiss "Gullah Geechee" because of its shock value, but that is not its intention. Lo' Kuntry demonstrates that he understands the severity and historical weight on the Gullah/Geechee people. He knows that atrocities like what the Gullahs and Geechees have faced cannot, and should not, be sugarcoated or ignored. In this way, "Gullah Geechee" uses contemporary popular music to teach younger generations about Gullah/Geechee culture through rap.

Dear Silas (real name Silas Stapleton III) equally presents an unusual track related to the Gullah/Geechee with "Gullah Gullah Island." A native of Mississippi, rapper and trumpeter Dear Silas obtained social media fame with the release of his song "Skrr Skrr" in 2018 when it became incorporated into a video meme via the 1990s cartoon *Dexter's Laboratory*.[353] "Gullah Gullah Isand," which appears

---

351 Lo' Kuntry. "Gullah Geechee," *Saute (House of Fengshui)*, Lo' Kuntry. 2015 (accessed December 9, 2019). https://open.spotify.com/album/7DedDliBKhcyXnmaKYUl6i. Tr. 2.

352 Lo' Kuntry, 2015.

353 Matt Collar, Rovi, "Dear Silas, About: Biography," Spotify (accessed December 16, 2019). https://open.spotify.com/artist/4C6vnglzmsWszcdp5WaX6O/about.

on the 2016 debut album *The Day I Died*, features another direct reference to 90s popular entertainment culture in the form of musical sampling. Dear Silas samples directly from the theme song to the Nick, Jr. program "Gullah Gullah Island" (1994-97). The original show, created by Ron and Natalie Daise, served to educate young children about Gullah/Geechee culture within the setting of a fictional island (Parts of the show were filmed on location in Beaufort, South Carolina).[354]

"Gullah Gullah Island"(the rap) captures the same sense of fiction, albeit with a more mature tone. Dear Silas perceives Gullah Gullah Island as Utopia: a perfect place with no problems, no broken families, and no social injustices against African Americans. Like Lo' Kuntry does in "Gullah Geechee," Silas provides listeners with vitriolic social commentary in the 2010s: in this case, themes about police brutality and racial discrimination—themes that persist in the 2020s through anti-racist protests advocated by the Black Lives Matter movement. These themes also manifest themselves in the accompanying music video, which functions as a musical response to the anti-Black massacre at the Mother Emmanuel church in Charleston, South Carolina in 2015.[355] In terms of the lyrics, the rap itself contains an abundance of profanity and racial epithets, including the use of the "n-word." "Gullah Gullah Island" functions as a creative metaphor for escapism: not as a rap that necessarily explores Gullah/Geechee history and culture.

Q Smalls, by contrast, candidly addresses and embraces Gullah/ Geechee culture. A native of Hilton Head Island, South Carolina, Q Smalls (real name Quinton Smalls) grew up Gullah Geechee and raps about the culture from the emic perspective. In a manner similar to what Lo' Kuntry does in "Gullah Geechee," Smalls applies his raps as tools to educate the public about Gullah/Geechee

---

[354] Defunctland. "DefunctTV: The History of Gullah Gullah Island, *YouTube* (November 30, 2019). https://www.youtube.com/watch?v=cm1TIe19cJs (accessed December 2, 2019).

[355] Dear Silas, "Gullah Gullah Island," *The Day I Died*. The Village. 2018 (accessed December 16, 2019). https://open.spotify.com/album/5f4l4lTL1QPLvTMD2R4Zqq; Dear Silas, "Dear Silas-Gullah Gullah Island (Official Video)" *YouTube* (February 16, 2016). https://www.youtube.com/watch?v=79fWDxPyLm0 (accessed December 19, 2019).

identity: whether it is through his solo work, or as part of the duo Spiritual Gangsters.[356] Smalls does rap about issues that concern the Gullah/Geechee way of life by concentrating on land, cultural preservation and suppression. However, Smalls also avoids the lyrical elements frequently associated with hip-hop and gangsta rap, He mostly does not use profanity or refer to violence when getting his messages across to listeners.[357]

---

[356] Wade Livingston, "These Gullah rappers have a stern message for Hilton Head—and America—in their new rhymes," *Island Packet* (October 13, 2017), https://www.islandpacket.com/news/local/article178666036.html (accessed February 19, 2020); Q Smalls, "Coast Boy King," *Gullah Life*, 1102323 Records DK, 2019, https://open.spotify.com/album/6LXWf3T5z5YvO1ROPMSghA (accessed February 19, 2020).

[357] Wade Livingston, 2017; Q Smalls, 2019.

Moving Towards the Future: The Legacy of Gullah/Geechee and Afro-Latin Cultures and Music

"That is true culture which helps us to work for the social betterment of all."

~Henry Ward Beecher

"The triumph of culture is to overpower nationality."

~Ralph Waldo Emerson

Cultural Preservation, Tourism, and Avoiding Exploitation

In the previous chapters, I demonstrated the ways in which ethnomusicologists and performing artists had approached Gullah/Geechee and Afro-Latin music cultures from the twentieth and twenty-first centuries. While cultural respect had served as a driving force for such work, recall that I also illustrated how these approaches did not always produce positive results. Preserving and drawing inspiration from these music cultures would call into question aspects about ownership and use, regardless of intent. What about more contemporary times, though? Besides pointing out artists in rap music who have directly or indirectly referred to Gullah culture in the 2010s, what else has been done in the Gullah/Geechee and Afro-Latin communities in recent years to preserve their legacy for the future? Most importantly, how can these cultures avoid exploitation and assimilation?

To effectively answer these questions, allow me to refer to aspects that I mentioned earlier in this investigation and presenting feedback from the members of the Gullah/Geechee. Think about the problems associated with mishandling Gullah culture. Cultural tourism has become a recurring problem in the twenty-first century for the Gullah/Geechee for several reasons, which has affected the visibility of the community due to racialized misinterpretations. Consider the frequent instances of land loss due to external modern development projects that infringe upon Gullah territory (eg., condominiums and gated communities). The Gullah/Geechee have also protested companies that create products that use the "Gullah" or "Geechee" names without their permission: products like alcohol and rice. These are all situations that I have previously discussed throughout this investigation. As I had demonstrated in those sections of this research, the Gullah/Geechee have sufficient reason to fight back to reclaim their identity. The continuous unauthorized commercial use of

Gullah/Geechee culture diminishes the history and legacy of the people.

The best approach to understanding Gullah/Geechee culture is to get feedback from the Gullah/Geechee people: not through interpretations of what other people say about the community. I demonstrated this many chapters earlier by explaining how younger Gullah/Geechee entrepreneurs, like Sonya Grant, run businesses while still respecting their heritage. This attitude is not limited to the youth demographic, but also includes the older generations of Gullah/Geechee who believe in preserving the culture through education. In my correspondence with Zenobia Harper, a tour guide at the The Rice Museum and Hopsewee Plantation in South Carolina, she provided the following:

> I thinks (sic.) that young people, (from early 20's - early 30's) have had different more positive views, understandings and experiences being Gullah, and at an earlier age. Many in my generation were encourage to "move on" from many things, Gullah especially the language. younger Gullah's have more pride and awareness, and are incorporating more of that heritage in their everyday life, and they live much of their lives on social media I can view this generation on social medias, using the language in poetry and music, Gullah Hastags (sic.), people are trying podcasting etc. to reach out to one another and create a larger Gullah community online.[358]

One can see from this quote that Harper acknowledges the importance of what the current generation of Gullah/Geechee people are doing: both in terms of applying technology *and* advancing the visibility of the culture in the twenty-first century. This point bears significance because she mentions forms of social media interactivity and podcasts: things that I have alluded to when talking about cultural appropriation and will expand upon in this current chapter. Notice, also, the stark contrast from what Zenobia Harper reveals about her generation. Based on what she says, the Gullah/Geechee in her time had been discouraged from practicing the culture and language ("Many from my generation were encourage to 'move on' from many things…").[359] This point should come as no surprise. Recall what I mentioned about Xavier Vatin and his interview with Queen Quet, in

---

[358] Zenobia Harper, "Correspondence E-mail to Zenobia Harper," (November 15, 2019).

[359] Zenobia Harper, 2019.

Figure 22: Close-up of Choir at First African Baptist Church—Hilton Head, South Carolina

Figure 23: Interview with Zenobia Harper (Left) at Hopsewee Plantation—Georgetown, South Carolina

Figure 24: Ring Shout Performance by the Geechee Gullah Ring Shouters at RiceFest (Riceboro, Georgia)

which she explained that the Gullah/Geechee in the past were forced to keep their cultural identity secret.[360]

What about Latin America and the Caribbean? What have they been doing? I had shown how Brazil, Cuba, and Puerto Rico have sought to maintain visibility despite racial discrimination. Like the Gullah/Geechee, Afro-Latin communities have had to combat cultural erasure by raising social awareness about their identity and customs. Like the Gullah/Geechee. the Afro-Latin communities have constantly fought against their cultural exploitation and commodification in tourism and other ventures.[361] They have also

---

[360] Xavier Vatin, "Memórias Afro-Atlânticas / Afro-Atlantic Legacies (Zumbi Series, CCADI, NY, 14/12/2020)," *YouTube* (Feb 1, 2021), https://www.youtube.com/watch?v=EaJi63AYscA (accessed June 23. 2021).

[361] Aleysia K. Whitmore, "CUBAN MUSIC IS AFRICAN MUSIC: NEGOTIATING AFRICA AND THE AFRICAN DIASPORA ON THE WORLD MUSIC STAGE," *African Music* 9, No. 3 (2013), http://www.jstor.org/stable/24877317 (accessed January 12, 2021); Rebecca M. Bodenheimer, "National Symbol or 'A Black Thing?': Rumba and Racial Politics in the Era of Cultural Tourism," *Black Music Research Journal* 33, No. 2 (2013), https://www.jstor.org/stable/10.5406/blacmusiresej.33.2.0177 (accessed January 12, 2021); Terrance Pitts, "The Leaders of Loiza, Afro-Puerto Ricans Struggle for Change," *Open Society Foundations* (August 8, 2012),

openly denounced the racial underpinning of "Latinidad." That specific terminology presents itself as racial diversity and equality, albeit under the guise of Whiteness. This problem, which still exists in the 2020s, has become especially noticeable when factoring in Latin American representation in media, where the Afro-Latin presence often gets excluded, presented as *mestizaje* (eg., being Black, but socially "passing" as White or the reverse) or trivialized.[362]

When talking about audio recording preservation, I encouraged readers and researchers to consider the purpose for such recordings (educational, for entertainment, or both). Perhaps, the same could be said about Gullah/Geechee festivals by thinking about the target audience for these events. Is the specific Gullah/Geechee festival necessarily *for* the Gullah/Geechee people? Is the event meant to educate everyone in attendance, regardless of racial background, or is the event meant strictly for visitors not affiliated with the Gullah/Geechee?

Recent scholarship from the 2000s and 2010s reveals that Gullah/Geechee tourism has become more prevalent. However, that has mostly been for the wrong reasons. The problem stems from how cultural tourism has been used to exploit the culture and people.[363] Ryan Thomson has addressed this topic through his ethnographic work with the Gullah/Geechee from 2019. Through his investigation on the commercialization of Gullah/Geechee land and culture,

---

https://www.opensocietyfoundations.org/voices/leaders-lo-za-afro-puerto-ricans-struggle-change. (accessed March 11, 2019).

[362] Astrid Galvan, "Controversy over 'In the Heights' raises awareness of colorism and racial inequity," *PBS News Hour* (June 18, 2021), https://www.pbs.org/newshour/arts/controversy-over-in-the-heights-raises-awareness-of-colorism-and-racial-inequity (accessed August 6, 2021); Maritza Quiñones Rivera, "From Trigueñita to Afro-Puerto Rican: Intersections of the Racialized, Gendered, and Sexualized Body in Puerto Rico and the U.S. Mainland," *Meridians* 7, No. 1 (2006). https://www.jstor.org/stable/40338721 (accessed March 23, 2020).

[363] Hargrove, Melissa. "Will the 'Fools' Always Live Off the 'Damn Fools?' The Politics of 'Lowcountry' Tourism." *Practicing Anthropology* 29, No. 3 (2007) https://www.jstor.org/stable/24782398?Search=yes&resultItemClick=true&searchText=gullah&searchText=geechee&searchUri=%2Faction%2FdoBasicSearch%3FQuery%3Dgullah%2Bgeechee&ab_segments=0%2Fdefault-2%2Fcontrol&refreqid=search%3A225a608139508a09c7894823ccf448ee&seq=1#page_scan_tab_contents, (accessed July 8, 2019).

Thomson notes that some Gullah festivals that generate visits from outsiders provide inaccurate representations of the Gullah/Geechee people and (to a certain extent) their music. [364] I include music as part of the problem not just because of what I mentioned in the previous chapters, but also because of what Thomson demonstrates in his research. For instance, I wrote about the group Ranky Tanky and how they combine Gullah/Geechee music with jazz. Some members of the Gullah/Geechee community, however, disapprove of the group and their efforts. Ryan Thomson highlights this problem in his ethnographic interview with Queen Quet of the Gullah/Geechee Nation, in which she takes umbrage at how she perceives that Ranky Tanky has tried to appeal to outsiders. [365]

This resentment proves logical when one remembers that the Gullah/Geechee people, culture, and language have been suppressed or misunderstood by those not affiliated with the community for decades. That attitude also elicits the problem of (in)authenticity because the context of the "Gullah" becomes racialized and politicized through dialectical stereotyping and cultural theft from people not from the Gullah/Geechee community. That approach distracts tourists by showing them an imagined version of the Gullah/Geechee while simultaneously denying the real people the opportunity to represent themselves to the public. [366]

Most audio recordings that I have found for this research derive from online sources. I previously discussed the availability of digital and intangible versions of ethnographic field recordings (both spoken interviews and music) from scholarly institutions, like the Library of Congress and the Association for Cultural Equity. This does not suggest that these are the *only* places where listeners or researchers interested in Gullah/Geechee and Afro-Latin music should look. They should also consider the impact of audio streaming services and radio in terms of the content available to listeners. I focus specifically on the accessibility (or lack thereof) of Gullah/Geechee Afro-Latin recordings on the audio streaming platform. I am primarily concerned about the type of content on these platforms that relate to these

---

[364] Ryan Thomson, "4. GATES AND FAKES: PERCEPTIONS OF THE SEA ISLAND INVASION," in *Destructionment: Gates & Fakes Invade the Sea Islands* (Gainesville, FL: University of Florida, 2019), 78-98, https://ufdc.ufl.edu/UFE0054389/00001 (accessed July 13, 2021).

[365] Ryan Thomson, 78-98.

[366] Ryan Thomson, 78-98.

cultures and how to locate them for research purposes. Readers should keep in mind the possibility of other currently available audio streaming services, like when searching for related materials. Concerning radio, I provide a brief observation of the content available to listeners and the kind of music broadcast to audiences.

There are three significant aspects to remember when using music streaming services to locate Gullah/Geechee and Afro-Latin music. The first stems from the fact that most platforms do not limit their scope to only music. They also contain podcasts with episodes that vary by topic. This includes podcast episodes that openly discuss the Gullah/Geechee and Latin American language, culture, music, and identity. This is best exemplified in "Episode 22" of *The Stoop*, a podcast hosted by Leila Day and Hana Baba dedicated to exploring the Black diaspora and culture.[367] The episode features interviews from coastal South Carolina with Queen Quet of the Gullah/Geechee Nation and Sunn m'Cheaux, a Harvard professor who specializes in teaching and preserving the Gullah/Geechee language. His interview stands out to me, because he talks about his initial struggle as a child speaking Gullah/Geechee in South Carolina and being alienated by the African American community because his classmates and teacher interpreted Gullah/Geechee as "regressive." "Episode 22" additionally presents moments of self-discovery. Part of that program involves Leila Day uncovering and appreciating her Gullah/Geechee heritage, albeit as someone who grew up not speaking the language.[368]

The Stoop is not the only podcast where Sunn m'Cheaux discusses Gullah/Geechee language. The *Subtitle* podcast features a similar episode from December 18, 2019, in which m'Cheaux discusses the significance of his language course. He also maintains a visible presence on social media. m'Cheaux has managed his social media content since the 2000s through lectures and discussions concerning Gullah/Geechee language and culture. More specifically, he uses his platforms to address the sociocultural and academic implications of English on creolized and marginalized people: mainly, that receiving

---

[367] Leila Day, "Episode 22," *The Stoop* (January 24, 2019) (accessed December 19, 2019). https://open.spotify.com/episode/0fnTupYVdd09IbrOcn24Nf.

[368] Leila Day, "Episode 22."

praise for speaking "proper" English denotes covert systemic racism and a continuation of colonialist practices.[369]

Most online music and podcast streaming services additionally contain free versions of desktop an d mobile smartphone applications. Listeners can search for music or podcasts quickly at the minor expense of sitting through advertisements. In certain cases, some albums do not appear in complete form unless listeners upgrade to the premium monthly subscription service. In terms of music related to Gullah/Geechee, these streaming services do not feature a wide selection of tracks or albums at the outset. People must know the names of the musical artists or groups in advance of their searches. I found the following artists whom I have referred to throughout this project:

- Moving Star Hall Singers
- Bessie Jones and the Georgia Sea Island Singers
- Queen Quet[370]
- Alan Lomax (as archivist)
- Ranky Tanky (as jazz)
- Lo' Kuntry (as rap, when typing the words "Gullah" or "Gullah/Geechee")
- Dear Silas (as rap, when typing the words "Gullah")
- McIntosh County Shouters[371]

Audio selections related to Latin America and the Caribbean, by contrast, present plentiful, if at times uneven, results. Locating music from one of these specific regions or countries largely depends on what is available on the streaming services. They feature many albums about Afro-Latin syncretic religious music from Cuba and Brazil in relation to the kinds of ceremonial songs performed for

---

[369] Patrick Cox and Kavita Pillay. "Gullah Geechee enters the academy," *Subtitle* (December 18, 2019). https://subtitlepod.com/gullah-geechee-enters-the-academy/ (accessed December 19, 2019); Sunn m'Cheaux, "The Inherent Ant-Blackness of 'Proper English' Conditioning," *YouTube* (March 8, 2020), https://www.youtube.com/watch?v=7K3rjOvkFTg (accessed October 23, 2020).

[370] Queen Quet, *Cum Een*, Queen Quet & De Gullah Cunneckshun. 2015. Accessed August 27, 2019. https://open.spotify.com/album/2jNkr92H4FgGboShxPx3MR.

[371] McIntosh County Shouters, *Slave Shout Songs from the Coast of Georgia*, Smithsonian Folkways Recordings/Folkways Records. 1984, 2004, Accessed August 28, 2019. https://open.spotify.com/album/6Ixz1rNhem4WILFGVqhCL9.

certain orishas.[372] The only drawback with these recording is that they only feature the audio and do not incorporate the visuals associated with the ceremonial practices. Listeners not familiar with Afro-Latin syncretic religious music will most likely become confused as to what is happening without using accompanying liner notes: something that music streaming services do not have. In the case of music from Puerto Rico, the results are mixed. It has no shortage of popular music from some of the top island and stateside artists like Residente, Lin-Manuel Miranda, and others. Some services also feature music from Puerto Rican classical composers and Afro-Puerto Rican performance ensembles. Of course, the only way to find groups like La Familia Cepeda[373] (The Cepeda Family) or composers like Roberto Sierra[374] is to find them online elsewhere in advance of searching.

What I have just presented demonstrates a small selection of music related to the Gullah/Geechee and Afro-Latin communities on music and podcast streaming platforms. However, listeners should also take into consideration that this is not a comprehensive list by any means. Some other Gullah/Geechee music ensembles appear online (like the Geechee Gullah Ring Shouters), but their album catalogs have not been made accessible to the public. Another problem stems from what I had discussed earlier in this project: the context of words like "Geechee" when searching for Gullah/Geechee music. Consider the jazz electronica piece "Geechee Pimp Strollin'" by the ensemble Avram Fefer's Rivers on Mars.[375] Listening to the futuristic track online reveals no direct clues or references to Gullah/Geechee music culture. Instead, it is possible that the title of the track refers to the derogatory slang and connotation of the word "Geechee" as

---

[372] Abbbilona y Tambor Yoruba, *Elegua, Ogun y Ochosi* (Havanna: Caribe Productions, Inc., 1999 Stockholm: Spotify), https://open.spotify.com/album/6PaZKP3MJOJBWzy12qQiGX (accessed September 22, 2021); Mavambo Trio, *Candomble Ketu, Angola E Jexa: Oba de Yoruba* (Brazil: DGD Records, 2015; Stockholm: Spotify), https://open.spotify.com/album/4Y1wgxtjQqWKSo35PLIVdL (accessed September 22, 2021).

[373] La Famila Cepeda, *Los Embajadores de la Bomba*, San Juan: Fundacion Folclorica Cultural Rafael Cepeda, Inc., 2015 (accessed October 23, 2020), https://open.spotify.com/album/25QrsiFlqREpnK0L0Pyfr9.

[374] Roberto Sierra, *Roberto Sierra: Cantare, Loiza & Triple Concerto*, Naxos, 2020 (accessed October 23, 2020), https://open.spotify.com/album/3UzzM04E3TL6gd05wGi46J.

[375] Avram Fefer's Rivers on Mars. "Geechee Pimp Strollin,'" *Deja Voodo*, Ropeadope, 2018. Tr. 6. https://open.spotify.com/album/5PidebY36lhYzYPAmHoHA0 (accessed January 2, 2020).

"backwards." The fact that it is also grouped with the sexually suggestive word "pimp" does not alleviate matters.

Concerning radio and the Gullah/Geechee, I have noticed two prominent stations available through initial online searches. The Gullah/Geechee Nation features their "Gullah Riddim Radio," created by Queen Quet, where members of the organization discuss topics concerning Gullah/Geechee culture and preservation. The other station derives from Beaufort, South Carolina via the Gullah Geechee Radio Network (GGRN): WKWQ 100.7 FM. This station, led by Jabari Moketsi, promotes Gullah/Geechee culture on the local level from within the community. In an interview that I conducted on January 29, 2020 with permission from Mr. Moketsi (See "Appendix E" for interview excerpt transcript and "Appendix F" for photograph), I asked him about the origins of the radio station and programming, among other relevant topics. He explained that he initially founded WKWQ 100.7 in 2015 as an offshoot of the now-defunct weekly newspaper, *The Gullah Sentinel.* In providing news to the Gullah/Geechee community in Beaufort, South Carolina, Moketsi offers a more global perspective that addresses both information that mainstream media outlets often miss and topics that affect African American and Gullah/Geechee communities:

> We call it the "Nine Areas of Human Activity" which we cover… Economics, Education, Labor; Law, Sex, War; Religion… And, those are the "Nine Areas of Human Activity" and how they affect us and how they affect us here. But, the main thing we're more concerned … with our radio station … is, uh, Land and Economics. You know? Land because … you cannot have a Gullah culture if the people continue to lose their land here.[376]

Much of the music performed on WKWQ 100.7 FM consists of modern songs and not necessarily those from the traditional Gullah/Geechee repertoire. The station primarily plays Gospel and secular R&B music: sometimes, as Gospel combined with hip-hop music to appeal to the younger generation of listeners. I asked Jabari Moketsi why, as a Gullah/Geechee radio station, he decided to program these musical genres. His answer stemmed from the lack of modern Gullah/Geechee performance groups who specialize in

---

[376] Jabari Moketsi and Anthony L. Sanchez, "Field Interview at WKWQ 100.7 FM in Beaufort, South Carolina: January 29, 2020."

traditional Gullah/Geechee music. Also, even though the station is Gullah/Geechee, Moketsi tries to include the Gullah/Geechee within a larger social scope. As he mentioned at one point earlier in the interview:

> See, now, everything that we do is not necessarily just totally "Gullah, Gullah, Gullah,"… because you can't live inside of a box. You know …You might be Gullah, but you still got to know what's going on in the world….[377]

WKWQ also serves a deeper purpose beyond simply providing the Gullah/Geechee and African Americans with news, entertainment, and sacred music. The radio station is locally owned and operated, with no connections to corporate mainstream radio stations whatsoever. This presents a good marketing tactic, according to Moketsi, because that means that it helps to prevent external cultural exploitation and control from mainstream radio corporations. Moketsi has admitted that his radio station has a short FM signal range that covers only Beaufort, South Carolina at the ground level. However, he has also taken advantage of the Internet as a practicable platform for WKWQ 100.7 FM.[378] Listeners from anywhere across the country and the world can access the radio station from home, thereby expanding the audience.

Using Twenty-First Century Technology to Preserve Gullah/Geechee and Afro-Latin Culture and Music for Future Generations

The research that I have covered in this book has addressed multiple facets of audio recording technology in terms of preserving Gullah/Geechee and Afro-Latin culture. I have discussed the analyzed the positive and negative ways in which people have used such technologies to understand and educate people about these cultures. I have also demonstrated how musical artists have applied different genres to interpret Gullah/Geechee music and speech, as well as how people can access audio materials related to the Gullah/Geechee and Afro-Latin communities in the twenty-first century.

These approaches represent valuable resources for gleaning and increasing knowledge about the Gullah/Geechee and Afro-Latin

---

[377] Jabari Moketsi and Anthony L. Sanchez, "Field Interview at WKWQ 100.7 FM in Beaufort, South Carolina: January 29, 2020."

[378] Jabari Moketsi and Anthony L. Sanchez, "Field Interview at WKWQ 100.7 FM in Beaufort, South Carolina: January 29, 2020."

American and Caribbean people. In the world of rapidly changing technology, however, how can people from within these communities further preserve the cultures for a generation of people that also encourages interactivity? The answer, perhaps, could lie in the creation of a smartphone application dedicated to teaching people about Gullah/Geechee and Afro-Latin cultures and music. The application could possibly concentrate on one or some of the following topics:

- A Gullah/Geechee or Afro-Latin language course with narrations provided by members of the respective communities in the native languages
- An interactive Gullah/Geechee or Afro-Latino dictionary, with "Gullah to English" translations and definitions by members of the Gullah/Geechee community
- An application focused on Gullah/Geechee or Afro-Latin music that provides audiovisual explanations and demonstration of genres, like the Ring Shout, performed by Gullah/Geechee music ensembles or instances of Africanized syncretic religion from people in Cuba, Brazil, and Puerto Rico
- Interactive tutorials about Gullah/Geechee or Afro-Latin culture and history from the perspective of people, possibly as interactive reenactments that address the presence of the people using the smartphone application
- An application dedicated to past and present Gullah/Geechee or Afro-Latin audio recording preservation: complete with an interactive map of relevant archival centers, digitized examples of music and speech, tips for conducting tactful ethnographic interviews in the respective communities, and a section on the pitfalls of cultural exploitation.

Why do I address these points? While conducting brief searches for anything related to the Gullah/Geechee through online smartphone application stores, I grew dissatisfied with what I found. Typing "Gullah/Geechee" in the search boxes revealed a small selection of aural media (all of which featured paywalls), a Gullah Bible, and an application devoted to Gullah cuisine. Additional searches that I conducted revealed that certain groups, like those in tourism, had tried to address the Gullah/Geechee language through online dictionaries. However, they are not accessible in mobile form.[379] An

---

[379] Ambrose E. Gonzales and Alphonso Brown, "Gullah Words," *Gullah Tours* (N.D.), https://gullahtours.com/gullah/gullah-words (accessed February 10, 2020).

application with features like what I had previously listed would prove necessary to push the Gullah/Geechee culture into contemporary times.

Searches for applications about Africanized syncretic religions fared slightly better. I initially ran into problems after typing in the words "Afro-Latino" (I kept getting unrelated results about social networking, which caused me to wonder how racialized—and racist—technology is becoming[380]). Searches improved somewhat as I narrowed the topic to syncretic religions by typing in the word "oricha." From then on, I encountered many applications designed to educate people about the African deities in both African and Afro-Latin syncretic religious practices. Most of these came in the form of encyclopedias or sources in Yoruba, English, Spanish, and Brazilian Portuguese. Perhaps, the most interesting application stemmed from *Yoruba 101*. This educational application functions as a game designed to teach children about the Yoruba language, culture, and religion. While some developers still refer to Africanized syncretism as a "cult" and while some applications contain visual errors, these attempts at teaching audiences about African and Afro-Latin religious customs demonstrate good efforts.

Figure 25: Dancers at MOJA Festival—Charleston, South Carolina

---

[380] Philip M. Boffey, "Baked-In How Racism is Coded into Technology," *Dana Foundation* (November 11, 2020), https://dana.org/article/baked-in-how-racism-is-coded-into-technology/ (accessed August 10, 2021).

Figure 26: Gullah/Geechee Dance

Figure 27: African Musicians in Concert—Conway, South Carolina

Such efforts must also apply to teaching people about the Gullah/Geechee through the creation of another technological application for smartphones. The process requires several important steps. First, a project of that magnitude would necessitate funding for it to come to fruition. Second, it would require some expertise in computer coding so that the features and visual presentation of the application could properly function (eg., It does not shut down and restart itself upon launching the program.) Programs like Android

168

Studio allow people to create applications from scratch, and multiple tutorials for this program are readily available online through social media. Third, creating an application about the Gullah/Geechee requires cooperation and figuring out the target audience. In this case, the application would need to be directed at the younger generation of people in the same way that developers have done with teaching Yoruba: by directing attention at audiences from children to adolescents. Even though the application could have academic potential, it could also be used by those curious about the Gullah/Geechee.

Lastly, and most important, this application would need to be created out of respect for the Gullah/Geechee people and culture. It would need to undergo preliminary testing to try and eliminate aspects of cultural exploitation, commodification, observational biases, ethnocentrism, and assimilation. It is for this reason that members of the Gullah/Geechee community would need to work together on this project to provide people with an impartial and accurate depiction of Gullah/Geechee cultural identity from emic perspectives. It could be possible to enlist assistance from Sunn m'Cheaux concerning the linguistic aspects of the application and ensembles like the Macintosh County Shouters for musical demonstrations. Other Gullah/Geechee scholars, like Althea Sumpter, could also contribute their knowledge about correctly approaching and combining Gullah/Geechee ethnography and media. Sumpter also views Gullah/Geechee culture from an emic standpoint, as a person who grew up in the culture, and applies media technology in ways that do not infringe upon the privacy of her informants.[381]

Conclusion

What I have presented throughout this book about the Gullah/Geechee and Afro-Latin connections demonstrates many sides of musicological and ethnomusicological research. Perhaps, the most important comes from realizing that such research never truly ends. The introduction of newer, credible information and forms of technology allow people to carefully reexamine and reinterpret these cultures, their religions, and their music throughout history. In terms of understanding the Gullah/Geechee and Afro-Latin communities, researchers still have a long way to go. The tone of the scholarship

---

[381] Althea Sumpter, "About," https://altheasumpter.com/about.html (accessed February 7, 2020).

about Gullah/Geechee and Afro-Latin communities has become more inclusive, self-conscious, and less condescending when compared to most resources from the early twentieth century. Part of that gradual change has to do with either the scholars coming from the cultures under study, or from external scholars who try to exercise tact and respect so as not to cause offense.

Audio recording technology has served as a valuable resource for uncovering details about the Geechee/Geechee and Afo-Latin people for nearly a century. As I have demonstrated, the applications of the evolving recording formats on the people have illustrated multiple purposes over time. Some attempt to demonstrate cultural respect, while others directly or indirectly take from their resources in the name of art without considering the possibility for sociocultural backlash. I have shown the consequences of working with musical materials from the Gullah/Geechee through transculturation and cultural appropriation. Bearing this in mind, preserving Gullah/Gullah recordings depends on whether cultural insiders or outsiders (the *Binya*s, or the *Comya*s) have control of the materials and how they use these materials.

I found it ironic that most of the past recordings and scholarship on the Gullah/Geechee and Afro-Latin communities that I encountered for this research derived from outsiders. Keeping these cultures alive in the twenty-first century through music and audio recording preservation means educating the younger generation of people via the technology that they have at their disposal today though accessible digitalization and mobile applications. It additionally involves reclaiming the Gullah/Geechee and Afro-Latin American narratives and music by concentrating more on the emic perspective of the culture and by openly acknowledging the missing or silenced parts of the past. In this way, future discussions concerning Gullah/Geechee and Afro-Latin preservation can demonstrate balanced perspectives.

Works Cited

Bibliography

Allen, Ray. "An American Folk Opera? Triangulating Folkness, Blackness and Africaness in Gershwin and Heyward's 'Porgy and Bess.'" *Journal of American Folklore* 117, No. 465 (2004), http://www-5.unipv.it/girardi/2020_DM/2004_Allen.pdf. Accessed January 16, 2020.

Baralt, Guillermo A. and Christine Ayorinde (English Transl.). *Slave Revolts in Puerto Rico: Conspiracies and Uprisings, 1795-1873.* Princeton: Markus Wiener Publishers. 2007.

Beats, Christopher. "CHAPTER THREE: BACKGROUND: ST. AUGUSTINE'S HISTORY AND TREATMENT OF SLAVES." In *African Religious Integration in the First Spanish Period.* Orlando: University of Central Florida, 2007, 32-51, M.A. Thesis, https://stars.library.ucf.edu/cgi/viewcontent.cgi?article=4076&context=etd. Accessed July 30, 2021.

Bodenheimer, Rebecca M. "National Symbol or 'A Black Thing?': Rumba and Racial Politics in the Era of Cultural Tourism." *Black Music Research Journal* 33, No. 2 (2013). https://www.jstor.org/stable/10.5406/blacmusiresej.33.2.0177. Accessed January 12, 2021.

Boffey, Philip M "Baked-In How Racism is Coded into Technology," *Dana Foundation* (November 11, 2020), https://dana.org/article/baked-in-how-racism-is-coded-into-technology/ (accessed August 10, 2021).

Boley, Bynum and Cassandra Johnson Gaither. "Exploring empowerment within the Gullah Geechee cultural heritage corridor: implications for heritage tourism development in the Lowcountry." *Journal of Heritage Tourism* (2015). http://dx.doi.org/10.1080/1743873X.2015.1080712. Accessed September 10, 2019.

Boon, Marcus. "On Appropriation." *CR: The New Centennial Review.* 7. 1. 2007. JSTOR. Web. 14 April 2016.

Braziel, Jana Evans and Anita Mannur. "Nation, Migration, Globalization: Points of Contention in Diaspora Studies." In *Theorizing Diaspora: A Reader.* Malden, MA: Blackwell Publishing Ltd, 2003. 1-21.

Briggs, Laura; Gladys McCormick and J.T. Way, "Transnationalism: A
Category of Analysis." *American Quarterly* 60. 3 (2008).
https://pages.ucsd.edu/~rfrank/class_web/ES-
200A/Week%207/60.3.briggs.pdf. Accessed February 5, 2020.

Brown, Kenneth L. "Ethnographic Analogy, Archaeology, and the African
Diaspora: Perspectives from a Tenant Community." *Historical
Archaeology* 38, No. 1 (2004).
https://www.jstor.org/stable/25617133?Search=yes&resultItemClic
k=true&searchText=gullah&searchText=geechee&searchText=musi
c&searchUri=%2Faction%2FdoBasicSearch%3FsearchType%3Dfac
etSearch%26amp%3Bcty_journal_facet%3Dam91cm5hbA%253D%
253D%26amp%3Bsd%3D%26amp%3Bed%3D%26amp%3BQuery
%3Dgullah%2Bgeechee%2Bmusic&ab_segments=0%2Fdefault-
2%2Fcontrol&seq=1#page_scan_tab_contents. Accessed July 8,
2018.

Cartagena, Juan "When Bomba Music Becomes the Music of the Nation…"
Centro Journal XVI, num. 1 (2004). 14-35.

Cartwright, Keith. "Voodoo Hermeneutics/The Crossroads Sublime: Soul
Musics, Mindful Body and Creole Consciousness." *Mississippi
Quarterly* 57, No. 1 (2003-04). https://www.jstor.org/stable/26466953.
Accessed January 11. 2021.

Clarkson, Thomas. *History of the Rise, Progress, and Accomplishment of the Abolition
of the African Slave Trade by the British Parliament.* London: John W.
Parker, West Strand, 1839, 1-615.

Cooper, Melissa. *"They Made Gullah": Modernist Primitivist and the Discovery and
Creation of Sapelo Island, Georgia's Gullah Community, 1915-1991.* New
Brunswick, NJ: Rutgers University, 2012. 33-65. PhD Dissertation.

Correa, Pablo and Brian Graves. "Articulating Cultural Belonging at the
Border of the Heritage Corridor: Public Communication and the
Preservation of North Florida's Gullah/Geechee Culture." *Florida
Communication Journal* 43, No. 1 (2015).
https://s3.amazonaws.com/academia.edu.documents/40858091/Flo
rida_Gullah_Geechee_FSU.pdf?response-content-
disposition=inline%3B%20filename%3DArticulating_Cultural_Belo
nging_at_the_B.pdf&X-Amz-Algorithm=AWS4-HMAC-
SHA256&X-Amz-
Credential=AKIAIWOWYYGZ2Y53UL3A%2F20191205%2Fus-

east-1%2Fs3%2Faws4_request&X-Amz-Date=20191205T163040Z&X-Amz-Expires=3600&X-Amz-SignedHeaders=host&X-Amz-Signature=377f6e41737c86ebf76b75f9f02ac2fa2a0d4fb55ada1205f90 03b682863c8cd. Accessed September 23, 2019.

Cromartie, J. Vern. "Gullah Strata People: Historical Notes on the Geechees." In *Supporting Cultural Differences Through Research: 2011 Monograph Series.* Scarborough, ME: NAAAS & Affiliates, 2011, 1164-1197. https://d1wqtxts1xzle7.cloudfront.net/8268585/2011monograph2.p df?1328290242=&response-content-disposition=inline%3B+filename%3DThe_Representation_of_Colo nial_Africa_in.pdf&Expires=1601050706&Signature=eZDbgQTOT-XYVRHsAhpJ~C6B-uJmrH4pQwlygZx3~wg71xuikZoTgWQFF-OXlHeF6Ipe9jIDugPGWJ9wRuYsQ5ufi6MRlJPZwk0-SHgVUiCjHiD2RLgZrKnNWbIGuuCUAONRM48l8j6xQtTZtvose qGSwc4WbXr8pylEBwQn9LeZjuf8HvAcmOA~eOXaLaOBQh2LF juDO7FSS0nmRY2Q-ay8oyC4IzQlBpS6bE6j3cRB7EoGT2JSXonqdWY2G3m8ipaeUF~E V2pAI4VTC0Zto5RgbADNG-2W7MPJSTVB31zZap-XQEhgGQ72bFIUwHihs6ODbZCIBNVbK30kd1lREg_&Key-Pair-Id=APKAJLOHF5GGSLRBV4ZA#page=1174. Accessed September 25, 2020.

Cruz-Jansen, Marta I. "Out of the Closet: Racial Amnesia, Avoidance, and Denial- Racism Among Puerto Ricans." *Race, Gender & Class* 10, No. 3 (2003). 64-81. https://www.jstor.org/stable/41675088. Accessed May 6, 2021.

Daise, Ronald. "Gullah Geechee Corridor's Management Plan is Meaningful to Many." *George Wright Forum* 32, No. 2 (2015). https://www.jstor.org/stable/43598416?Search=yes&resultItemClic k=true&searchText=gullah&searchText=geechee&searchUri=%2Fa ction%2FdoBasicSearch%3FQuery%3Dgullah%2Bgeechee&ab_seg ments=0%2Fdefault-2%2Fcontrol&refreqid=search%3Aaa737f6364a36c45af0a39df3f2fe5 d2&seq=1#page_scan_tab_contents. Accessed July 8, 2019.

Diaz, Javier. *Meaning Beyond Words A Musical Analysis of Afro-Cuban Bata Drumming.* New York: CUNY Academic Works. 2019.

https://academicworks.cuny.edu/cgi/viewcontent.cgi?article=4024&
context=gc_etds. Accessed June 22, 2021.

Díaz Quiñones, Arcadio. "Fernando Ortiz and Allan Kardec: Transmigration
and Transculturation." In *Cultures of the Hispanic Caribbean*, Edited by
James Conrad and John Perivolaris. Gainesville, FL: University Press
of Florida, 2000. 9-27.

Dixon, Anthony E. *Black Seminole Involvement and Leadership During the Second
Seminole War, 1835-1842*. Bloomington: Indiana University, 2010.
PhD Dissertation,
https://scholarworks.iu.edu/dspace/bitstream/handle/2022/7603/u
mi-indiana-1694.pdf?sequence=1. Accessed September 25, 2020.

Duany, Jorge and Patricia Silver. "The 'Puerto Ricanization' of Florida:
Historical Background and Current Status." *Centro Journal* XXII, No.
1 (2010). https://www.redalyc.org/html/377/37721077001/
Accessed March 25, 2019.

Edison, Thomas A. "The Perfected Phonograph." 146, No. 379 (1888).
https://www.jstor.org/stable/pdf/25101531.pdf. Accessed January
4, 2020.

__. "The Phonograph and its Future." *North American Review* 126, No. 262
(1878). https://www.jstor.org/stable/pdf/25110210.pdf (accessed
January 4, 2020).

Ferreras, Salvador E. *Solo Drumming in the Puerto Rican Bomba: An Analysis of
Musical Processes and Improvisational Strategies*. Vancouver, BC, CA:
University of British Columbia, 2005. PhD. Dissertation.
https://open.library.ubc.ca/cIRcle/collections/ubctheses/831/items
/1.0092337#downloadfiles Accessed August 28, 2019.

Figueroa, Luis A. *Sugar, Slavery, and Freedom in Nineteenth-Century Puerto Rico*.
Chapel Hill, NC: University of North Carolina Press, 2005.

Fuller, Sharon. *Gullah Geechee Indigenous Articulation in the Americas*. Berkley,
CA. University of California, Berkley. 2015. PhD. Dissertation.
https://escholarship.org/content/qt42x916c0/qt42x916c0.pdf.
Accessed September 16, 2019.

Gates, Henry Louis, Jr. *Black in Latin America*. New York: New York University Press, 2011.

___. *Stony the Road: Reconstruction, White Supremacy, and the Rise of Jim Crow*. New York, Penguin Press, 2019.

Grabbatin, Brian. "Co-producing Space Along the Basket Makers' Highway in Mount Pleasant, South Carolina." *Southeastern Geographer* 52, No. 3 (2012). https://www.jstor.org/stable/26229016?Search=yes&resultItemClick=true&searchText=gullah&searchText=geechee&searchUri=%2Faction%2FdoBasicSearch%3FsearchType%3DfacetSearch%26amp%3Bsd%3D%26amp%3Bed%3D%26amp%3BQuery%3Dgullah%2Bgeechee%26amp%3Bpagemark%3DcGFnZU1hcms9Mw%253D%253D&ab_segments=0%2Fdefault-2%2Fcontrol&seq=1#page_scan_tab_contents. Accessed July 8, 2019.

Graden, Dale T. "An Act 'Even of Public Security': Slave Resistance, Social Tensions, and the End of the International Slave Trade to Brazil: 1835-1856." *Hispanic American Historical Review* 6, 2 (1996). 249-282.

Gutierrez, Mariela A. "Y yo, ¿Dónde me pongo? El negro en la sociedad cubana desde la trata (1451-1870) hasta el Nuevo Orden (1898-1912)." Warsaw: *Revista del CESLA* Num. 9 (2006). 101-113. https://www.revistadelcesla.com/index.php/revistadelcesla/article/view/219/217. Accessed February 13, 2021.

Hackert, Stephanie and John A. Holm. "Southern Bahamian: Transported African American Vernacular English, Or Transplanted Gullah?" *College of the Bahamas Research Journal* (2009). https://pdfs.semanticscholar.org/b876/10aadbcfc9683dbdd6bd400c790703a05e67.pdf. Accessed September 24, 2020.

Halbert, Barton. "A Challenge to Puerto Rican Music: How to Build a Soberao for Bomba." *Centro Journal XVI, num. 1* (2004). 68-89.

Hamilton, Kendra. "Mother Tongues and Captive Identities: Celebrating and 'Disapearing' the Gullah/Geechee Coast." *Mississippi Quarterly* 65, No. 1 (2012). https://www.jstor.org/stable/26467170?Search=yes&resultItemClick=true&searchText=gullah&searchText=geechee&searchText=musi

c&searchUri=%2Faction%2FdoBasicSearch%3FsearchType%3Dfac
etSearch%26amp%3Bcty_journal_facet%3Dam91cm5hbA%253D%
253D%26amp%3Bsd%3D%26amp%3Bed%3D%26amp%3BQuery
%3Dgullah%2Bgeechee%2Bmusic&ab_segments=0%2Fdefault-
2%2Fcontrol&refreqid=search%3A42dff46f866b6678b1dd5f90ccec0
f74&seq=1#page_scan_tab_contents. Accessed July 8, 2019.

Hargrove, Melissa. "Will the 'Fools' Always Live Off the 'Damn Fools?' The
Politics of 'Lowcountry' Tourism." *Practicing Anthropology* 29, No. 3
(2007).
https://www.jstor.org/stable/24782398?Search=yes&resultItemClic
k=true&searchText=gullah&searchText=geechee&searchUri=%2Fa
ction%2FdoBasicSearch%3FQuery%3Dgullah%2Bgeechee&ab_seg
ments=0%2Fdefault-
2%2Fcontrol&refreqid=search%3A225a608139508a09c7894823ccf4
48ee&seq=1#page_scan_tab_contents. Accessed July 8, 2019.

Hazzard, Dominique T. "The Gullah People, Justice, and the Land on Hilton
Head Island: A Historical Perspective." *Honors Thesis Collection*. 60.
https://repository.wellesley.edu/thesiscollection/60/?utm_source=r
epository.wellesley.edu%2Fthesiscollection%2F60&utm_medium=P
DF&utm_campaign=PDFCoverPages. Accessed September 10,
2019.

Hazzard-Donald, Katrina. "Hoodoo religion and American dance traditions:
rethinking the ring shout." *Journal of Pan African Studies* 4, No. 6
(2011). p. 194+. http://www.jpanafrican.org/docs/vol4no6/4.6-
11HoodooReligion.pdf. Accessed October 13, 2020.

Kartomi, Margaret J. "The Processes and Result of Musical Culture Contact:
A Discussion of Terminology and Concepts." *Ethnomusicology* 25, No.
2 (1981), 227-249. http://www.jstor.org/stable/851273 (accessed
December 1, 2019).

Library of Congress. *Slave Narratives from the Federal Writers' Project, 1936-1938:
Georgia*, (Bedford, MA; Washington, D.C.: Applewood Books, Library
of Congress, 2005), 1-159.

Lindau, Elizabeth Ann. "Avant-gardism, 'Africa,' and Appropriation in *My
Life in the Bush of Ghosts*," In *Brian Eno: Oblique Music*, Edited by Sean

Albiez and David Pattie. London: Bloomsbury Academic, 2016. 193-210.

Lipski, John M. "On the Construction ta + Infinitive in Caribbean 'Bozal' Spanish," *Romance Philology* 40, No. 4 (1987), https://www.jstor.org/stable/44942858 . Accessed October 16, 2020.

__. "Chapter 20: Where and how does *bozal* Spanish survive?" In *Spanish in Contact: Policy, Social, and Linguistic Inquiries.* Edited by Kim Potowski and Richard Cameron. Amsterdam: John Benjamins Publishing Company, 2007. 359-375. http://php.scripts.psu.edu/faculty/j/m/jml34/newbozal.pdf. Accessed October 16, 2020.

Matory, J. Lorand. "The Illusion of Isolation: The Gullah/Geechee and the Political Economy of African Culture in Americas." *Comparative Studies in Society and History* 50, No. 4 (2008). 949-980. https://www.jstor.org/stable/27563714?seq=1#page_scan_tab_contents. Accessed January 30, 2019.

Matthes, Erich Hatala. "Cultural Appropriation Without Cultural Essentialism?" *Social Theory and Practice* 42, No. 2 (2016). https://www.jstor.org/stable/24871347. Accessed September 24, 2020.

Melissaris, Emmanuel. "The Concept of Appropriation and the Offence of Theft." *Modern Law Review.* 70, No. 1 (2007). https://www.jstor.org/stable/4543155. Accessed December 30, 2019.

Miles, Robert and Malcolm Brown. *Racism (Second Edition).* London: Routledge, 2003.

Mille, Katherine Wyly and Michael B. Montgomery (Editors.). "Introduction." In *Africanisms in the Gullah Dialect.* Columbia, SC: University of South Carolina Press, 1949, 2002. xi-xlix.

Moore, Robin. "Representations of Afrocuban Expressive Culture in the Writings of Fernando Ortiz." *Latin American Music Review* 15, No. 1 (1994). http://www.jstor.com/stable/3085947. Accessed December 28, 2019.

National Park Service. *Low Country Gullah Culture Special Resource Study and Final Environmental Impact Statement.* Atlanta, GA: NPS Southeast Regional Office, 2005

Nettl, Bruno. *The Study of Ethnomusicology: Thirty-Three Discussions.* Urbana, IL: University of Illinois Press, 2015, 141-156.

Ortiz, Fernando. *Hampa Afro-Cubana: Los Negros Brujos (Apuntes para un estudio de etnología criminal).* Madrid: Librería de Fernando Fé, 1906.

__ and Harriet de Onís (English Translation). *Cuban Counterpoint, Tobacco and Sugar* (Durham, NC: Duke University Press, 1995). 97-103.

Osborne, Richard. "'Blackface. Minstrelsy from Melville to Moby." *Critical Quarterly* 48, No. 1 (2006). https://s3.amazonaws.com/academia.edu.documents/32119407/Richard_Osborne_Blackface_Minstrelsy_from_Melville_to_Moby.pdf?response-content-disposition=inline%3B%20filename%3DBlackface_Minstrelsy_from_Melville_to_M.pdf&X-Amz-Algorithm=AWS4-HMAC-SHA256&X-Amz-Credential=AKIAIWOWYYGZ2Y53UL3A%2F20190916%2Fus-east-1%2Fs3%2Faws4_request&X-Amz-Date=20190916T205515Z&X-Amz-Expires=3600&X-Amz-SignedHeaders=host&X-Amz-Signature=f4e11bc13126f1daa51a10f9fc257c8be60c1eb5efebb3cc15a1bd498d1f6dc2. Accessed September 16, 2019.

Pizarro. Errol L. Montes. *Más ramas que raíces: Diálogos musicales entre el Caribe y el continente africano.* San Juan: Ediciones Callejón, 2018.

Ramos, Miguel. *Lucumí (Yoruba) Culture in Cuba: A Reevaluation (1830s-1840s).* (Miami: Florida International University FIU Digital Commons, 2013), https://digitalcommons.fiu.edu/cgi/viewcontent.cgi?article=2083&context=etd. Accessed February 11, 2021.

Rausenberger, J. "Santurismo: The Commodification of Santeria and the Touristic Value of Afro-Cuban Derived Religions in Cuba." *Almatourism Special Issue* N. 8 (2018). 150-171. https://almatourism.unibo.it/article/view/7775. Accessed June 22, 2021.

Rivera, Maritza Quiñones. "From Trigueñita to Afro-Puerto Rican: Intersections of the Racialized, Gendered, and Sexualized Body in Puerto Rico and the U.S. Mainland." *Meridians* 7, No. 1 (2006). https://www.jstor.org/stable/40338721. Accessed March 23, 2020.

Roberts, Amy Lotson and Patrick J. Holladay. *Gullah Geechee Heritage in the Golden.* Stroud, UK (?): HISTORY Press, 2019.

Rogers, Richard A. "From Cultural Exchange to Transculturation: A Review and Reconceptualization of Cultural Appropriation." *Communication Theory* 16 (2006). http://jan.ucc.nau.edu/~rar/papers/RogersCT2006.pdf. Accessed October 8, 2019.

Román, Reinaldo. "Governing Man-Gods: Spiritism and the Struggle for Progress in Republican Cuba." *Journal of Religion in Africa* 37 (2007). 212-241, https://www.jstor.org/stable/27594414. Accessed June 23, 2021.

Rosenbaum, Art and Lydia Parish "Foreword." In *Slave Songs of the Georgia Sea Islands.* Athens, GA: Brown Thrasher Books, University of Georgia Press, 1992. xiii-xx.

Runyon, Shane Alan "3. FLORIDA'S FUGUTUVE SLAVE POLICY AND FORT MOSE." In *Fort Mose: The Free African Community and Militia of Spanish St. Augustine.* Bozeman, MT: Montana State University-Bozeman, 1999. Master's Thesis. 36-68. https://scholarworks.montana.edu/xmlui/bitstream/handle/1/8563/31762104216096.pdf?sequence=1&isAllowed=y. Accessed October 29, 2021.

Sanchez, Anthony L. *The Jíbaro and the Gaucho United in Music and Song* (English Translation), Vancouver, BC: Ditrie Marie Bowie, 2019.

__. *The Puerto Rican Cuatro as a Device for Transculturation: A Contemporary Compositional Approach in Estampas de La Isla del Encanto.* University of Georgia. D.M.A. Dissertation. http://dbs.galib.uga.edu/cgi-bin/getd.cgi?userid=galileo&serverno=18&instcode=publ&_cc=1. Accessed December 30, 2019.

Santana, José "An Absent History: The Marks of Africa on Puerto Rican Popular Catholicism. Dayton, OH: University of Dayton, 2017. 1-104. Master's Thesis. https://etd.ohiolink.edu/apexprod/rws_etd/send_file/send?accession=dayton1500482261688046&disposition=inline. Accessed June 25, 2021.

Schmidt, Bettina E. "The Power of the Spirits: The Formation of Identity based on Puerto Rican Spiritism." *Revista de Estudos da Religiao* No. 2 (2006), 127-154.

https://www.pucsp.br/rever/rv2_2006/p_schmidt.pdf. Accessed February 25, 2021.

__. "Spirit Possession in Brazil: The Perception of the (Possessed) Body." *Anthropos* 109, H1 (2014). https://www.jstor.org/stable/43861689. Accessed February 17, 2021.

Shaw, Lisa. "*São Coisas Nossas*: Samba and Identity in the Vargas Era (1930-45). *Portuguese Studies* 14 (198), 152-169. https://www.jstor.org/stable/41105089. Accessed June 24, 2021.

Smart, Andrew et al. *Identity Politics and the New Genetics: Re/Creating Categories of Difference and Belonging.* Edited by Katharina Schramm. David Skinner, and Richard Rottenburg. New York: Berghann, 2012.

Stanley, William. *Fear and Rebellion in South Carolina: The 1739 Stono Rebellion and Colonial Slave Society.* Harrisonburg, VA: James Madison University, 2020. Master's Thesis. https://commons.lib.jmu.edu/cgi/viewcontent.cgi?article=1019&context=masters202029. Accessed February 12, 2021.

Starke, David M. "Rescued from Their Invisibility: The Afro-Puerto Ricans of Seventeenth-and Eighteenth-Century San Mateo de Cangrejos, Puerto Rico." *Americas* 63, No. 4 (2007). https://www.jstor.org/stable/4491299. Accessed October 2, 2020.

Sutter. Paul S. and Paul M. Pressly. *Coastal Nature, Coastal Culture: Environmental Histories of the Georgia Coast.* Athens, GA: University of Georgia Press, 2018. https://www.jstor.org/stable/j.ctt1vhtr90?turn_away=true&Search=yes&resultItemClick=true&searchText=gullah&searchText=geechee&searchText=music&searchUri=%2Faction%2FdoBasicSearch%3FQuery%3Dgullah%2Bgeechee%2Bmusic%26amp%3Bfilter%3D&ab_segments=0%2Fdefault-2%2Fcontrol. Accessed July 8, 2019.

Sutton, Robert K. and John A. Latschar (Editors). *The Reconstruction Era.* Fort Washington, PA: Eastern Natoinal, 2016.

Swed, John. *Alan Lomax: The Man Who Recorded the World.* New York: Penguin. 2010.

Sweet, James H. "Reimagining the African-Atlantic Archive: Method, Concept, Epistemology, Ontology." *Journal of American History* 30, No.

1 (2014). https://www.jstor.org/stable/43305182. Accessed January 12, 2021.

Thomson, Ryan. "4. GATES AND FAKES: PERCEPTIONS OF THE SEA ISLAND INVASION." In *Destructionment: Gates & Fakes Invade the Sea Islands* (Gainesville, FL: University of Florida, 2019),. 78-98. PhD. Dissertation. https://ufdc.ufl.edu/UFE0054389/00001. Accessed July 13, 2021.

Thornton, John K. "African Dimensions of the Stono Rebellion." *American Historical Review* 96, No. 4 (1991), 1101-1113. https://www.jstor.org/stable/2164997. Accessed February 12, 2021.

Trinkley, Michael. "The Lifestyle of Freedmen at Mitchelville, Hilton Head Island: Evidence of a Changing Pattern of Afro-American Archaeological Visibility." Columbia, SC: Chicora Foundation, 1987, 1-11. https://dc.statelibrary.sc.gov/bitstream/handle/10827/33293/Chicora_Research_Contributions_021_1987.pdf?sequence=1. Accessed May 20, 2021.

Turner, Lorenzo Dow. *Africanisms in the Gullah Dialect.* Columbia, SC: University of South Carolina Press, 1949, 2002.

Viala, Fabienne. "Chapter 1: Transculturation as Commemoration: Fernando Ortiz, The Cuban *longue duree*, and the Role of Columbus." In *The Post-Columbus Syndrome: Identities, Cultural Nationalism, and Commemorations in the Caribbean.* (New York: Palgrave Macmillan, 2014), 21-39.

Vogel, Peggy MacLeod. *Biculturalism and Identity in Contemporary Gullah Families.* Blacksburg, VA: Virginia Tech, 2000. https://vtechworks.lib.vt.edu/bitstream/handle/10919/37496/dissert2.pdf?sequence=1. Accessed October 13, 2020. PhD. Dissertation.

Wade, Bonnie C. *Thinking Musically: Experiencing Music, Expressing Culture.* New York: Oxford University Press, 2013.

Wade, Peter. *Race and Ethnicity in Latin America.* Sterling, VA: Pluto Press, 1997, 5-24.

Walker, Cam. *Corinth: The Story of a Contraband Camp.* Fort Washington, PA: Eastern National, 2020.

Washington, Erica Lanice. *"Shabach Hallelujah!": The Continuity of the Ring Shout Tradition as a Site of Music and Dance in Black American Worship.* Bowling Green, OH. Bowling Green State University, 2005. Master's Thesis. https://etd.ohiolink.edu/!etd.send_file?accession=bgsu1131054976&disposition=inline. Accessed August 28, 2019.

Whitmore, Aleysia K. "CUBAN MUSIC IS AFRICAN MUSIC: NEGOTIATING AFRICA AND THE AFRICAN DIASPORA ON THE WORLD MUSIC STAGE," *African Music* 9, No. 3 (2013). https://www.jstor.org/stable/24877317. Accessed January 12, 2021.

Wirtz, Kristina. "Divining the Past: The Linguistic Reconstruction of 'African' Roots in Diasporic Ritual Registers and Songs. *Journal of Religion in Africa* 37, Facs. 2 (2007). https://www.jstor.org/stable/27594415. Accessed January 12. 2021.

Young, James O. "Authenticity and Appropriation." *Frontiers of Philosophy in China.* 1 3. 2006. JSTOR. Web. 14 April 2016.

Webography

Adams, Sanford. *Beyond Barbados: The Carolina Connection*, etv, 2019. https://www.scetv.org/beyond-barbados-carolina-connection?fbclid=IwAR3W61J-NNcHyJ6_US5BOihBkY9AFlSjKOWruPbWApYXei-IhlXHnEGXr0. Accessed June 18, 2021.

Archivo Virtual Instituto de Cultura Puertorriqueña (2020). https://www.archivoicp.com/coleccion-por-series. Accessed October 26, 2020.

Association for Cultural Equity (ACE). http://www.culturalequity.org/. Accessed September 16, 2019.

__. "Alan Lomax: About Alan." http://www.culturalequity.org/alan-lomax/about-alan. Accessed September 16, 2019.

__. "Global Jukebox". http://www.culturalequity.org/resources/gjb. Accessed September 16, 2019.

Alvarez, Jorge. "El Código Negro y la Real Cédula de 1789, los reglamentos esclavistas de Francia y España." *La Brujula Verde* (September 1,

2016). https://www.labrujulaverde.com/2016/09/el-codigo-negro-y-la-real-cedula-de-1789-los-reglamentos-esclavistas-de-francia-y-espana. Accessed April 5, 2019.

Barreiro, Everton. "Alba Darabi in Candomble/Brazil, the untold story. " *YouTube* (February 26, 2021). https://www.youtube.com/watch?v=4kaSZ5KVEII. Accessed August 2, 2021.

Benavides, Nicolas Lell. "Out of Context #8: Privilege and Creative Consequence." New York: *I CARE IF YOU LISTEN* (August 26, 2020). https://www.icareifyoulisten.com/2020/08/out-of-context-8-privilege-and-creative-consequence/. Accessed September 24, 2020.

Berliner, Emile. "Gramophone, &c." US Patent 637, 197 (January 25, 1899). *Google Patents.* https://patents.google.com/patent/US637197A/en. Accessed January 3, 2020.

Charles Joyner Institute (Coastal Carolina University). "Projects and Research," (Conway, SC: Coastal Carolina University, 2021), https://www.coastal.edu/joynerinstitute/projects/. Accessed August 24, 2021.

Coffey, Brandon. "Spiritual Society Field Recordings, 1936-39." *YouTube* (December 4, 2016). https://www.youtube.com/watch?v=1-MU6lIzGSw&t=103s. Accessed March 23, 2020.

Colección Gladys Palmera, (2018). https://gladyspalmera.com/coleccion/. Accessed August 19, 2021.

Collar, Matt, Rovi, "Dear Silas, About: Biography," Spotify. Accessed December 16, 2019. https://open.spotify.com/artist/4C6vnglzmsWszcdp5WaX6O/about.

Connick, Tom. "Bruno Mars accused of cultural appropriation." *NME* (March 13, 2018). https://www.nme.com/news/music/bruno-mars-accused-cultural-appropriation-2261789. Accessed December 30, 2019.

Couraca Criações, "Memorias Afro Atlánticas: as gravações do Lorenzo Dow Turner na Bahia 1940 1941 Vol.1 (Full Album)." *YouTube* (Nov 21, 2017), https://www.youtube.com/watch?v=hG3yBT9oq84. Accessed June 23, 2021.

Cowell, Sydney Robertson and Aurora Calderon. "Bolero sentimental." *Library of Congress* (1939). https://www.loc.gov/item/2017701673/. Accessed October 22. 2020.

___. "La terruca." *Library of Congress* (1939). https://www.loc.gov/item/2017701610/. Accessed October 22, 2020.

___. "San Sererin." *Library of Congress* (1939). https://www.loc.gov/item/2017701612/. Accessed October 22, 2020.

___. "Si me dan pasteles = If you give me pasteles…" *Library of Congress* (1939). https://www.loc.gov/item/2017700903/. Accessed October 22. 2020.

___. "Venid pastores = Come, shepherds." *Library of Congress* (1939). https://www.loc.gov/item/2017701611/. Accessed October 22, 2020.

Crowe, Michelle. "'Precious' 1940s recordings travel back to Brazil." *Indiana University Bloomington Archives of Traditional Music* (November 5, 2019). https://libraries.indiana.edu/precious-1940s-recordings-travel-back-brazil. Accessed June 23, 2021.

DiCrescenzo, Brent. "Moby *Play* Album Review." *Pitchfork* (June 1, 1999). https://pitchfork.com/reviews/albums/5344-play/. Accessed December 18, 2019.

Donohue, Caitlin, "Meet Gladys Palmera, the Woman Who Has Collected 50,000 Latin Music Records," *Remeszcla* (April 10, 2017), https://remezcla.com/music/gladys-palmera-record-collection/. Accessed August 19, 2021.

Duany, Jorge. "Mickey Ricans? The Recent Puerto Rican Diaspora to Florida." (Miami, Florida International University, 2012), 1-43. https://scholarcommons.usf.edu/cgi/viewcontent.cgi?article=1019&context=las_hhfc. Accessed February 17, 2021. Conference Paper.

Edison, Thomas A. "Improvement in phonograph or speaking machines." US Patent 200, 521 (February 19, 1878), *Google Patents.* https://patents.google.com/patent/US200521A/en. Accessed January 4, 2020.

Ellison, Sarah. "How the 1619 Project Took Over 2020." *Washington Post* (October 13, 2020). https://www.washingtonpost.com/lifestyle/style/1619-project-took-over-2020-inside-story/2020/10/13/af537092-00df-11eb-897d-3a6201d6643f_story.html. Accessed June 28, 2021.

Federal Bureau of Prisons, "Orisha Manual," https://www.bop.gov/foia/docs/orishamanual.pdf (accessed February 23.2021).

Feria del Barrio, "Ballet Folklorico Hermanos Ayala." *Feria del Barrio* (August 8, 2019) https://feriadelbarrio.org/2019/08/08/ballet-folklorico-hermanos-ayala/. Accessed November 5, 2021.

Florida Public Archaeology Network, "Where is Cosmo?" *Going Public* (December 9, 2019). https://fpangoingpublic.blogspot.com/2019/12/where-is-cosmo.html. Accessed February 4, 2021.

Fox, Margalit. "RING SHOUT" (oldest surviving African-American performance tradition of any kind). Original People (April 1, 2013). https://originalpeople.org/ring-shout-oldest-surviving-african-american-performance-tradition-kind/?fbclid=IwAR3IPkWCt-gv58RsSyvweZllcKehhDu4Zj4bu4ODlhBFUTuJb8rVKU_iN68. Accessed October 13, 2020.

Freeman, Samuel G. "A Black Cultural Tradition and Its Unlikely Keepers." *New York Times* (June 17. 2011). https://www.nytimes.com/2011/06/18/us/18religion.html. Accessed March 20. 2020.

Galvan, Astrid. "Controversy over 'In the Heights' raises awareness of colorism and racial inequity." *PBS News Hour* (June 18, 2021). https://www.pbs.org/newshour/arts/controversy-over-in-the-heights-raises-awareness-of-colorism-and-racial-inequity. Accessed August 6, 2021.

Geechee Gullah Ring Shouters. "Home." *Geechee Gullah Ring Shouters* (N.D.). https://www.geecheegullahringshouters.com/. Accessed January 15, 2020.

Geechee Kunda Cultural Arts Center & Museum. "Home." *Geechee Kunda Cultural Arts Center & Museum.* https://www.geecheekunda.org/home. Accessed January 19, 2022.

Geneaology Adventures Live. S03 E02 Genealogy Adventures Live Gullah
    Geechee Genealogy with Althea Sumpter" *YouTube* (September 16,
    2019), https://www.youtube.com/watch?v=qV-RxvDv4eo.
    Accessed February 8, 2020.

George, Philip B. et al. "Recording of performance by Conjunto de Cuerdas
    Tipicas de Puerto Rico at El Romance Club, Chicago, Illinois, part
    1," *Library of Congress* (1977)."
    https://www.loc.gov/item/afc1981004_afs20754/. Accessed July 28,
    2021.

Gonzales, Ambrose E. and Alphonso Brown, "Gullah Words," *Gullah Tours*
    (N.D.). https://gullahtours.com/gullah/gullah-words. Accessed
    February 10, 2020.

Gross, Terry and Alan Lomax. "Folklorist Alan Lomax: Everyone Has a
    Story." *Fresh Air* (January 7, 2011, Rebroadcast).
    https://www.npr.org/2011/01/07/132733850/folklorist-alan-
    lomax-everyone-has-a-story. Accessed January 15, 2020).

__ and Ranky Tanky. "Ranky Tanky Builds on the Music and Culture of
    Slave Descendants. *Fresh Air* (July 26, 2019).
    https://www.npr.org/2019/07/26/745583378/ranky-tanky-builds-
    on-the-music-and-culture-of-slave-descendants. Accessed August 22,
    2019.

Guasco, Michael. "The Misguided Focus on 1619 as the Beginning of Slavery
    in the U.S. Damages Our Understanding of American History."
    Smithsonian (September 13, 2017).
    https://www.smithsonianmag.com/history/misguided-focus-1619-
    beginning-slavery-us-damages-our-understanding-american-history-
    180964873/. Accessed June 19, 2019.

Gullah Geechee Chamber of Commerce. "Covid-19," (2020). *Gullah Geechee
    Chamber of Commerce*,
    https://www.gullahgeecheechamber.org/corona-virus-covid-19/.
    Accessed July 23, 2021.

Gullah/Geechee Nation (June 2012-   ). https://gullahgeecheenation.com/
    Accessed April 5, 2019. Blog.

Gullah Hilton Head Island. "The Mitchelville Story." *Hilton Head Island-
    Bluffton Chamber of Commerce & Visitor and Convention Bureau* (2019).

https://www.hiltonheadisland.org/gullah/the-mitchelville-story/.
Accessed June 19, 2019.

Gusby, Kim. "Geechee Kunda: Preserving, celebrating Gullah-Geechee culture." *WSAV 3* (February 14, 2019). https://www.wsav.com/events/celebrating-black-history/geechee-kunda-preserving-celebrating-gullah-geechee-culture/1783268009. Accessed March 13. 2019.

Hansen, Zachary. "Rescue of St. Simons schoolhouse also protects Gullah-Geechee culture." *Atlanta Journal Constitution* (January 23, 2017). https://www.ajc.com/lifestyles/rescue-simons-schoolhouse-also-protects-gullah-geechee-culture/JHh6FtuyQiQXDKiWzSOCPM/. Accessed April 28, 2019.

Harvey, Todd. "Gullah/Geechee collections at the American Folklife Center." *Library of Congress*, February 25, 2019. https://guides.loc.gov/gullah-geechee-folklife, (Accessed January 7, 2020). Archival Collection Guide.

__ and Riley Calcagno. "Gullah/Geechee collections at the American Folklife Center, Library of Congress." *Gullah-Geechee Corridor* (February 2018). https://www.gullahgeecheecorridor.org/wp-content/uploads/2018/02/Gullah-Geechee-Finders-Guide.pdf., (accessed October 1, 2019). Draft Document.

Hendry, Erica R. "Holding On to Gullah Culture" *Smithsonian Magazine* (2011). https://www.smithsonianmag.com/arts-culture/holding-on-to-gullah-culture-185296/. Accessed September 10, 2019.

Herschthal, Eric. "What we get wrong about the roots of slavery in America." *Washington Post* (February 19, 2019). https://www.washingtonpost.com/outlook/2019/02/19/what-we-get-wrong-about-roots-slavery-america/?noredirect=on&utm_term=.d5ff7f59d5ff. Accessed June 19, 2019.

Hiatt, Brian "David Byrne on Trump, Cultural Appropriation and Why He Won't Reunite Talking Heads." *Rolling Stone* (February 1, 2018). https://www.rollingstone.com/music/music-features/david-byrne-on-trump-cultural-appropriation-and-why-he-wont-reunite-talking-heads-203033/. Accessed December 30, 2019.

Hinz, Kristina et al. "The rise of Brazil's neo-Pentecostal narco militia." *Open Democracy* (May 6, 2021). https://www.opendemocracy.net/en/democraciaabierta/rise-narco-militia-pentecostal-brazil-en/. Accessed August 2, 2021.

Historic Mitchellville Freedom Park. http://exploremitchelville.org/. Acccessed June 19, 2019. Historic Site.

History with No Chaser, "THE GULLAH WARS!!!" *YouTube* (August 17, 2020). https://www.youtube.com/watch?v=pUOf7Z0b6KE. Accessed May 6, 2021.

House of Representatives, "H.R. 694 Gullah/Geechee Cultural Heritage Act," *Congress*, 2005-2006, https://www.congress.gov/bill/109th-congress/house-bill/694. Accessed February 14, 2020. Public Domain.

__. "H.R.3004 - To amend the Gullah/Geechee Cultural Heritage Act to extend the authorization for the Gullah/Geechee Cultural Heritage Corridor Commission." *Congress*, 2015-2016. https://www.congress.gov/bill/114th-congress/house-bill/3004. Accessed February 14, 2020. Public Domain.

__. "Recognizing the Song 'Kumbaya' Congressional Record Vol. 163, No. 200 (December 7, 2017). *Congress*. https://www.congress.gov/congressional-record/2017/12/07/house-section/article/H9714-1. Accessed January 7, 2020. Public Domain.

Jenkins, Amanda. "Copyright Breakdown: The Music Modernization Act." *Library of Congress*. February 5, 2019. https://blogs.loc.gov/now-see-hear/2019/02/copyright-breakdown-the-music-modernization-act/. Accessed December 9, 2019.

Jerome, Cristina. "Bad Bunny's Latin Trap is Cultural Appreciation, Not Appropriation," Miami: *Miami New Times* (March 7, 2019). https://www.miaminewtimes.com/music/things-to-do-miami-bad-bunny-at-american-airlines-arena-march-16-11103116. Accessed September 24, 2020.

Johnson, Ahmed and Sabrina Thomas. "Gullah/Geechee History and Culture." *Library of Congress: Research Guides* (October 1, 2018, March 5, 2019). https://guides.loc.gov/gullah-geechee-history/introduction. Accessed April 30. 2019.

Johnson, Ellen. "Brush Up on Your Folk History with This Rare Bessie Jones Performance from 1963." *Paste* (June 20,2019). https://www.pastemagazine.com/articles/2019/06/bessie-jones-georgia-sea-island-singers.html. Accessed August 22, 2019.

Jones, Bessie, Alan Lomax, and Antoinette Marchand. "Bessie Jones I, 10/61: 8. Commentary by Bessie Jones on homemade musical instruments." *Association for Cultural Equity* (2018). http://research.culturalequity.org/get-audio-detailed-recording.do?recordingId=23065. Accessed October 1, 2019.

Jones, David. "Living History: Freedom Park will memorialize local Gullah Geechee people, veterans with PTSD in Jacksonville." *First Coast News* (March 14. 2020). https://www.firstcoastnews.com/article/news/local/living-history-freedom-park-will-memorialize-local-gullah-geechee-people-veterans-with-ptsd-in-jacksonville/77-9a2ad817-1c33-4967-9f77-e57d48d3b766. Accessed February 4, 2021.

Klein, Thomas B. "Consciousness and linguistic agency in Creole: Evidence from Gullah and Geechee." *TRANS* 16 (2006). http://www.inst.at/trans/16Nr/03_2/klein16.htm. Accessed September 10. 2019.

Lao-Montes, Agustin. "Afro-Boricua Agency: Against the Myth of the Whitest of the Antilles." *ReVista: Harvard Review of Latin America* (2018). https://revista.drclas.harvard.edu/book/afro-boricua-agency-against-myth-whitest-antilles. Accessed March 11, 2019.

Library of Congress, "About This Collection." *Southern Mosaic: The John and Ruby Lomax 1939 Southern States Recording Trip.* https://www.loc.gov/collections/john-and-ruby-lomax/about-this-collection/. Accessed January 7, 2020.

___. *Born in Slavery: Slave Narratives from the Federal Writers Project, 1936-1938.* https://www.loc.gov/collections/slave-narratives-from-the-federal-writers-project-1936-to-1938/about-this-collection/?&loclr=reclnk. Accessed July 20, 2021. Archival Resource.

___. "Collection: California Gold: Northern California Folk Music from the Thirties Collected by Sydney Robertson Cowell," *Library of Congress.* https://www.loc.gov/collections/sidney-robertson-cowell-northern-california-folk-music/articles-and-essays/wpa-california-folk-music-project/. Accessed October 21, 2020.

Livingston, Wade. "These Gullah rappers have a stern message for Hilton Head—and America—in their new rhymes." *Island Packet* (October 13, 2017). https://www.islandpacket.com/news/local/article178666036.html. Accessed February 19, 2020.

Lomax, Alan. Alan Lomax Collection, Manuscripts, Georgia Sea Island Singers. 1958-1987. https://www.loc.gov/item/afc2004004.ms180333/. Accessed August 26, 2019. Manuscript/Mixed Material.

__, Zora Neal Hurston and Mary Elizabeth Barnicle. "Interview with Wallace Quarterman, Fort Frederica, St. Simons Island, Georgia, June 1935 (part 1 of 2)." Library of Congress, 1935. https://www.loc.gov/item/afc1935001_afs00342a/. Accessed January 16, 2020.

__. "Interview with Wallace Quarterman, Fort Frederica, St. Simons Island, Georgia, June 1935 (part 2 of 2)." Library of Congress, 1935. https://www.loc.gov/item/afc1935001_afs00342b/. Accessed January 16, 2020.

Lomax, John A. and Ethel Best. "Come by Here," (May 1936). *John A. Lomax Southern States Collection, 1933-1937.* https://www.loc.gov/item/ihas.200197362/. Accessed January 7, 2020.

Lopez, Julyssa. "One of the World's Largest Private Collection of Latin American Music Just Hit the Web." *Remezcla* (May 7, 2018). https://remezcla.com/music/gladys-palmera-collection-online-archive/. Accessed August 19, 2021.

Matos, Narlan. "The Malê Rebellion in Bahia: Brazil's African Muslim Uprising." Smithsonian Folklife Festival (May 19, 2020). https://festival.si.edu/blog/male-rebellion-african-muslim-brazilian-uprising. Accessed August 4, 2021.

m'Cheaux, Sunn. "Congrats RANKY TANKY, Grammy Award Winners," *YouTube* (January 26, 2020), https://www.youtube.com/watch?v=d0tCeoCD1GA. Accessed October 23. 2020.

__. "The Pros and Cons of Code-Switching for Creole Speakers." *YouTube* (October 7, 2020). https://www.youtube.com/watch?v=movQMdB7hY0. Accessed October 13, 2020.

Momodu, Samuel. "Igbo Landing Mass Suicide (1803)." *Black Past* (October 25, 2016). https://www.blackpast.org/african-american-history/events-african-american-history/igbo-landing-mass-suicide-1803/. Accessed October 19, 2021.

Montoya, Orlando. "Remembering Jim Bacote." *Connect Savannah* (June 6, 2018). https://www.connectsavannah.com/savannah/remembering-jim-bacote/Content?oid=8618900. Accessed March 13, 2019.

Moreira-Almeida, Alexander. "Spiritism: The Work of Allan Kardec and Its Implications for Spiritual Transformation." *metanexus* (September 2, 2008). https://metanexus.net/spiritism-work-allan-kardec-and-its-implications-spiritual-transformation/. Accessed October 19, 2021.

Morejón, Jorge Luis "From the *Areito* to the *Cordon*: indigenous healing dances." *Revista Brasileira de Estudos da Presença* 8, No. 3 (2018). 563-591. https://www.scielo.br/j/rbep/a/WS5vKQPZPp9D454fj8NkFKx/?format=pdf&lang=en (accessed October 18, 2021)

Nagashima, Kaito, Matthew Bellury and Trevon Johson. "Plena: A Music of the Puerto Rican People." *The Classic Journal* (April 10, 2017). http://theclassicjournal.uga.edu/index.php/2017/04/10/plena-a-music-of-the-puerto-rican-people/. Accessed April 28, 2019.

Newsday. "Descendants of African slaves trace the origins of Kumbaya." *BBC* (February 13, 2018). https://www.bbc.co.uk/programmes/p05xzmx5. Accessed November 15, 2019.

Núñez Molina, Mario A. "Community healing among Puerto Ricans: Espiritismo as a therapy for the soul." *Healing Cultures* (2001), https://academic.uprm.edu/~marion/SOULHEAL.htm. Accessed October 18, 2021.

Otterbourg, Ken. "Being Gullah or Geechee, Once Looked Down On, Now a Treasured Heritage." *National Geographic* (October 16, 2014).

https://www.nationalgeographic.com/news/2014/10/141017-gullah-geechee-heritage-corridor-lowcountry-coast-sea-islands-sweetgrass/. Accessed January 4, 2020.

Parelles, John. "My Life in the Bush of Ghosts." *Rolling Stone* (April 2, 1981). https://www.rollingstone.com/music/music-album-reviews/my-life-in-the-bush-of-ghosts-252823/. Accessed January 22, 2020.

PBS. "What Trump is saying about 1619 Project, teaching U.S. history." *PBS News Hour* (September 17, 2020). https://www.pbs.org/newshour/show/what-trump-is-saying-about-1619-project-teaching-u-s-history. Accessed October 21, 2020. Transcript.

Pitts, Terrance. "The Leaders of Loiza, Afro-Puerto Ricans Struggle for Change." *Open Society Foundations* (August 8, 2012). https://www.opensocietyfoundations.org/voices/leaders-lo-za-afro-puerto-ricans-struggle-change. Accessed March 11, 2019.

Poplar Grove Plantation, "Gullah Geechee Corridor." http://poplargrove.org/discover/gullah-geechee-2/. Accessed August 16, 2021.

"Seven African Powers." *Occult World*, 2020, http://occult-world.com/seven-african-powers. Accessed February 23. 2021.

Schatz, Lake. "David Byrne Apologizes for Wearing Blackface in 1984 Stop Making Sense Promo Video." *Consequence of Sound* (September 1, 2020). https://consequenceofsound.net/2020/09/david-byrne-apology-blackface-video/amp/. Accessed October 23, 2020.

Sherbro Foundation. "Connecting the Dots: Sierra Leone—US Shared History," 2013 (?). https://sherbrofoundation.org/2014/02/17/connecting-the-dots-sierra-leone-us-shared-history/amp/?fbclid=IwAR2GP7RmqS_AeK3eq1Vd9eXvQv1WxI57o7Hs-5sO39IZWenIisGiuo7xiEM. Accessed November 1, 2019.

Smithsonian Folkways Recordings. "Puerto Rican *Bomba* and *Plena*: Shared Traditions—Distinct Rhythms." *Smithsonian Folkways Recordings* (2019?). https://folkways.si.edu/puerto-rican-bomba-plena-shared-

traditions-distinct-rhythms/latin-world/music/article/smithsonian.
Accessed March 12, 2019.

Society for the Preservation of Spirituals (Website).
http://gullahspirituals.org/. Accessed March 20. 2020.

Springston, Rick "Much of what we've been told about Virginia's 1619 first
Africans is wrong." *Virginia Mercury* (August 11, 2019).
https://www.virginiamercury.com/2019/08/11/what-are-we-
commemorating-much-of-what-weve-been-told-about-virginias-
1619-first-africans-is-wrong/. Accessed December 30, 2019.

Stewart, Mason. "The Story of the Shout." *Elegant Island Living Media Group*
(January 27, 2017). http://www.elegantislandliving.net/ssi-
archives/the-story-of-the-shout/. Accessed October 13, 2020.

Swift, M. "El Código Negro and the Royal Decree of Graces of 1789." *Black
Then* (July 7, 2018). https://blackthen.com/el-codigo-negro-royal-
decree-graces-1789/ Accessed April 5, 2019.

Temple, Alex. "The Appropriation Problem." *NewMusicBox*, January 23,
2014. https://nmbx.newmusicusa.org/the-appropriation-problem/.
Accessed December 6, 2019.

Torres, Kristina. "Good Lord: Georgia lawmakers are recognizing
'Kumbaya.'" *Atlanta Journal Constitution* (February 23, 2017).
https://www.ajc.com/news/state--regional-govt--politics/good-lord-
georgia-lawmakers-are-recognizing-
kumbaya/dTCImxIonvY2I7bod9TtFP/. Accessed January 7, 2020.

tucidides. "Andre Pierre Ledru en Puerto Rico 1797" *Asociacion Estudiantil de
Historia: Recinto de Rio Piedras, Universidad de Puerto Rico* (2 abril 2010).
https://aehuprrp.wordpress.com/2010/04/02/andre-pierre-ledru-
en-puerto-rico-1797/. Accessed August 18, 2021.

Turner, Lorenzo. "Interview with Ann Scott, St. Helena Island, South
Carolina, June 27, 1932 (part 1 of 2)." Library of Congress.
https://www.loc.gov/item/afc1984011_afs25657a. Accessed
October 5, 2020.

__. "Interview with Ann Scott, St. Helena Island, South Carolina, June 27,
1932 (part 2 of 2)." Library of Congress.
https://hdl.loc.gov/loc.afc/afc9999001.25657b. Accessed October 5,
2020.

__. "Interview with Dave White, St. Simons Island, Georgia, July 26, 1933
        (part 1 of 2)." Library of Congress.
        https://www.loc.gov/item/afc1984011_afs25666a/. Accessed
        October 5, 2020.

__. "Interview with Dave White, St. Simons Island, Georgia, July 26, 1933
        (part 2 of 2)." Library of Congress.
        https://www.loc.gov/item/afc1984011_afs25666b. Accessed
        October 5, 2020.

__. "Interview with Samuel Polite, St. Helena Island, South Carolina
        (Gullah), June 27, 1932 (part 1 of 2)." Library of Congress.
        https://www.loc.gov/item/afc1984011_afs25656a/. Accessed
        October 5, 2020.

__. "Interview with Samuel Polite, St. Helena Island, South Carolina
        (Gullah), June 27, 1932 (part 2 of 2)." Library of Congress.
        https://www.loc.gov/item/afc1984011_afs25656b/. Accessed
        October 5, 2020.

__. "Interview with Susan A. Quall, St. Johns Island, South Carolina, May 16,
        1932 (part 1 of 2)." : Library of Congress.
        https://www.loc.gov/item/afc1984011_afs25665a/. Accessed
        October 5, 2020.

__. "Interview with Susan A. Quall, St. Johns Island, South Carolina, May 16,
        1932 (part 2 of 2)." Library of Congress.
        https://www.loc.gov/item/afc1984011_afs25659b/. Accessed
        October 5, 2020.

__. "Interview with Wallace Quarterman, St. Simons Island, Georgia, August
        5, 1933 (part 1 of 2)." Library of Congress.
        https://www.loc.gov/item/afc1984011_afs25665a. Accessed
        October 5, 2020.

__. "Interview with Wallace Quarterman, St. Simons Island, Georgia, August
        5, 1933 (part 2 of 2)." Library of Congress.
        https://www.loc.gov/item/afc1984011_afs25665b/. Accessed
        October 5, 2020.

University of Nebraska Lincoln. *The Good Person: Excerpt from the Yorùbá
        Proverb Treasury,* http://yoruba.unl.edu/yoruba.php-
        text=1b&view=0&uni=1&l=1.htm. Accessed July 28, 2021.

Vatin, Xavier. "Memórias Afro-Atlânticas / Afro-Atlantic Legacies (Zumbi Series, CCADI, NY, 14/12/2020)." *YouTube* (Feb 1, 2021). https://www.youtube.com/watch?v=EaJi63AYscA. Accessed June 23. 2021.

Vice News. "A Vanishing History: Gullah Geechee Nation," *YouTube* (January 6, 2016). https://www.youtube.com/watch?v=SqDTJogdWmA. Accessed October 13, 2020.

Voices in Time. "American Folk Music (Southern): You Gots to Move." *YouTube* (May 16, 2016). https://www.youtube.com/watch?v=IzHDuQrdvMk. Accessed January 7, 2020.

Weeks, Linton. "When Did 'Kumbaya' Become Such a Bad Thing?" *National Public Radio (NPR)* (January 13, 2012). https://www.npr.org/2012/01/13/145059502/when-did-kumbaya-become-such-a-bad-thing. Accessed January 16, 2020.

Weeping Time Commemoration Primus, "The 162nd Commemoration of The Weeping Time," *YouTube* (March 6, 2021), https://www.youtube.com/watch?v=X-9k5fIdDdw. Accessed March 18, 2021.

Williams, Emily. "Charleston businesses using 'Gullah' and 'Geechee' in brands say they'll change names." Charleston, SC: *Post and Courier* (July 20-September 14, 2020). https://www.postandcourier.com/business/charleston-businesses-using-gullah-and-geechee-in-brands-say-theyll-change-names/article_6854de70-c051-11ea-9dd9-eb93b822e43c.html. Accessed September 24, 2020.

Wilson, Cristin. "Remembering Cosmo: For about 100 Years, families of former slaves made a life on East Arlington Land." *Florida Times Union* (January 18, 2015). https://www.jacksonville.com/article/20150118/NEWS/801237613. Accessed February 4, 2021.

Winnick, Stephen "Kumbaya: History of an Old Song." *Library of Congress* (February 6, 2018). https://blogs.loc.gov/folklife/2018/02/kumbaya-history-of-an-old-song/. Accessed December 16, 2019.

Discography

Abbbilona y Tambor Yoruba. *Elegua, Ogun y Ochosi*. Havanna: Caribe
Productions, Inc., 1999 Stockholm: Spotify.
https://open.spotify.com/album/6PaZKP3MJOJBWzy12qQiGX
Accessed September 22, 2021.

Avram Fefer's Rivers on Mars. *Deja Voodo*. Ropeadope. 2018. Accessed
January 2, 2020.
https://open.spotify.com/album/5PidebY36lhYzYPAmHoHA0.

Dear Silas. *The Day I Died*. The Village. 2018. Accessed December 9, 2019.
https://open.spotify.com/album/5f4l4lTL1QPLvTMD2R4Zqq.

Eno, Brian and David Byrne. *My Life in the Bush of Ghosts*. Nonesuch Records,
Inc. 2006. Accessed October 18, 2019.
https://open.spotify.com/album/0uWpq6h99OaylNLXe2KPTR.

Familia Cepeda. *Los Embajadores de la Bomba*. Fundacion Folclorica Cultural
Rafael Cepeda, Inc. 2015.Accessed August 27, 2019.
https://open.spotify.com/album/25QrsiFlqREpnK0L0Pyfr9.

Georgia Sea Island Singers. *Join the Band*. Odyssey Productions, Inc. 2012.
Accessed October 1, 2019.
https://open.spotify.com/album/0BOwYcp6kwTlLH9UaZiMDj.

Hermanos Ayala. *Bomba de Loiza*. Blue Jackel Entertainment. 2006. Accessed
August 27, 2019.
https://open.spotify.com/album/3vGGMqUHgOQv3aOsom3plI.

Jones, Bessie and Alan Lomax. "Bessie Jones 1961-1962." *Association for
Cultural Equity* (2018). http://research.culturalequity.org/get-audio-
ix.do?ix=session&id=BJ61&idType=abbrev&sortBy=abc. Accessed
November 1, 2019.

Lo' Kuntry. *Saute (House of Fengshui)*. Lo' Kuntry. 2015. Accessed December
9, 2019.
https://open.spotify.com/album/7DedDliBKhcyXnmaKYUl6i.

Mavambo Trio. *Candomble Ketu, Angola E Jexa: Oba de Yoruba*. DGD Records,
2015. Accessed September 22, 2021.
https://open.spotify.com/album/4Y1wgxtjQqWKSo35PLIVdL

Mestres Navagantes, *Candomble Ketu (Edicao Bahia/vol.2)*. Vila Mariana, Sao Paolo, BR: Zapipa Producoes, 2019. Stockholm: Spotify, 2019. https://open.spotify.com/album/3ylcymg08wg6iOBr0AsWHJ. Accessed June 22, 2021.

McIntosh County Shouters. *Slave Shout Songs from the Coast of Georgia*. Smithsonian Folkways Recordings/Folkways Records. 1984, 2004. Accessed August 28, 2019. https://open.spotify.com/album/6Ixz1rNhem4WILFGVqhCL9.

___. *Spirituals and Shout Songs from the Georgia Coast*. Smithsonian Folkways Recordings. 2016. Accessed August 28, 2019. https://open.spotify.com/album/7xcZ936R6lUc2VUQgFEZ6C.

Miranda, Lin-Manuel et al. "A Forgotten Spot (Olvidado)." New York: Hamilton Uptown Limited Liability Company/Atlantic/WEA; Stockholm: Spotify, 2018. Single. https://open.spotify.com/album/6J74LJVGaniegVuVcX9tna. Accessed August 19, 2021.

Moby. *Play and Play: The B-Sides*. Little Idiot, 2014. Accessed October 18, 2019. https://open.spotify.com/album/0t4ItMJbYMYLzvEO7tzt0B.

Moving Star Hall Singers. *Been in the Storm So Long: Spirituals & Shouts, Children's Game Songs, and Folk*. Smithsonian Folkways Recordings/Folkways Records. 1967, 2004. Accessed August 27, 2019. https://open.spotify.com/album/7EKB4qhYtMtny8cDxfoqEw.

___. *Moving Star Hall Singers Live in San Fransisco 1967*. Westside. 2016. Accessed August 27, 2019. https://open.spotify.com/album/2cAbzWsCHQJ6aodzqEvX5d.

___ and Alan Lomax. *Sea Island Folk Festival: Moving Star Hall Singers and Alan Lomax*. Smithsonian Folkways Recordings/Folkways Records. 1964, 2004. Accessed August 27, 2019. https://open.spotify.com/album/63mDe1DpOANi3he5WwrKhT.

Plena Combativa. "Candela," *Plena Combativa*. San Juan(?): Plena Combativa; Stolkhom: Spotify, 2020. Tr. 3 https://open.spotify.com/album/0hueG0Ly9bLV4qkJQ43iuD. Accessed August 19. 2021.

Queen Quet. *Cum Een.* Queen Quet & De Gullah Cunneckshun. 2015.
Accessed August 27, 2019.
https://open.spotify.com/album/2jNkr92H4FgGboShxPx3MR.

Residente. "Antes Que el Mundo Se Acabe." Miami: Sony Music
Entertainment Latin US LLC; Stockholm: Spotify, 2020. Single,
https://open.spotify.com/album/6w0POUCEoPxwGYM7tLOLG
M. Accessed August 19, 2021.

Seeger, Pete "Kumbaya." *Pete Seeger: The Smithsonian Folkways Collection*, Smithsonian
Folkways, 2019. Accessed January 15, 2020.
https://open.spotify.com/album/2D3VqXZRrje1UzRBDwLNas?highlight
=spotify:track:52dweof0R55C5KgR7QaYzX..

Seekers, "Kumbaya—Remastered." *Kumbaya (Remastered)*. Caribe Sound.
2018. Accessed January 15, 2020.
https://open.spotify.com/album/3yABmKDU9PBX4VodAKHRY
m.

Various Artists. *Sounds of the South.* Atlantic Records. 1993. Accessed October
18, 2019.
https://open.spotify.com/album/2MQMLFDBfgm3CNM24sK0TT.

Podcasts

Cox, Patrick and Kavita Pillay. "Gullah Geechee enters the academy." *Subtitle*
(December 18, 2019). https://subtitlepod.com/gullah-geechee-enters-the-
academy/. Accessed December 19, 2019.

Day, Leila. "Episode 22," *The Stoop* (January 24, 2019).
https://open.spotify.com/episode/0fnTupYVdd09IbrOcn24Nf. Accessed
December 19, 2019.

Correspondence E-mails

Grant, Sonya, "Correspondence E-mail to Sonya Grant." February 23, 2021.

Harper, Zenobia. "Correspondence Letter to Zenobia Harper." September 20,
2019.

__. "Correspondence E-mail to Zenobia Harper." November 15, 2019.

Lotson, Griffin. "Correspondence E-mail to Griffin Lotson." November 21, 2019.

Queen Quet,"Correspondence E-mail to Gullah/Geechee Sea Island Coalition."
    July 2, 2019.

<u>Ethnographic Field Interviews</u>

Moketsi, Jabari and Anthony L. Sanchez, "Field Interview at WKWQ 100.7 FM
    in Beaufort, South Carolina: January 29, 2020."

Appendices

Appendix A:

Gullah/Geechee Music Playlist

Note: The following list stems from tracks discovered and compiled through online music streaming services. I do not include additional ethnographic field recordings derived from the Library of Congress, Association for Cultural Equity and YouTube.

1) D.W. White, "Gonna' Take a Ride on the Chariot Wheel"—*Deep River of Song: South Carolina, Got the Keys to the Kingdom—The Alan Lomax Collection* (Compiled, 2002)

2) Hannah Besselieu, " Heaven is a Beautiful Place, I Know"—*Deep River of Song: South Carolina, Got the Keys to the Kingdom—The Alan Lomax Collection* (Compiled, 2002)

3) Pete Seeger, "Kumbaya"—*Pete Seeger: The Smithsonian Folkways Collection* (Compiled 2019)

4) The Seekers, "Kumbaya (Remastered)"—*Kumbaya (Remastered)* (Remastered, 2018)

5) The Moving Star Hall Singers, "See God's Ark A-Moving"—*Sea Island Folk Festival: Moving Star Hall Singers and Alan Lomax* (1964)

6) The Moving Star Hall Singers, "Moonlight in Glory"—*Sea Island Folk Festival: Moving Star Hall Singers and Alan Lomax* (1964)

7) The Moving Star Hall Singers, "Gullah Folk Tale: Barney McCabe"—*Sea Island Folk Festival: Moving Star Hall Singers and Alan Lomax* (1964)

8) Brian Eno and David Byrne, "Moonlight in Glory"—*My Life in the Bush of Ghosts* (1981, 2006)

9) Bessie Jones, "Sometimes"—*Sounds of the South* (Compiled, 1993)

10) Moby, "Honey"—*Play and Play: The B-Sides"* (1999, 2014)

11) Avram Fefer's Rivers on Mars, "Geechee Pimp Strollin'"—*Deja Voodoo* (2018)

12) Ranky Tanky, "Shoo Lie Loo"—*Good Time* (2019)

13) Ranky Tanky, "Freedom"—*Good Time* (2019)

14) Ranky Tanky, "Pay Me My Money Down"—*Good Time* (2019)

15) Lo' Kuntry, "Gullah Geechee"—*Saute (House of Fengshui)* (2015)

16) Dear Silas, "Gullah Gullah Island"—*The Day I Died* (2016)

Sample Project Interview Questions for Correspondence E-mails

1) What is your role in interpreting and disseminating information about the Gullah/Geechee?

2) How does your role incorporate the entire Gullah/Geechee Heritage Corridor?

3) What approaches do you use to educate the general public and younger generation of people about the Gullah/Geechee?

4) If applicable, what has been your experience with making audio recordings of Gullah/Geechee music or speech?

5) How do you think that the Gullah/Geechee maintain relevance in the twenty-first century through social media platforms or collaborations with organizations related to Gullah/Geechee culture?

6) How have the Gullah/Geechee expanded their musical presence to areas outside of the Corridor: either across the country, or the world?

7) What has been the overall critical reception of the Gullah/Geechee in helping audiences learn Gullah/Geechee culture?

Appendix C:

List of Selected Gullah/Geechee and Puerto Rican Audio Field Recordings at the Library of Congress Website: 1920s-1930s

Folklorist(s)/ Ethnomusicologist(s)	Recording Title	Performer(s) /Informant	Year	Recording Format
Robert Winslow Gordon	"Come By Here"	Henry Wiley	1926	Wax cylinder
Lorenzo Dow Turner	"Interview with Susan A. Quall, Johns Island, South Carolina, May 16, 1932"	Susan A. Quall	1932	Acetate disc
	"Interview with Ann Scott, St. Helena Island, South Carolina, June 27, 1932"	Ann Scott	1932	Acetate disc
	"Interview with Samuel Polite, St. Helena Island, South Carolina, June 27, 1932"	Samuel Polite	1932	Acetate disc
	"Interview with Dave White, St. Simons Island, Georgia, July 26, 1933"	Dave White	1933	Acetate disc
	"Interview with Wallace Quarterman, St. Simons Island, Georgia, August 5, 1933"	Wallace Quarterman	1933	Acetate disc

Alan Lomax, Zora Neale Hurston, and Mary Elizabeth Barnicle	Interview with Wallace Quarterman, Fort Frederica, St. Simons Island, Georgia, June 1935	Wallace Quarterman	1935	Analog Sound disc
John and Ruby Lomax	"Come By Here"	Ethel Best	1936	Analog Sound disc
	"You Gots to Move"	Annie Holmes	1939	Analog Sound disc
Stetson Kennedy and Herbert Halpert	"Church Door-Opening Song"	Rev. Harden W. Stuckey	1939	Analog Sound disc
Sidney Robertson Cowell	"La terruca"	Aurora Calderón	1939	Analog Sound disc
	"Bolero sentimental"	Elinor Rodriquez	1939	Analog Sound disc
	"San sererin"	Aurora Calderón	1939	Analog Sound disc
	"Venid pastores = Come Shepherds"	Aurora Calderón	1939	Analog Sound disc
	"Si me dan pasteles = If you give me pasteles …"	Aurora Calderón	1939	Analog Sound disc

Interview with Jabari Moketsi of WKWQ 100.7 FM (Beaufort, SC)

I conducted the following interview with Jabari Moketsi on January 29, 2020 at approximately 3:30 pm at the WKWQ 100.7 FM radio station in Beaufort, South Carolina. With permission from Mr. Moketsi, I have provided readers with a textual transcription of what transpired during the interview. The text derives from what I recorded through my smartphone. Maria Goretti Sanchez Cruz was also present and occasionally intervened by asking questions or providing additional commentary related to either the Gullah/Geechee or Mr. Moketsi and his profession.

While I initially recorded over twenty minutes of the interview, this event lasted over one hour. I decided against recording the remainder of the interview out of concerns that it would veer off-topic. The interview transcription provided in this appendix features the first fourteen or fifteen minutes of what happened. Additionally, for the sake of consistency and to reduce redundancies, I do not present the text to this interview in its raw form word for word. I have had to omit certain passages, specifically towards the end, to concentrate on what Mr. Moketsi says concerning his role in preserving and promoting Gullah/Geechee culture through his radio station. Where appropriate, I provide descriptions in parentheses that attempt to clarify the references, mannerisms of the participants, and pauses.

Anthony Luis Sanchez: Okay, so... (Pause) Pleased to meet you. I am Anthony Sanchez. Dr. Anthony Luis Sanchez. Um, your name is?

Jabari Moketsi: (States his name)

Anthony Luis Sanchez: Jabari Moketsi.

Jabari Moketsi: (Repeats his name, for clarification)

Anthony Luis Sanchez: Okay, and, um... (Pause, thinking) When did you establish this radio station (WKWQ 100.7 FM)?

Jabari Moketsi: Well, this radio station was established about five years ago as out of the... It's the outgrowth. We had a newspaper here for about eighteen years called, *The Gullah Sentinel.*

Anthony Luis Sanchez: (Intrigued) Ah!

Jabari Moketsi: *The Gullah Sentinel* newspaper...

Maria Goretti Sanchez: (Listening, intrigued) Hmm...

Jabari Moketsi: … And, uh, we had it here for about eighteen years, and we just transitioned from *The Gullah Sentinel* to *Gullah Radio.* So, we don't do the newspaper, anymore.

Anthony Luis Sanchez: Okay, so, *The Gullah Sentinel.* Could you elaborate a little more on what it (that newspaper) covered?

Jabari Moketsi: Well, it was… It was a newspaper. You know, as a newspaper that handled, I always say that we, uh, handled news that the mainstream media kind of neglect.

Anthony Luis Sanchez: Mm-hm.

Jabari Moketsi: See, now, everything that we do is not necessarily just totally "Gullah, Gullah, Gullah,"…

Maria Goretti Sanchez: Mm-Hm…

Jabari Moketsi: … because you can't live inside of a box. You know … (inaudible)… You might be Gullah, but you still got to know what's going on in the world. You see what I'm sayin'?

Anthony Luis Sanchez: Yes.

Jabari Moketsi: So, uh, we ha--, we, uh… We handle a lot of the local news around here (Beaufort, South Carolina) that, uh, the mainstream, uh, so-called "mainstream" newspapers, uh, tend to neglect, uh… We handle national and international stories, especially as (it…?) affect… (Pause)… African people, I put it that way.

Anthony Luis Sanchez: (Listening)Yes. So… (Pause, thinking) Um, what is the overall goal of this radio station (WKWQ 100.7 FM)? What are some programs that you have here? What are some topics that you cover, if any?

Jabari Moketsi: Well, you know, we, uh, … You know, we ca—(laughs or coughs?) We call it the "Nine Areas of Human Activity" which we cover… uh, uh, like, uh, we call it a, say like, um, … (Pause, begins to list the topics)

Economics, Education, Labor, Law, Sex, War, Religion… And, those are the "Nine Areas of Human Activity" and how they affect us and how they affect us here. But, the main thing we're more concerned with, you know, with our radio station—(clears throat)—is, uh, Land and Economics. You know? Land because, uh, you know, you cannot have a Gullah culture if the people continue to lose their land here.

Anthony Luis Sanchez: Mm-hm.

Jabari Moketsi: There'll be no Gullah culture. And, there was a time prior to, I guess, the 1950s, you know. Everything was "Gullah, Gullah, Gullah," until, you know, the development came on Hilton Head (in South Carolina). And, once the Hilton Head development came, you know, the "Flood Gates" were open.

Anthony Luis Sanchez: I had seen in previous research that, by about 1956, with the expansion of bridges, you know, there was that… as you said, development going on in Hilton Head and other parts of the "Corridor" (referring to the Gullah/Geechee Heritage Corridor)… you know, affecting and interloping across the "Corridor" and infringing upon Gullah/Geechee territory.

Jabari Moketsi: Exactly, exactly. And that's why, prior to the bridges, you know, people used, uh—when I was just a small child, you know like, seven years old, I remember—they used to use, um… (Thinking) … What do they call those things? When you go up from, uh—

Maria Goretti Sanchez: Ferry.

Jabari Moketsi: Ferry, yeah! They used to use ferries to move from one island to the other island. So, you know, and the people, the people in this area—I'm sure you know that—they are kinda' like a… Being isolated on these islands, they were able to kinda' maintain a lot of that West African—

Maria Goretti Sanchez: The purest, the pure (???)

Jabari Moketsi: … culture.

Anthony Luis Sanchez: Yes.

Jabari Moketsi: Yeah. Yeah, the pure West African culture. But, then, the coming of the bridges, you know, that kinda' brought, uh, modern—

Anthony Luis Sanchez: Modernization.

Jabari Moketsi: Modernization, yeah.

Anthony Luis Sanchez: In terms of the music that you play on the radio station, what types of music do you play? Is it modern? Is it a mixture of modern and traditional Gullah to educate audiences, or, you know, something different?

Jabari Moketsi: Well, we do play music that's traditionally Gullah, but there are not that many groups that just sing Gullah music or Gullah hymns or whatever. But, we do *one* thing. We play Gospel music. Gospel. You familiar with Gospel?

Anthony Luis Sanchez: Yes.

Jabari Moketsi: And Gospel is kind of indigenous, you know, to Gullah culture. Gospel music.

Anthony Luis Sanchez: Yes.

Jabari Moketsi: But, we also play modern music, or what we call R&B. I don't know if your familiar with that term.

Anthony Luis Sanchez: R&B.

Jabari Moketsi: Rhythm and Blues. R&B music. And, that's our main thrust is r&b music and Gospel music, you know. But, yeah. Not that many people who just sing, say, old Gullah tunes and things like that. It's not that much.

Anthony Luis Sanchez: Okay. Are there any cultural events related to the Gullah/Geechee that your station has sponsored over the past few years since your organization had founded?

Jabari Moketsi: Well, they have three events here. Three events here in this area here. You have what is, we have… Each year, you have what is called the … (Pause, thinking) Heritage Festival.

Maria Goretti Sanchez Cruz: Mm-Hm…

Jabari Moketsi: The Heritage Festival.

Anthony Luis Sanchez: Mm-Hm.

Maria Goretti Sanchez: We've been in one of those…

Jabari Moketsi: You have the Gullah Festival… (Pause, thinking) Uh, and you have the Lands End Festival. Land's End.

Anthony Luis Sanchez: Land's End.

Jabari Moketsi: (Spells the event name for clarification) Land's End Festival. And those festivals, you know, are… They kind of, uh, showcase and highlight a lot of the kinda' little traditional Gullah dances, the Gullah spoken word…

Maria Goretti Sanchez Cruz: The folk…

Jabari Moketsi: Uh, you know, the food. You know, that kinda' thing like that. And they do that three times. Those are three big events that happen here in this area here, as far as festivals. And… And, occasionally, you'll have little plays and whatnot like that. And they have a big thing around Christmastime. You know, (we) have one of our local stars around here. She does, like "A Gullah Christmas," or what it may have been like on the plantation here…

Anthony Luis Sanchez: Mm-Hm.

Jabari Moketsi: … during the Christmas season. (Like that)

Anthony Luis Sanchez: In terms of helping the future generations of people, what does your station …? (Thinking) … What has your station done, or what can it do to help the future generation: specifically, the youths of today to understand and, well… (Pause, thinking)… keep the culture, Gullah/Geechee culture alive for years and decades to come?

Jabari Moketsi: Well, what we do here (at the radio station), our kind of … (Pause) … model is that we entertain, we educate, and we inform. We entertain, educate, and inform. We have three … (Pause, thinking) … Let's see, well really four, radio talk shows on this radio station.

Anthony Luis Sanchez: Okay.

Jabari Moketsi: Well, as a matter of fact, we have four that's local. And of course, I don't know if you're familiar with—which is a national show— *Democracy Now!* Are you familiar with that one?

Anthony Luis Sanchez: I am not.

Jabari Moketsi: Okay. Any Goodman. Her (???) name is *Democracy Now!* And that comes on every day, and we air that show every day from 2 until 3 o'clock (pm).

Anthony Luis Sanchez: Okay.

Jabari Moketsi: Yeah, every day. It's called *Democracy Now!*, and they kinda' cover… (Pause) … It's kinda' like, um… (Pause)… I don't wanna' use the word "Left-Wing," but it's, you know, "Left." "Left to Center" kind of news agency. And they cover a lot of news that's often left out of mainstream newspapers, or they give you (the audience) another way to look at it (the news), you see?

Anthony Luis Sanchez: Okay.

Jabari Moketsi: And we have a program here (at the radio station) called *Education Spectrum*. Now, *Education Spectrum*, it deals with educational issues here locally across the state.

Anthony Luis Sanchez: Mm-Hm.

Jabari Moketsi: … And across the nation and internationally and how all of that plays into… (Pause) … Well, not necessarily Gullah culture, but the survival of a people. Because the people can't survive unless they are informed.

Anthony Luis Sanchez: Mm-Hm.

Jabari Moketsi: We have another program we call *Open Mic*, and all these programs are programs where listeners can call in and voice their opinions based on the… (Pause) … the topic or the subject for the program for that day. We have another program called *Freedom Road*, you know, and I am the host of this program called *Freedom Road*. You know, I'm a trained journalist, you know what I mean…

Anthony Luis Sanchez: Yeah.

Jabari Moketsi: I'm a trained journalist. I was a publisher of a newspaper

Anthony Luis Sanchez: Okay.

Jabari Moketsi: So, I keep up with a lot of things in terms of Politics: especially Economics, Politics, and those things that's going on in the social arena… (Pause) … to keep the people here informed about that. And all of these things, you know, by being informed, you are empowered, you see. So, that's what I do. And we have one more program. You know, its… (Long Pause, finding the words)… It's a Gospel program, but it's, um, … (Pause, Chuckles) Let me see how we explain it… But, it's what they call "Hip Hop Gospel"

Anthony Luis Sanchez and Maria Goretti Sanchez Cruz: Hmmm…

Maria Goretti Sanchez Cruz: Have to be a new era.

Anthony Luis Sanchez: Yeah.

Jabari Moketsi: Yeah, hip hop. You know, for younger people who like Gospel music. But, at the same time, they like that hip hop music. So, somehow or another, they make the Gospel music hip hop…

Anthony Luis Sanchez: Yes.

Jabari Moketsi: … And if you're not really listening, you really can't tell that what they call "the beats," you know "the beats" (?) It sounds just like music that they would like, but they're talking about issues…

Anthony Luis Sanchez and Maria Goretti Sanchez Cruz: Issues and topics…

Jabari Moketsi: … like that. But, yeah, those are some of the programs that we have. We also have … ministers. They have these, like, different churches. Like, on Sunday, you know, they come on and they do their Church ministry programs on Sunday. And with these programs… (Pause) … you can hear a lot the… (Pause, thinking) … you know, the "Gullah take," because these people are local, you know, and not all that educated and whatnot (Moketsi's words). And you can hear a lot of the language and whatnot like that. But, that's not… why they're there, to teach their language, It's that they just happen to speak it, that's all I'm saying.

Anthony Luis Sanchez: Okay. I was going to ask about, you know, whether those programs that you mentioned incorporate elements where they can educate listeners about the Gullah/Geechee language, because I've seen a lot of scholarship about the significance of Gullah/Geechee language and preservation of that language: specifically, through audio recordings and speech.

Jabari Moketsi: Well, we don't … set out to say: "This is the way you say, uh, 'you.' You say 'ya.' You know what I'm saying? We don't set out to do that. Some things just come natural. In other words (?), there's no script where we hear, uh, teaching, say, "Gullah Language." You know, I mean, I'm not prepared to do that anyway, you know. But sometimes, you know, we just get to talking: especially if we get into a, uh (with emphasis) *fast dialogue* with someone or a heated dialogue. Then, all of a sudden, all this stuff just (???)…

Anthony Luis Sanchez and Maria Goretti Sanchez Cruz: (Laughing)

Jabari Moketsi: … It just started comin' out, you see? Now, when we not in that dialogue, of course we gonna' try to be more articulate. You see what I'm sayin'?

Maria Goretti Sanchez Cruz: Sure (?).

Jabari Moketsi: …But then, once we get into a heated dialogue or a debate about something, you know, and then all of a sudden…

Maria Goretti Sanchez Cruz: It come out. (Laughs)

Jabari Moketsi: … It just comes out, you know, because you just wanna’ get your word out. And you kinda’ start speaking what’s kind of indigenous to you.

Maria Goretti Sanchez Cruz: Sure.

Anthony Luis Sanchez: So, … (Clears throat) … So, excuse me. Um, so… Knowing that this station has been around for five years, …

Jabari Moketsi: Five years.

Anthony Luis Sanchez: Um… Do you have plans for, you know, expansion of this radio station? Like, what are your plans for the future to, you know, keep this station going?

Jabari Moketsi: Well, I hope, you know, I hope that … You know, I have a daughter that’s comin’. She works with me, you know, I have a daughter, and I hope more, uh, and I’m… And I try very hard to get young people in here, a lot of young people in, to kinda’ pick it up a little bit, you know, because I ain’t gonna’ be here forever, you know, That kind of a thing. So, we try to get a lotta’ young people. We also, you know, we stream this station “live.”

Anthony Luis Sanchez: Yes.

Jabari Moketsi: And you can pick it up, you know, whether youre in Germany or whether you’re in New York…

Anthony Luis Sanchez: That’s, that’s how I found this station. And I noticed that a lot of radio stations, a lot of programs related to the Gullah/Geechee are also available through online streaming services and podcasts.

Jabari Moketsi: Right.

Anthony Luis Sanchez: I was wondering what your… take on, you know, incorporating this station as, personally as a podcast, what your thoughts would be on that.

Jabari Moketsi: When you said “the podcasts,” you mean to bring, like, uh, someone, say, if you had a podcast to bring them and broadcast them on this station? Is that what you’re saying?

Anthony Luis Sanchez: Or, you know, have an expansion or an extended version of this station, but in podcast episodes.

Jabari Moketsi: Yeah. Yeah… I would love that, but you see, again, you know, I… (Laughs) … (A) being that is what we might call—I don't know if you're familiar with the terminology— "Old School?"

Anthony Luis Sanchez and Maria Goretti Sanchez Cruz: Mm-hm.

Jabari Moketsi: Being that I'm like a "Old School" guy, there a lot of the technology that I'm just not totally up on, and that technology is moving (just) so fast. You know, it's just, once you learn this today, now it's old tomorrow.

Acknowledgements

The years of research comprised in this book demonstrate the importance of humanity and understanding in ethnographic fieldwork. I have met many people from all walks of life throughout this journey: people with the passion and motivation to both learn from the past and to preserve the cultural heritage of the Gullah/Geechee and Afro-Latin America for future generations of people. It is to them that I extend my sincerest thanks and appreciation. It is because of their firsthand insight and invaluable guidance that audiences in the twenty-first century can seek to uncover and (re)discover more about these communities and their indelible impact on the world.

I would like to extend my gratitude to those who aided me in providing feedback through correspondence e-mails and interviews: Griffin Lotson, Zenobia Harper, the Gullah Geechee Cultural Heritage Corridor Commission, the Gullah/Geechee Nation, Sonya Grant, and Jabari Moketsi. Your input enabled me to shed more light on the impact of the Gullah/Geechee community in the twenty-first century from emic perspectives. I also thank the authors and researchers I have met throughout this project via lectures and symposia, whom I have mentioned throughout this book: Melissa Cooper, Henry Louis Gates, Jr. Althea Sumpter, Patrick J. Holladay, and countless others. Finally, I would like to thank my fieldwork photographer, Maria G. Sánchez Cruz, for carefully and ethically capturing valuable moments for this research.

RICE FEST
COOK-OFF

WKWQ - FM
100.7
Gullah People's Radio
gullahradio.net

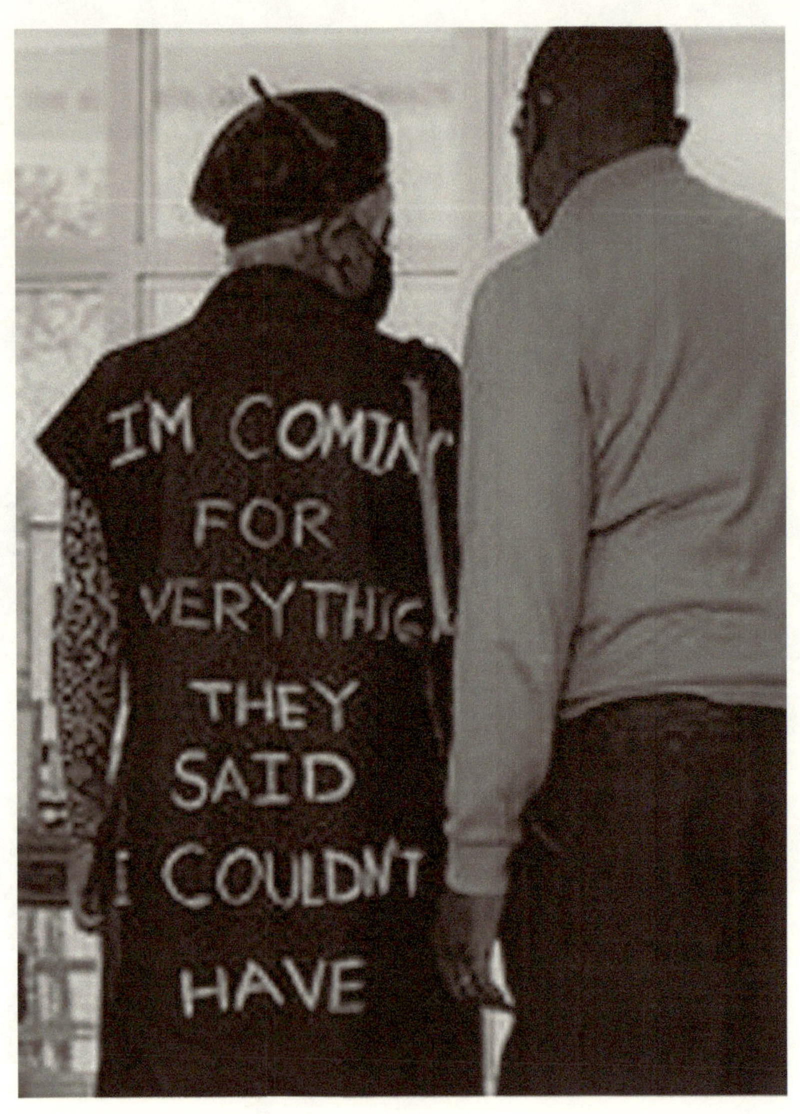

IM COMIN
FOR
VERYTHI
THEY
SAID
I COULDNT
HAVE